Papers in International Studies
Africa Series No. 37

ORAL TRADITIONS FROM THE GAMBIA
Volume I
Mandinka Griots

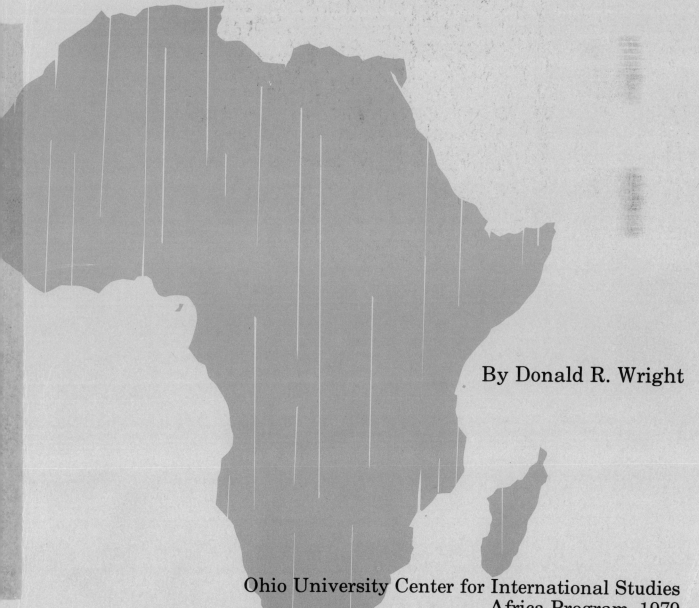

By Donald R. Wright

Ohio University Center for International Studies
Africa Program, 1979
Athens, Ohio

CENTER FOR INTERNATIONAL STUDIE
OHIO UNIVERSIT

PAPERS IN INTERNATIONAL STUDIES

Director of Publications: Gifford B. Doxsee

Africa Series
Editor: Gifford B. Doxsee
Department of History
Ohio University

Latin American Series
Editor: Lynden S. Williams
Department of Geography
Ohio University

Southeast Asia Series
Acting Editor: K. Mulliner
International Studies
Ohio University

Managing Editor: K. Mulliner
Editorial Assistants: Tom McLaughlin
John Mulligan

Individuals or institutions may become patrons of the Africa Series, the
Latin America Series, or the Southeast Asia Series by making a contribution to the Ohio University Fund, Inc., and specifying that it be used
for projects of the Publications Office, Center for International Studies.
Such contributions are fully tax-deductible. Patrons will receive compli-
mentary copies of any papers in the preferred Series published during
the year in which their contribution is made. A minimum contribution
of $50.00 per Series is requested.

The views expressed in the Papers in International Studies are those of the author
(s) and should not be considered to represent the policies or beliefs of the Center
Staff, the editors, or Ohio University.

For papers published and forthcoming, see colored pages at back.

ORAL TRADITIONS FROM THE GAMBIA

Volume I

Mandinka *Griots*

Map 1

Modern Political Map: Senegambia and Guinea-Bissau

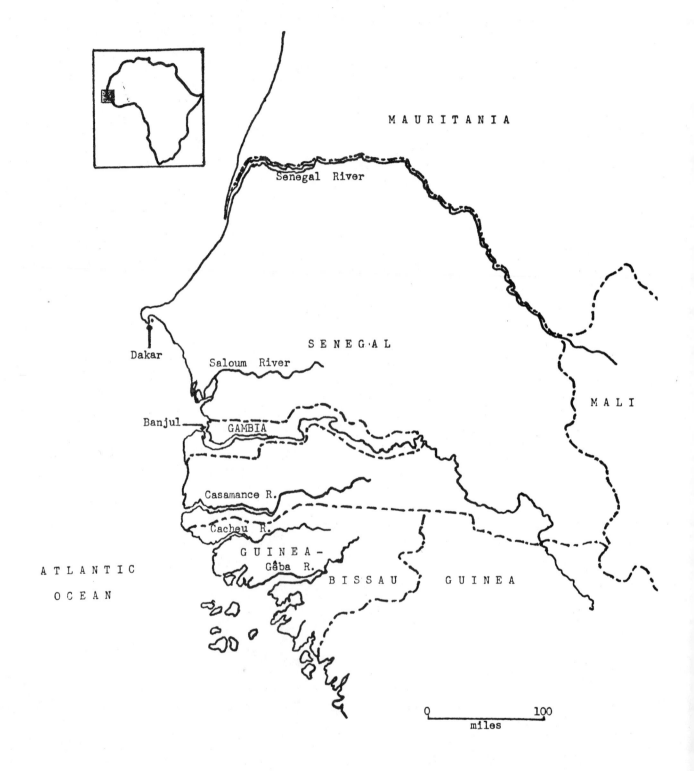

ORAL TRADITIONS FROM THE GAMBIA

Volume I

Mandinka *Griot*s

by

Donald R. Wright

Ohio University
Center for International Studies
Papers in International Studies
Africa Series No. 37
1979

Library of Congress Cataloging in Publication Data
Main entry under title:

Oral traditions from the Gambia.

(Papers in international studies : Africa series ;
no. 37-   )
Includes bibliographical references.
CONTENTS: v. 1. Mandinka griots.
1. Gambia--History--Sources. 2. Oral history.
I. Wright, Donald R. II. Series.
DT1.P33 no. 37, etc.   [DT509.A3]   966'.51'0072 79-14855
ISBN 0-89680-083-0

ISBN: 0-89680-083-0

TABLE OF CONTENTS

ACKNOWLEDGEMENTS

Of course, my greatest debt is to the one hundred six informants living in The Gambia and Senegal, who provided me with the wealth of oral traditions relating to the precolonial history of the lower Gambia from which material in these two volumes is taken. Without such individuals deeply interested in their cultural history, we would know considerably less about precolonial Africa. My gratitude to them equals my admiration for them.

I am grageful to the United States Department of Health, Education, and Welfare for the Fulbright-Hays Fellowship that sponsored my collection of these materials, and to the State University of New York Research Foundation for the Faculty Research Fellowship that supported a summer's work of preparing the materials for publication. I am grateful, too, to the government of The Gambia for permitting my lengthy stay and for lending me support at various stages of my work.

A seemingly endless list of individuals provided me with assitance at various stages of the project. Persons reading the introduction can tell how important Bakary Sidibe, Binta Jammeh, Mamadou Gasama, Winifred Galloway, and George Brooks were to the success of my research. Several Gambians, including Alhaji Maranta Sonko, M.P.; Landing Sali Sonko, Chief of Lower Niumi District; Alhaji Landing Omar Sonko, former Chief of Upper Niumi District; Alhaji Abu Khan, Chief of Jokadu District; and Ibrahima Njie, Imam of Berending, all gave my study their official blessings and gave me assistance in the form of food, lodging, and introductions on many occasions.

And finally, I owe a great deal to my family, Ginny, John, and Benjamin Wright, for their encouragement, help, and understanding throughout the entire project. I appreciate them most of all.

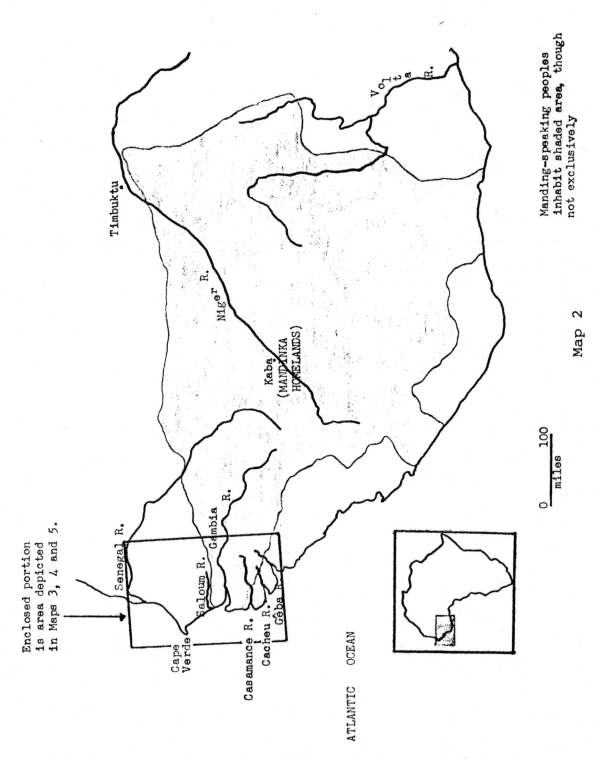

Map 2

The Western Sudan and the Manding World

Map 3

General Distribution of Ethnic Groups
in the Senegambia

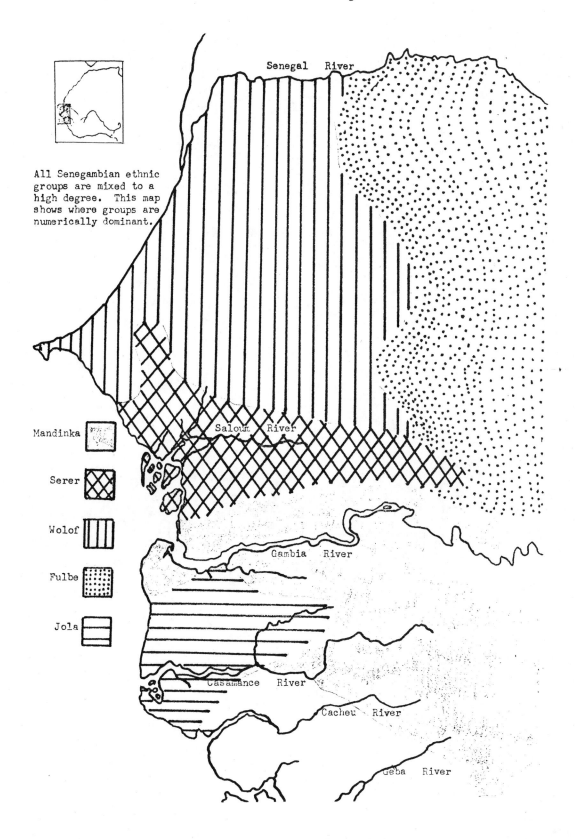

All Senegambian ethnic
groups are mixed to a
high degree. This map
shows where groups are
numerically dominant.

Senegal   River

Mandinka

Serer

Wolof

Fulbe

Jola

Saloum   River

Gambia   River

Casamance   River

Cacheu   River

Geba   River

Map 4

Precolonial States of the Senegambia and Guinea-Bissau

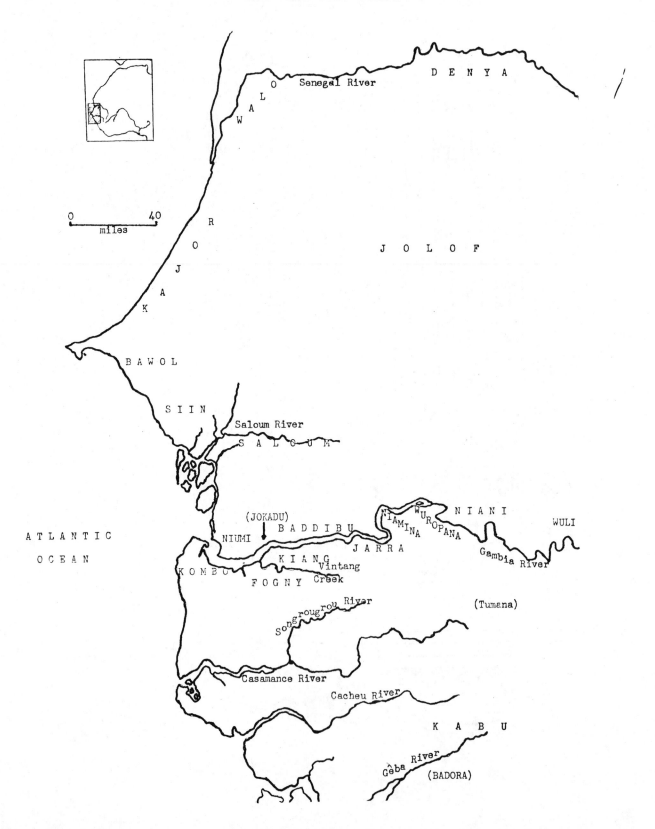

Map 5

Senegambia and Guinea-Bissau, Showing
Futa Toro and Select Villages
from the Text

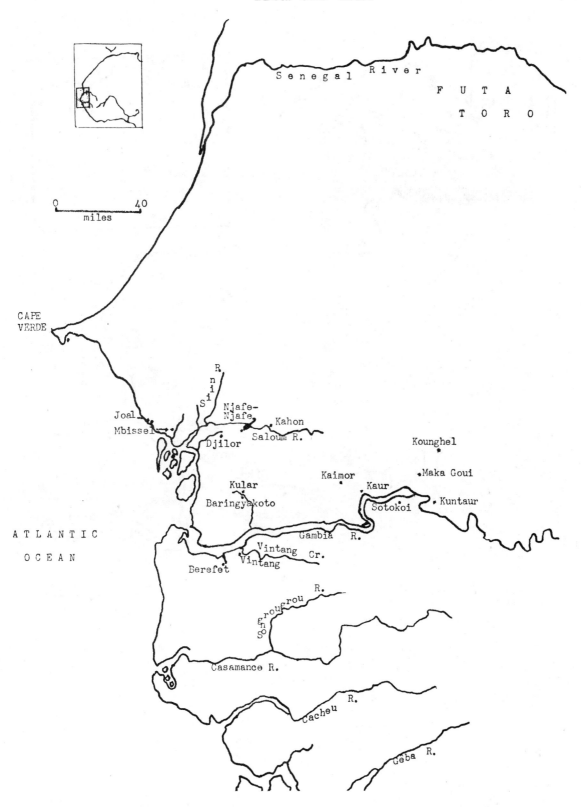

Map 6

The Lower Gambia River

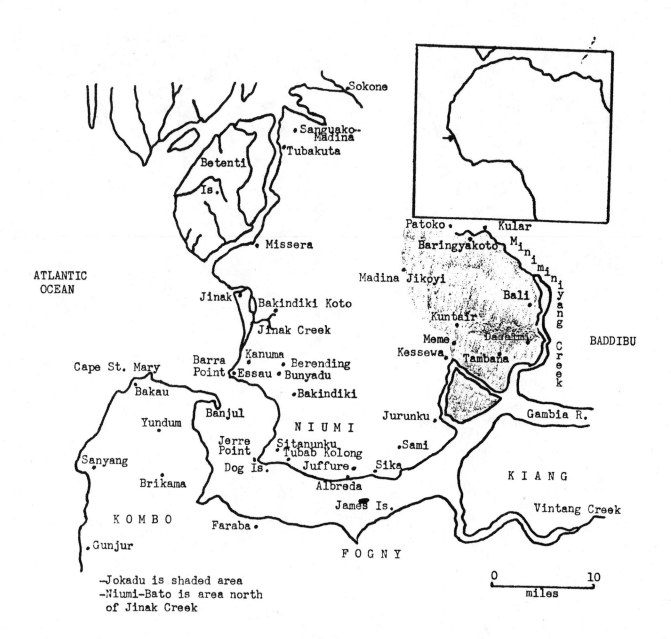

ATLANTIC
OCEAN

−Jokadu is shaded area
−Niumi-Bato is area north
 of Jinak Creek

0   10
  miles

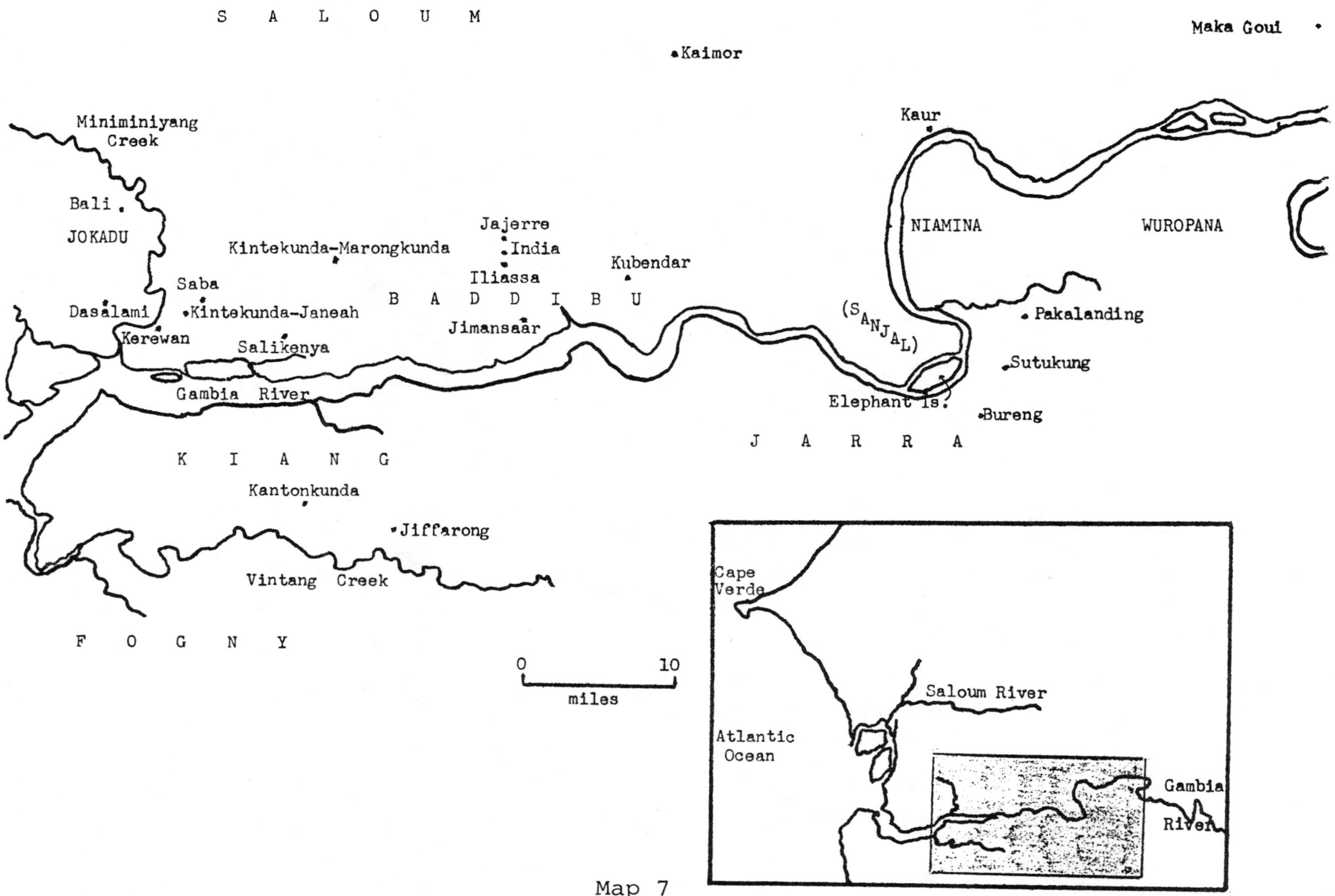

Map 7

The Lower-Middle Gambia River

INTRODUCTION

This is a book of primary source materials suited for the study of precolonial African history but also useful for studying African folklore, anthropology, political science, and some of the other disciplines commonly associated with African studies. The first of a two-volume set, this volume consists of translated, transcribed, edited, and annotated oral traditions[1] of professional Senegambian musicians and storytellers, called *jali* in Mandinka but known more widely as *griots*[2] throughout much of West Africa and beyond. The second volume (to appear as Africa Series No. 38) will contain oral traditions of non-professionals, who in most instances are respected lineage elders knowing something of the oral history of their families, villages, or even larger social or political groups. Together these volumes will provide what I consider to be a usable, representative sample of the best oral traditions available in the mid-1970s in and around the lower Gambia River in The Gambia and neighboring parts of Senegal, West Africa.

With the exception of one interview, which the Gambian Cultural Archives recorded and has graciously allowed me to publish, I recorded these oral histories between September 1974 and April 1975 when I was in The Gambia and Senegal conducting field work for my doctoral dissertation.[3] For several years since that time I have wanted to publish some of the best traditions in the collection--the ones I considered most fascinating and knew to be important source materials for African history. To my good fortune, beginning in 1977 Gifford Doxsee and Suzanne Miers of Ohio University's African Studies Program began to encourage me strongly to do so, and the State University of New York Research Foundation provided a grant to allow me the time during the summer of 1978 to work on the project. This book is the initial result. I hope it is not merely my personal bias that makes me believe this type of publication is long overdue.

Although individuals have recognized the value of African oral traditions for many years, the systematic collection and use of such materials to study and write precolonial African history is a relatively recent phenomenon. It was only in the mid-1950s that one of the acknowledged pioneers of African oral history, Jan Vansina, collected a large number of traditions from societies in Central Africa; it was not until 1961 that Vansina published his valuable theoretical approach to the interpretation of oral traditions, *De la tradition orale: Essai de méthode historique*; and it was several years after that before historians in any numbers accepted even part of the challenge Oxford's Colin Newbury issued in a review of Vansina's book: "All that is needed, as quickly as possible, is a massive collection of tradition and critical annotation and interpretation along the lines suggested by Dr. Vansina."[4]

From the time of publication of Vansina's own *Kingdoms of the Savanna* in 1966, important studies of precolonial African history, based primarily upon oral data, began appearing. In the late 1960s and early 1970s some of today's most noted historians of precolonial Africa made systematic, intensive collections of African oral traditions, each refining techniques of collection and methods of interpretation. Several recent studies, which have been the most careful interpretations of oral traditions, have received considerable acclaim from outside the history profession as well as from within.[5]

As Africanists became increasingly familiar with the effects of the forces of modernization upon African societies, many came to realize that the present generation might well be the last to have direct access to a true wealth of traditional history and lore. They recognized that this generation would have an obligation not merely to use the existing traditions but to preserve them with care and to leave them in their most usable form for the future. But from the very beginning a trend among collectors was to treat their collections of African oral data as private archives, prohibiting other interested scholars from using them. In an attempt to remedy this practice and to insure that valuable oral traditions would be preserved properly and made available for use many years hence, the Oral Data Committee of the African Studies Association designated a Center for African Oral Data at Indiana University. By the early 1970s, many, though still not all, Africanists deposited original recordings or copies of their taped collections in the Center upon return from their field work.[6]

Yet serious problems confront the person wishing to use even those oral materials deposited in the Center. Depositors are allowed to restrict access to their collections, and over half of them have done so. A person visiting the Center to use materials from a specific collection would have less than an even chance of being allowed to do so without first obtaining special permission from the depositor. Furthermore, nearly all of the materials in the Center remain on magnetic tape (which is more difficult to work with than transcribed data) in one of a number of African languages from Pulaar to Swahili, untranslated. To efficiently use most of this material, a person would have to know well the language and cultural setting of the narrator.

Several Africanists have made useful suggestions of ways to increase access to and use of these collections. One of the most complete suggestions has come from Philip Curtin, a collector of African oral data himself and a member of the Oral Data Committee of the African Studies Association.[7] Besides collecting, Curtin proposes a systematic process that involves translating, transcribing, editing, annotating, and finally publishing the most valuable of the written, annotated translations. Translating and transcribing are necessary, Curtin suggests to render the materials into their most usable form, and editing prevents the amassing of a great deal of material "with a very low yield in usable data, almost no organization, and a consequent multiplication of the work to be done before the material can be reduced to a useful collection of sources." Annotation also is vitally important, he believes, for through annocation the collector can clarify points in the narratives that would not be clear to persons less familiar with the original language and culture. The final step in Curtin's process involves the writing of introductory notes to each interview, which contain the full circumstances of the narration itself, and the arranging of previously made annotations into footnotes. The result, he concludes will be "an annotated historical source, complete with the full apparatus of normal historical scholarship." Ideally, completion of this process, or one similar, should be an early goal of every collector of African oral traditions.

Unfortunately for African studies, collectors have not followed Curtin's suggestions to their desired ends. While the collection in the Center for African Oral Data grows annually, virtually no material from this collection has been published other than an occasional appendix to a monograph.

This work, then, is an attempt to disseminate as widely as possible (and importantly, I think, as inexpensively as possible without sacrificing quality in the publication) the most valuable portions of my interviews with Senegambian, primarily Mandinka-speaking, oral historians. I prepared the material with Curtin's suggestions in mind as the headnotes and annotations, in footnotes, will attest. I regret I have not been able to make these materials of more value to African linguists by including transcriptions of the narrations in their original Mandinka or Wolof language. Ideally, published narratives would print the entire translation process--the narration in the African language, the word-for-word translation of the narration, and then the translation into colloquial English. However, because my translations are not in such form, because getting them into such form would have taken considerable time and expense, and because publishing in that way would require three times the space of the single, colloquial translation, I decided it was impractical to arrange the translated interviews in such a way. Otherwise, I think the material is published in its most useful fashion.

I did not translate the interviews myself. Quite frankly, I could not understand and speak Mandinka well enough to do so. With the exception of three interviews in the two volumes, all have been translated by Binta Jammeh, a resident of Banjul, The Gambia's capital, who was enrolled in her first year of Sixth Form, the uppermost level of secondary school, when she was doing the translating. I doubt that I could have found a better translator. In the fall of 1975 Charles Bird, a linguist at Indiana University, brought Binta Jammeh to Indiana to attend college while working on Bird's large, comparative project on the Mande languages, the language family of which Mandinka is a member. Binta Jammeh graduated from Indiana University in three years and in so doing she excelled in English, among other things, though Mandinka is her first language. Ayo Bayo translated the three interviews Binta Jammeh did not. Bayo completed the Fifth Form about four months before she translated for me. Her husband, B. K. Sidibe, Research Officer in charge of the Gambia Cultural Archives, a student of linguistics at London University for four years and later a Headmaster of junior secondary schools in The Gambia, assisted Bayo and looked over each of her translations upon completion. In short, I am convinced the translations of these narrations are accurate renditions of the original Mandinka (or Wolof) into good, colloquial English.

Actual recordings of the interviews published herein, along with the others in the collection not selected for publication, exist in three separate locations. The original recordings are on deposit in Indiana University's Archives of Traditional Music, the Center for African Oral Data of the African Studies Association, under catalogue number 75-185-F. Copies of the original recordings exist in the Gambia Cultural Archives in Banjul and in my home in Homer, New York.

With each interview I provide the circumstances of the narration, along with information on the narrator and other data deemed helpful to the reader. However, for better understanding of the material it is obviously necessary to know more. I tried placing myself in the position of reading these interviews without much background in oral history methodology or in the appropriate people and places, and then asking myself what kinds of information I needed most to improve my understanding of them. I decided a reader should know something of the circumstances of the entire project, or, more precisely, what brought the collector to do the work in the first place. A reader would benefit also from knowing how the collector went about locating good informants and conducting the interviews, as well as what basic kinds of problems he encountered in working with oral materials relating to precolonial Africa. Finally, and most importantly, a reader would need to know something of the general geographical setting and historical background for the narratives. With these considerations in mind, I include the following information.

The Project

I was fortunate in many ways to have the opportunity to study African history under George Brooks at Indiana University. Among other things, Brooks insists that all of his doctoral students begin early in their graduate careers to focus upon areas of Africa for their dissertation research and then progressively narrow that focus until, by the time they reach doctoral candidacy, they have reasonably good ideas of what the topics of their dissertations will be. I had narrowed my focus to the Mandinka and the Senegambia after two years of graduate education and a master's degree. I remember receiving a letter from Brooks early in 1969 in which he suggested some considerations for my future dissertation. I was then in the military, having been summoned after my second year of graduate school, and Brooks helped keep me involved in African history by mail. His major suggestion had to do with studying and writing the history of Niumi, a precolonial Mandinka state located at the mouth of the Gambia River. Niumi was particularly important historically because it was located at a point where Africans, Afro-Europeans, and Europeans long met to conduct a portion of the Atlantic slave trade. In terms of source materials there was much to say for study of Niumi. Portuguese, English, and French explorers, traders, and government officials had been in fairly regular contact with the lower Gambia for several precolonial centuries, and they had left reasonably good records. Equally important, Mandinka-speakers are among the most careful preservers of oral traditions relating to their family, clan, village, and state histories. The subject interested me, it seemed to hold potential value for the history profession, and I thought realistically that I could do it. Thus, I began thinking of narrowing my focus.

When I returned to Indiana University in 1972 I had direction. I studied the Mandinka language for two years, worked to improve my ability to read French and Portuguese, took the appropriate courses, passed the appropriate exams, and through it all read dutifully in the published sources relating to my project. To prepare myself to collect and study oral history, I read books on methodology and studies based significantly upon African oral materials, and I consulted individuals coming back to Indiana and other schools from African field work. During one summer, too, I was fortunate enough to be able to work with Sidibe, then a visiting scholar in the University's African Studies Program, translating Mandinka oral traditions and discussing how to collect and study such materials. In 1974 I won a Fulbright-Hays Doctoral Dissertation Research Abroad Fellowship, supportive of a year's study of the political, economic, and social history of precolonial Niumi.

Nearly all of the Indiana University doctoral candidates who had preceded me in projects at all similar to mine had gone first to various European countries to read in relevant archival

collections before going to Africa for their field work. Brooks
suggested I reverse the procedure so I could learn first from
the Mandinka residents of the lower Gambia what was most important to them in their history and then go to the archival material
to search for corroborative evidence. I agreed, realizing the
benefits of getting the African perspective first. Therefore,
in August of 1974 I left for The Gambia.

The Collecting

My first few weeks in and around Banjul, capital of The
Gambia, were busy ones filled with finding somewhere to live,
getting approval of various government agencies of my research
project (having been able to secure only tentative approval in
advance), and making necessary contacts with assorted people.
During this time, too, I began reading through relevant records
in the country's national archives, something I would do continually when I found time between collecting and processing oral data.
But it was not long before I was ready to begin collecting the
important oral histories and traditions upon which my project
would be based, so I soon faced the task of finding good informants and distinguishing between individuals whom it would be
profitable to interview and ones whom it would not. Of course,
using these research methods, there were no bibliographies to
consult, no card catalogues of local holdings of oral historians.
I knew I would have to find other sources of reference.

Thanks to information provided by Sidibe and Winifred
Galloway, who had spent several years in The Gambia studying the
history of one of the upriver Mandinka states, I knew something
of the oral history situation in the area before I arrived. In
the lower Gambia, the portion of the oddly-shaped, long and narrow country wherein residents feel most strongly the influence
of the capital city, there remain relatively few practicing,
traditional *griot*s who have the ideal narrow and deep knowledge
of history and lore. Most members of former *griot* families in
this region have found other, less traditional occupations more
lucrative. Nearly all those who remain practicing *griot*s have
"gone commercial," perfecting their instrumental skills and truly
specializing in little besides their abilities to sing or recite
the generally known information about most topics upon request
and payment. Some even perform for large audiences in local clubs
and night spots. Therefore, with a few exceptions the *griot*s and
traditionalists I would encounter in and around Banjul would tend
to be the least likely to provide me with the kind of information
I needed.

Again I was fortunate that Sidibe, able to rely upon his
experience in the Cultural Archives, was there to help. He knew
many who were "*chosan*" informants--the *griot*s who remained true

to their traditional calling and the family elders and others who were respected among the African population for their knowledge of the histories of their families, villages, or social groups--and it was with these individuals, who lived within reasonable distance of the capital, that I conducted my first interviews. With them I got my cultural and linguistic feet under me before I looked farther afield.

Some of the best potential informants, however, lived a good distance away from the more Western, cosmopolitan capital, and it was in hopes of finding such sources as these that I traveled throughout much of The Gambia and parts of southern and western Senegal. To my pleasant surprise, I discovered that turning up the oral historians once in a more remote village was not so difficult as getting there. Upon arriving my interpreter and I would go invariably to the compound--the series of dwellings arranged around an open yard--of the head of the village. We would greet this man and talk for a few minutes before making our intentions known. Such was being polite, and acting otherwise was being brash. Once the village head found out what we wanted, he would summon others; once a group in the village realized our intentions, there was seldom disagreement over whom we should interview. Residents of a village commonly know their best "generalist" narrator. They know also which individuals are best informed and able to speak on specific historical topics. We did not often get misdirected. Occasionally we would visit a village where residents admitted they did not have a good historical narrator, and interviewing someone from the village almost always proved them correct. When this was the result of a good narrator having moved away, as was frequently the case, we tried to find the recommended informant in his new location and to interview him there. Also, in a few instances we found village residents reluctant or even entirely unwilling to have us conduct any interviews in their village. In one case this was because of political difficulties brewing in the area; in another it was because an American student who had preceded me there by several years had alledgedly purchased an important religious and political symbol of the people of the region, which should not have been for sale, and had taken the symbol with him back to the United States.

But nearly always the "ask-and-ye-shall-find" technique of identifying informants reaped dividends. It was particularly valuable in identifying individuals with truly vast knowledge, for they were usually known outside their own locales. We always took special note whenever a village resident would pull one of us aside and say something like, "If you *really* want to find out about the history of this area, go to [a particular village] and speak to [a certain individual]." Often by the time we had arrived in the village of referral we had received several references to the same person, and almost always these people turned out to be gifted narrators and, with almost equal frequency, knowledgeable sources.[8]

We conducted most of our interviews in similar fashion. Before each one began, usually as I was being introduced to the informant, I would give the individual a small present, as was polite and customary. Nearly always I took along kola nuts--the small pale red or white nuts chewed fairly generally in West Africa for their stimulant and thirst-quenching qualities, and commonly offered from one to another as tokens of greetings and good will--or small packages of sugar for this purpose. Also, before the interviewing began, I would jot down briefly in a notebook the circumstances of the interview: names, dates, locations, persons in attendance, and circumstances that I considered beyond the ordinary. It is this information, along with whatever notes to myself I spoke into the tape recorder, that appears in the headnotes of the interviews.

Though my interviews normally were with a single individual there were nearly always other persons present. Sometimes I found it necessary or most convenient to interview two, three, or four people at once. I would have preferred the ideal setting of individual interviews without audience, because the presence of listeners known to the narrator may prejudice what he says. But I rationalized that such an ideal was practically impossible to attain--and with the normal village-wide interest our interviews created, it was--and I took consolation in the fact that listeners might keep the informant "honest" and on occasion some person in the audience would interject a valuable statement. In fact, now and then I began interviewing one person and, finding someone in the audience having what seemed to be more knowledge of subjects of my direct interest, finished interviewing another.

I had decided long before I went into the field that I wanted to take along a tape recorder and make recordings of my interviews. This would serve my interest in preserving the oral history (and make possible such a project as this) and would facilitate the kind of interviewing I wanted to do.

African historians are not in complete agreement about how best to go about collecting oral data in the field. Their thoughts on the matter lie somewhere along a continuum from getting the informant to speak at length on general topics, with as little interruption as possible, and with translation occurring after the interview is completed, to asking the informant direct, specific questions, the answers to which the interpreter, if used, translates verbally on the spot. With slight variation I used the get-them-talking-and-work-with-it-later method for my initial interviews with informants. This proved especially good for me, since I wanted to find out what things out of the narrators' knowledge of history were most important to them.[9] Obviously, for this method a tape recorder was essential. I used a Sony TC-110A, which had a rechargeable battery pack, and it was completely reliable. In every instance I used the remote microphone instead of the unit's built-in "condenser microphone" because it gave me a much better recording of the individual narrator's voice, without extraneous background noise, and because not one narrator seemed to mind it.

Normally, I would turn on the tape recorder and then, through my interpreter, I would begin by telling the narrator of my general interests as well as the more specific topics I hoped he would discuss. If I wanted information on the local village or on a specific family or families therein, I would say so. Then I would let the informant speak at length on those subjects or others he deemed important (of course, within reason). I would ask questions only when the narrator reached a point of having little more to say on the subject. This could be frequent in some instances; in others, particularly in interviews with *griots*, I would go through a whole side of a cassette, forty-five minutes of narration, without saying a word.

When I decided to interview persons a second time, something I did frequently with my best informants, I would go into the interview with a longer list of more specific questions. These were usually questions designed to get the narrator to elaborate upon points made in an earlier interview or to speak on some fresh topic that the first interview led me to believe he could speak on knowledgeably. Naturally, using this method I ended up with some information on tape that was considerably less valuable to me than other, though I continued to try to record data that might be of value to students of other disciplines and I did manage, usually discreetly, to turn off the recorder when I could tell I was hearing information that would be of little value to anyone. But I obtained some of the best information of the whole project on subjects about which I might never have thought to ask by merely starting an informant talking about some aspect of his own or other local cultural history. On my nearly sixty hours of magnetic tape, which is filled with interviews of slightly over one hundred individuals, I find I have much more wheat than chaff and I am continually realizing new value in information I considered extraneous.

When the formal interviews were over, I faced the question of whether or not to offer the informant something in payment. This was always a quandary for me when dealing with informants who were not *griots*. With *griots*, who did this sort of thing for a living, there was seldom a choice. In fact, I most often had to strike a bargain with a *griot*--so much for an interview at what appeared to be a fairly standard rate--before he would begin playing and talking or singing. But with non-*griots* it was a different story. These individuals were proud of their family or village histories and usually pleased that I was interested in them. Nearly all of these interviews passed without mention of payment, and those that did not were seldom worth much. Sidibe, who often served as my interpreter, was of the impression that I should give these individuals something at the end of the interview to show my appreciation and respect for their knowledge. I tried to follow his wishes with some small payment, in cash or in kind. When I took photographs of the informants, as I regularly did, I tried to take or send prints of the picture to the individuals.

In terms of conducting interviews and obtaining translations, I did things in batches. Because informants were often a long distance from my residence and widely separated at that, I tried to interview a number of people on a single trip, traveling from village to village in a given area, going with leads and references, and interviewing people as I found appropriate. These trips lasted anywhere from one to ten days, depending on the proximity of an area of interest to my residence, my prospects for returning, and my usual desire to make a reasonably exhaustive canvass of the good informants in an area.

Upon my return from one of these interviewing trips, I would turn my tapes over to Binta Jammeh, who would begin translating and transcribing them, from Mandinka (or Wolof) on tape into English in longhand. She was remarkably diligent in her work, seldom keeping any tape longer than a week. She would give me the translations when completed, along with the original recordings, and I would then type her translation, word-for-word, making a copy for the Gambia Cultural Archives in the process. At the beginning of each typed translation I would write appropriate headnotes, in a standard format, from those I had taken (and spoken into the tape) at the interview. This left me, relatively soon after I had conducted the interview, with a workable manuscript, which was much easier for me to study than a translation on another tape would have been. After studying these translations, I could identify particularly promising informants and unanswered questions, necessary information with which to make plans for a second interview.

When I was caught up with typing the translations, I would carry the processing of the materials one step farther by making indexed notes on each translated and transcribed interview. Over time, as the pages of typescript mounted, I came to consider this step a vital one for anyone planning to use a collection of oral data for a reasonably large research and writing project. Once I had worked out a system, with advice from Tom Hunter, I kept the notes on sheets of typing paper with a separate sheet for each topic heading. When I was finished with my field work I had seventy-four headings and sub-headings for my notes, consisting of everything from individual epic heroes to specific families and villages, from Islam (with sub-heads) to intermarriage, from kingship to the slave trade, with an average of about five pages of typed notes for each heading. I indexed each entry under the headings so I knew where to find it among my typed translations. And again, such note-making, however tedious, proved of immense value when it came time to organize my research materials and to begin writing my dissertation.

Though many times I did not relish the idea of doing so, I kept up with my typing and note-making throughout my days of

field work. When I left The Gambia for Dakar and the beginning
of the archival phase of my project, I was only four tapes behind
out of the forty-five in the collection.

The Problems

Lest to this point I have made collecting, processing, and
working with African oral data sound like a simple procedure, let
me here take a few paragraphs to suggest that it was not entirely
so. Mere traveling about in a foreign country can sometimes be
difficult. But traveling and residing in a less developed country
such as The Gambia, having to conduct a research project relying
largely upon the close cooperation of residents of the country,
who are initially strangers speaking a language one knows only
through formal study, and then having to study and interpret
African oral data to form the basis of a meaningful historical
study brought problems of greater or lesser magnitude. The fact
that I solved many of these problems and was able to carry out
my research and eventually write my dissertation should neither
diminish the significance of the problems in retrospect nor preclude their mention for when they arose, they loomed quite large.

I had anticipated one of the problems, that of language,
though I had underestimated its degree of seriousness. In preparation for my field work I had studied Bambara, the language
offered at Indiana University most relevant to my research. Bambara is the portion of the Mande family of languages that is
spoken in Mali. In The Gambia most residents speak another Mande
language, Mandinka. I had high hopes that Bambara and Mandinka
would be mutually intelligible, but soon after my arrival in Banjul
my hopes were dashed. The two languages seem to be about as
closely related as Spanish and Portuguese, meaning that I could not
immediately understand what Mandinka-speakers were saying and I
could not even greet someone in Mandinka without being recognized
as a "*tilebonka*," a person from the East. During my stay in West
Africa I worked to learn Mandinka, and eventually I could understand much of what was being said in interviews and narrations.
Still, for cultural as well as linguistic reasons, I always relied on an interpreter to accompany me on interviews, to help
make necessary arrangements, and to pose my questions.

Problems of getting about in The Gambia and Senegal also re-
curred with regularity. Many times I bemoaned the fact that there
was nothing like an interlibrary loan service for oral historians;
one had to go to the narrator, wherever he was located. My Fellowship was sufficient to provide for my basic necessities for the
year of overseas study, and it even included some funds for local
travel, but it did not provide nearly enough to allow me to buy
and maintain a car. Therefore, I had to travel as best I could.
Both Senegal and The Gambia have good taxi service in urban areas.
Outside of these regions they have taxis, too, which often consist

of French-manufactured Peugeot vehicles resembling small partially-covered pickup trucks, but the service these vehicles provide tends by nature to frustrate the person of Western mental set, who is used simply to hopping in and taking off. Drivers of these vehicles remain at designated "taxi-parks" until they are full, or nearly so. This could mean a wait of but a few minutes, as it sometimes did, or it could mean waiting patiently for half a day, depending on the situation. It turned out I spent many hours waiting for taxis to fill. And once under say the taxis proved most unreliable. Breakdowns were commonplace. I once took a taxi (with cord tellingly showing through the rubber of its tires) along the main road paralleling the Gambia River's north bank, intent upon traveling but six miles from a ferry dock to the village of Berending. Within four miles the taxi experienced two flat tires--blowouts, in fact--neither of which its driver could fix without assistance, for he had no jack and but one spare, itself of dubious reliability. Following the second I struck out on foot for my destination, a small rebate on the original fare being my only consolation. Fourtunately, through his position with the Gambia Cultural Archives, Sidibe was able to arrange for me to use government Land Rovers on several occasions. I used these to reach most of the informants living far upriver and off the most frequented roads.

Not being fluent enough in the language to make local arrangements and to conduct interviews with ease brought the potential for difficulty with interpreters. Good ones, it turned out, would be worth whole countries full of poor ones. I used no more than two interpreters, once each, who did not have what I considered to be full command of both languages, but I encountered other, less obvious problems with some who did. One individual, a highly educated, well-read man, who knew some African history as well as local oral history, could not restrain himself from asking leading questions. I would request him, for example, to ask an informant to tell us what he knew about the history of his village. The interpreter would then say, "He wants to know about the founding of this village--you know, how the Sonko family came here from Denya and made this their first village in the state, how they later split apart and founded other villages, and so on." To my chagrin, the informant would do as asked. I might as well have been interviewing my own interpreter. This same man could not understand why I wanted to hear two different informants talk about the same subject. He would try to cut narrators short if they began to touch upon specific subjects of previous interviews. Within a short time I simply had to find a different interpreter, however fine had been this man's command of the language.

Another individual, a devout and learned Muslim, refused to pose several of my questions that concerned Islamic or even non-Islamic religious practices. "They won't tell you," he would say, and then he would refuse adamantly to proceed with that line of questioning.

   With these experiences in mind, I came to realize how fortunate I was to have been able to rely almost exclusively upon
three individuals: Sidibe, Binta Jammeh, and Mamadou Gasama,
the last a Headmaster of a junior secondary school in a rural
district. After a short time these people knew the methods I
wanted to employ and the questions I hoped to have answered.
They knew when to speak and when not to, when to interrupt if
narrators strayed from topics of even the most minute historical relevance (as one did continually with one informant, who
very badly wanted to expound on the upcoming soccer match between The Gambia's national team and Morocco), and altogether
they made my interviewing procedures effective and efficient.

   Yet the best interpreters could not prevent some informants
from being sources of consternation. This was particulary true in
my dealings with *griot*s, who have a reputation for being a mercenary,
wily lot. Because of their intense pride in their knowledge and
because they are so accomplished at narrating stories--any stories--
I seldom found a *griot* who would admit that he did not know the answer to one of my questions or that the information he had on a
subject was not what had been passed down to him from reliable,
traditional sources. Consequently, I asked many a *griot* a specific
question, to which I received an artfully narrated answer, only to
find sometime later that the *griot* had likely fabricated the answer
out of whole cloth or had adpated several scraps of local folklore
to meet his needs in a pressing situation. My notes to the Unus
Jata interviews in the text of this volume may be most instructive
on this matter. Suffice it to say that *griot*s have the potential
to provide data that can be almost terminally confusing for a large
project.

   Non-*griot*s created interviewing problems, too. Their narrations could be full of information from less reliable sources--such
being the nature of informal African oral traditions--and frequently
they simply did not know the answers to many of even my most general
questions. Some of these informants were clearly better informed
on their history than others; nearly all admitted when they did not
have information, from any source, on the topic of my interest. But
the most perplexing problem posed by the non-professional informant
was an occasional, out-and-out refusal to speak about a specific
topic, something I sensed they knew a great deal about, for reasons
that remained entirely their own. One informant might decline to
disucss relationships between his family and another, some refused
to talk about the ways their ancestors practiced religion, and some
few appeared to be of that nature that led them to argue and fuss
considerably before they would provide information on almost anything. Sometimes when patient coaxing did not work, I was forced
to give up and leave, retiring with the knowledge that a stone had
been unturned in my collecting canvass.

The Oral Traditions[10]

Informants from much of the lower Senegambia (and certainly far beyond) provide historical information from two general periods of time: the recent past and the distant past. They recognize little as coming from a period in between. Those narrating on the recent past talk of events that happened in their own lifetimes and about which they have personal or second-hand knowledge, or they speak of happenings in the lifetimes of others who told the stories to them, often fathers or grandfathers. Consequently, the recent past in this sense seldom stretches back before the beginning of the colonial period or, roughly speaking, before the 1890s. These informants tend to provide fairly factual information, though personal biases are evident. Frequently they can discuss what life was like during the recent past, even identifying changes that took place in economic conditions or the political structure of their society. But, by definition, only a small portion of this information falls under the classification of oral tradition.

Informants narrating on the distant past speak of events that occurred a long time ago--they never know exactly when. Most of the information they have has been passed down orally, from generation to generation, over many years. They, too, talk about what life was like in the distant past, though they do so synchronically, as if nothing changed over the decades and even centuries of the precolonial period, at least not until the coming of the recent past. Much of this kind of data consists of traditions of origin, which are fairly standard stories about the origins of clans, the migrations of ancestral clan members, and the final establishment of the narrator's branch of the clan where it is at the time of the narration. Examples of other kinds of data obtainable out of the distant past are narratives of how one family came to rule a precolonial state, stories of individual wars or eras of warfare, or epics involving individuals, usually local cultural heroes. Of course, it is to these authentic traditions relating to the distant past that the historian must turn for evidence supporting studies of precolonial African history.

Senegambian traditions are frequently large bodies of myth having but small skeletons of historical truth. For most residents of the Senegambia who hear these traditions, the history is all the more meaningful when combined with mythology because they are aware of the cosmology underlying the myth. But for the non-African historian it takes a great deal of cautious analysis, using traditional evidence collected from a wide area, even to attempt to separate history from mythology and then to say something reasonably accurate and meaningful about the precolonial history of the area.[11]

Cautious analysis is necessary, too, before one comes to realize (and accept the fact) that oral traditions change, sometimes drastically, over time. [Griots are continually adding new embellishments to their tales which, when heard by other traditionalists, are adopted and spoken again more widely. Furthermore, in at least one instance, and probably more, members of a segment of a Senegambian clan, the Sonko have purposefully altered their traditions of origin and early history for what seem clearly to have been political reasons.[12] Whether purposeful or not, whether recent or not, unrecognized changes in oral traditions lead directly to misconceptions and confusion for the African historian.]

Compounding problems of altered oral histories is the fact that new traditions or new versions of old traditions are picked up and passed along (while the old traditions or old versions are forgotten) among members of a society with startling rapidity. The factual basis of the story or the reliability of the informant is not always a factor in the dissemination of Senegambian traditions. Though alteration of the oral history of the Sonko clan (mentioned above) occurred most likely in the early decades of this century, every informant I could find who was able to speak of early Sonko history, whether related to the Sonko or not, within a radius of one hundred miles of the two major Sonko villages in the lower Gambia, narrated the new, altered version of the clan's history. Not one of these individuals could recognize the names of major figures of the formerly accepted Sonko history. In fact, I had to travel about 120 miles upriver to a fairly remote village to find an informant who could recite the old story, and it turned out he had not heard the new one.[13]

Thus, the obstacles that oral traditions by their nature place in the historian's path appear formidable. In fact, in writing this I feel slightly fearful that knowledge of these obstacles--the misinformation from griots, the mythology that constitutes the body of Mandinka oral traditions, the regularly changing oral histories, and the rapid and wide acceptance of new or altered traditions--is likely to discourage would-be African historians long before they reach the stage of field work. But readers should know of my strong conviction that the obstacles mentioned above are ones that historians can overcome through patience, diligence, and careful selection of informants. Indeed, the best advice I received relating to collecting and analyzing African oral data was to be patient and to collect and process oral traditions from as many good informants over as wide an area as possible, taking special care to ask informants about members of families, villages, social classes, or states other than their own. Detached, disinterested parties even (or often especially) those physically removed by long distances from subjects of interest, often provided better information on the subjects than did nearby residents or those with special interest in the subject. By collecting widely, by rendering collected oral data into its most usable form, and by comparing many versions of the same events and themes, [it is possible to recognize history within the mythology, to see why the myth is included and what it adds to the story, and to make meaningful statements about pre-colonial African history. If the patient and sometimes tedious hard work tries the soul, the success that it is apt to bring truly rewards the spirit.

The Setting

With the exception of a few tangential traditions, most of the material in these volumes pertains to persons living and events taking place in the southwestern portion of the region known as the Senegambia. More precisely, the focus is on an area lying between the Saloum River on the north, the southern boundary of The Gambia on the south, the Atlantic Ocean on the west, and the first great northward bend of the Gambia River about 150 miles upriver from the mouth on the east. Geographically, the area is fairly uniform culturally, if not linguistically.

Most of the Gambia-Saloum River region is the westernmost extension of the savannas that stretch out across the entire Western Sudan. The countryside is flat, or barely rolling, with grasses and trees, many short, scrubby ones but many tall silk-cottons and fat baobabs as well, growing where people have not altered nature's course by planting peanuts or millet, cutting roads, or building villages. Only in the extreme southwest portion of the region, along the banks of the lower Gambia, and on the Atlantic coast and offshore islands north of the Gambia is the wooded grassland pattern broken. In the southwest along the river there is a more truly forested landscape. In fact, in the rainy summer months parts of these areas have the heavy undergrowth and full canopy associated with a rainforest. North of the Gambia, between that river and the Saloum along the Atlantic, is a stretch of low, mangrove-lined sandy islands through which the tides ebb and flow, creating a veritable maze of vegetation, land, and water. Palm trees dot the forested regions along the coast, but they are not seen more than a dozen miles inland except in isolated spots near the river.

The major determinants of these vegetation patterns and of the life styles of the people of the region are climate and rain-fall. Lying between thirteen and fourteen degrees north latitude, the country has a climate that is truly tropical. Temperatures range between seventy and ninety-five degrees Fahrenheit during the humid summer and between fifty-five and eighty-five in the winter, when the wind comes down from the drier regions to the north and northeast. The average annual rainfall varies several inches from the Saloum River to the southern Gambian border and annual deviations from the norm are frequent, but speaking for the whole, the region lies in an east-west belt that receives between thirty and forty-five inches of rain each year. This is about as much as some of the most agriculturally productive parts of the American mid-west. But precipitation does not fall regularly throughout

the year as it does in Illinois or Wisconsin; it falls in four or
five months, no more, creating distinct wet and dry seasons. During the summer months of heavy rainfall the land is lush and the
savanna grasses are tall and green. After October, when it stops
raining for more than half a year, the land grows progressively
dryer. By April a coating of reddish dust covers grasses and the
leaves of trees, and small fires burn rapidly out of control.

Residents of the area adapt their lives to the seasonal pattern. In the wet summer they remain close to home, tending crops
and doing domestic chores. In the dry season, after harvesting,
they do their traveling, and it was in this period that *griots*
traveled among their patrons, singing the praise songs and reciting the traditions that provided them a livelihood.

At first glance it would appear that the lower Gambia region
is an area of extreme cultural diversity. Its population is a
mixture of no fewer than five different ethnic and linguistic
groups: Mandinka, Serer, Wolof, Fulbe, and Jola.

The largest ethnic group in the region is the Mandinka, the
westernmost portion of the large Sudanic ethnic and linguistic
group called the Manding which with Mandinka, Bambara, and Dyula
linguistic divisions probably consists of over ten million. Mandinka live throughout most of the lower Gambia and adjacent parts
of Senegal, and they inhabit an area southward through Guinea-
Bissau and Guinea.

Directly north of the Gambia's mouth and estuary, from the
Gambia-Senegal border northward through the region of the lower
Saloum River to one hundred miles or more beyond, live the Serer.
They moved into the area many centuries ago as part of a larger
north-to-south movement that brought Wolof and Fulbe out of the
Senegal River valley and into the better-watered regions of the
Senegambia.

The centuries-long habitation of the Wolof, and indeed where
most Wolof are found today, is the western portion of Senegal immediately north of the Serer or, roughly speaking, between Cape
Verde and the Senegal River. The center of the once-powerful
Jolof Empire was located in the eastern part of this Wolof area.
Today scattered Wolof settlements exist along the north bank of
the Gambia River about half-way up the length of the country, and
influence of the Wolof language and culture is noticeable in and
around Banjul and even more strongly in the vicinity of the upper
reaches of the Saloum River. But much of the spread of this influence has been a relatively recent phenomenon.

The Fulbe have long been a confusing element for West African
historians because they differ from most other West Africans in
physical characteristics, in that some Fulbe are sedentary agriculturalists and some are semi-nomadic pastoralists, and because

today they are spread across the Western Sudan from Senegal to Cameroun.[14] The pastoralist Fulbe lend a touch of ethnic confusion to the lower Senegambia as well because they live scattered among members of the numerically dominant ethnic groups mentioned above, where they practice their pastoral life style and maintain their ethnic identity. The agricultural Fulbe live along the middle Senegal River and in parts of eastern Senegal and beyond.

Finally, the Jola occupy part of the south bank of the extreme lower Gambia, between that river and the Casamance, for about seventy-five miles inland from the Atlantic. Only as one approaches Banjul and the region south of Cape St. Mary, where the capital's influence is felt most strongly, are Jola less prevalent than Mandinka along the river's lower south bank.

Yet in spite of the ethnic and linguistic diversity in the region, culturally and socially many of the people living there shared much in common. The basis of the economies of most of the area was agriculture. Millet formed the staple crop for Mandinka, Serer, and Wolof, though each grew different varieties in different ways. Along the Gambia, Mandinka women supplemented the diet with rice; Serer and Wolof grew cotton and some maize as well. Cattle to all three groups were of secondary importance. The Serer managed their own cows, keeping them in penned areas where they could fertilize areas that would become tomorrow's maize fields. The Mandinka and Wolof had Fulbe herdsmen care for their cattle, moving them north and south with the rains in a cycle of trans-humance. Members of these two groups relied more on letting fields lie fallow than on their animals' fertilizer to improve production. The growing of peanuts as a cash crop, which members of all three ethnic groups do today, was begun in the 1830s and grew in importance throughout the rest of the nineteenth and early twentieth centuries.

The Jola are agriculturalists, too, though they specialize in growing rice in their wetter, southern region. They are efficient cultivators. In places today they support a population of more than eight persons per square mile. Only the pastoral Fulbe deviate from the general agricultural pattern, and frequently they associate themselves with Mandinka, Serer, or Wolof farming communities, living in a state of symbiosis with the agriculturalists.

Holding together Mandinka, Serer, Wolof, and Fulbe society and lending unity to the wider Senegambian social and cultural region were a tripartite social structure and strong kinship relations. Where Jola came into heaviest contact with Mandinka they, too, were influenced by this social organization. Freemen, artisans, and slaves were the three major class divisions throughout much of the Western Sudan. Philip Curtin explains the relationships among the divisions:

> In a broad sense, the three major divisions
> were a hierarchy of rank, but wealth, status,
> and power did not line up neatly in the ranked
> order. Many finer lines and divisions could ex-
> ist within any of the three divisions, so that
> in fact they overlapped. Those who were best
> off in either of the lower groups, in terms of
> wealth, status, and power, were better off
> than the lowest ranks of free men.[15]

In many areas ruling lineages of warriors set themselves apart
from the rest of society to the extent that they formed an elite
surclass among themselves, making the remaining freemen a second,
lesser rank below them. Among the Mandinka these ruling lineages
were called *mansakunda*; from them came the *mansa*, the rulers, of
the states.

Uniting persons in different parts of the Senegambia, giving
individuals the framework for their own identity, and providing a
measure of the sense of unity that tied together the various ethnic
groups was kinship. Mandinka normally traced their kinship patri-
lineally, whereas pre-Islamic Serer, Wolof, and Fulbe were matrilineal. The largest common descent group, called a clan, included
all persons with the same surname who traced their ancestry to the
same person. Usually members of the same clan were of the same
ethnic group, but in places where intermarriage brought widespread
mixing, members of the different groups shared surnames. The geographically dispersed clans were much too broad to be effective
social units; the effective units were made up of relatives living
together in the same village in extended families. An extended
family had a leader, usually the eldest male member, who presided
over social and religious rites, mediated differences, and over-
saw collection and redistribution of income.

The similarity of institutions among the major ethnic groups
of the Senegambia had profound effects upon the history of the
region, especially on the ease of movement of peoples and on the
widespread mixing of peoples there over the centuries. Class and
status seem to have played more important roles than ethnicity in
the establishment of settlements, interpersonal relations, and
intermarriage. The only restriction on marriage seems clearly to
have been one of class: a Mandinka freeman would only marry a
"free" person from any ethnic group, an artisan would only marry
another artisan, and so on. Members of the different groups did
intermarry on a wide scale, and this intermarriage and the subsequent mixture of ethnic groups seems to have been a key element
in the development and long-term stability of political institutions in the area.[16]

The Historical Setting

Studies of the history of the western portion of the Western Sudan have long conentrated on the large Sahelian and Sudanic Empires, Ghana and Mali. The former, centered in what is now the southeastern part of Mauritania, was a creation of people called Sarakolle. Ghana existed from the middle centuries of the first millennium A.D., down into the early centuries of the second, with some hiatuses and one notable period of conquest. It embraced a horizontal stretch of the Sahel thereby controlling and rationalizing the trade of gold out of the Buré gold fields on the upper Senegal into the trans-Saharan trade. Mali succeeded Ghana, though not directly, increasing in importance as merchants opened sources of gold further south toward the edge of West Africa's rainforests. From the thirteenth to the seventeenth centuries, with the peak of its influence seemingly in the fourteenth century, this Mandinka state with its center on the upper reaches of the Niger River, the traditional Mandinka homelands, dominated a considerable amount of the Western Sudan. At its height its control in some form reached the Atlantic coast between the Gambia and Senegal Rivers. Therefore, it is necessary to view at least part of the early history of the Senegambia with the influence of these large, powerful empires, Mali especially, in mind.[17]

The precolonial history of the lower Gambia-Saloum River region that historians so far have been able to reconstruct is largely the history of extensive population movement and mixing and the formation of long-standing political units. The leadership of these states came to dominate social, economic, and political events in the area into the nineteenth century.

It is not possible to tell much about the earliest people who lived in the lower Gambia beyond the facts that their numbers were small and their social structures were similar to those of other savanna dwellers. But from the beginning of the second millennium there clearly seem to have been two important general movements of population into the Senegambia along two axes. Serer, Wolof, and Fulbe moved southward from the Senegal River valley, fleeing the combined threats of Berber pastoralists and marginal agricultural conditions in their homelands. By the thirteenth century their migrations had taken them into the lands where one finds them today. Beginning even earlier, Mandinka hunters, farmers, and traders moved west out of their upper Niger River homelands and pushed along the extension of the savanna. They settled in villages near the Atlantic north of the Gambia, along the middle and upper Gambia, and between the upper Casamance and Gêba Rivers. The peoples indigenous to these areas accepted them, valuing their symbiotic relationships. Continual contact with Mandinka hunters and traders from the Mandinka homelands allowed the Mandinka language, life style, and cultural traditions to persist. Then, following Mali's emergence in the thirteenth century, still more

Mandinka--this time ambitious warriors with their families and
retainers as well as more hunters, farmers, and traders--moved
west and increased Mandinka influence among other peoples.

In the region of the upper Casamance, Cacheu, and Gêba Rivers
where Mandinka influence was initially more pervasive, Mandinka
hunters and warriors combined with different groups in the area
to form a ruling-warrior elite called the *nyancho*. Adopting mores
and customs based upon those of Mandinka hunters' association, the
nyancho glorified ritualistic "macho" behavior, adherence to animist
(as opposed to Islamic) regligious practices, expert horsemanship,
warfare and, above all, attainment of leadership (*mansaya*) over
a Mandinka-type state. By what was probably the early fourteenth
century *nyancho* began providing *mansa*--rulers--for the state of
Kabu, which later became one of the largest and most influential
of all the western Mandinka states.

The *nyancho* not only dominated life in Kabu; they came to
have a strong influence, direct and indirect, on populations living throughout most of southwestern Senegambia. From the fourteenth
century *nyancho* and their relatives, frustrated by the impossibi-
lity for all ambitious warriors to achieve political rule in one
of the sub-states of Kabu and lured by reports of growing trade
and opportunities for conquest in the lower Gambia and nearby
coastal regions, moved north and west, conquered, mixed, and
intermarried with peoples already settled, thus populating parts
of the area between Kabu and the Saloum River. Mixed Mandinka-
Serer (and other) families resulting from this population movement eventually formed the states of Siin, Saloum, Niumi, Baddibu,
Jarra, Kiang, Fogny, and Kombo. In the northernmost area, in Siin
and Saloum, where *nyancho* and other Mandinka were small in numeri-
cal comparison to the Serer, the result was the grafting of the
nyancho surclass (called *guelowar* in Siin and Saloum) and Mandinka
state structure onto what remained otherwise Serer (or Serer-Wolof)
societies. South of the Gambia, in Fogny and to a lesser extent
in Kombo, the strong Jola presence cast its form upon the societies that emerged, though again the Mandinka state structure took
shape. But along the rest of the lower Gambia, in Niumi, Baddibu,
Jarra, and Kiang, populations of mixed heritage but speaking
Mandinka and following what was basically the Mandinka culture
and life style, joined other Mandinka states farther upriver
and to the southwest to form a solid arm of Mandinka social and
political units reaching westward from the Mandinka homelands
to the Atlantic.

Because of the *nyancho*-Mandinka influence upon their formation, the states of the lower Gambia-Saloum River region had a
great deal in common. At the head of the state was a single individual, the *mansa* (called the *bur* in Siin and Saloum). In the
predominantly Serer states in the north a council representing
the most important lineages in the state selected the ruler, but
among the more heavily Mandinka states along the Gambia (with
few exceptions in the states farthest upriver) leadership of the
state (*mansaya*) was rotated in what was ordinarily a fixed order

among several "royal" lineages (*mansakunda*) living in the state. In none of the states was the *mansa* omnipotent. He had to consult a council on major decisions and if things did not go well he could be deposed. Where the rotational system of succession functioned *mansa* tended to have short reigns. Rivalry was great and intrigue among contenders for rule was common.

In the state of Niumi, the primary subject of many of the interviews in these two volumes, seven branches of three different lineages rotated *mansaya* among themselves. Two branches of the Jammeh lineage, a family of mixed Serer-Mandinka heritage; two of the Manneh, a lineage with Kabu-Mandinka roots; and three of the Sonko, another basically Mandinka lineage whose ancestors came from Kabu, were Niumi's *mansakunda*. Male members of the *mansakunda* adopted something of the *nyancho* life style. They rode horses, raided other people, and dominated the other lineages in their states to the extent possible. And, importantly the *mansakunda* of Niumi had widely-ranging links through marriage. They remained closely tied to the leadership of Baddibu and Jarra through clan ties—a Jammeh lineage in Baddibu and a Sonko lineage in Jarra shared *mansaya* in each state with other lineages—and they solidified these relationships with appropriate marriages. But Niumi's *mansakunda* were careful to maintain marriage ties with all of their neighbors. Different ones of Niumi's *mansakunda* regularly married sons or daughters into specific important families in Siin, Saloum, Kiang, Fogny, and Kombo, and they married an occasional family member into a ruling family of Kabu. As noted, the reciprocity such marriage ties entailed lent political and social stability to the entire region.

Of course, the political stability was occasionally disturbed when one state or another found the wherewithal to conquer others and levy some sort of tribute on the conquered peoples. The Wolof state of Jolof, centered in central Senegal, took on imperial characteristics some time before Europeans came to West Africa. When the first Portuguese arrived, Jolof may have controlled much of the land along the north bank of the Gambia River, between there and the Senegal River, or much of the present country of Senegal. Saloum, too, collected tribute from Niumi and Baddibu from time to time, and Kabu held political authority over many of the states along the Gambia's south bank and southward from there during what may have been a long period of time. But the European presence along the Atlantic coast and up the major rivers enabled rulers of nearby states to improve their positions through trade and thereby to gain the power to exert their independence.

The first Europeans in the lower Gambia were Portuguese mariners who in the mid-fifteenth century hoped to begin a lively shipboard trade. However, against the wishes of the Portuguese Crown, shipboard trading gave way to Portuguese settlement on the coast and along the estuaries of navigable rivers, and these settlers mixed with the local populations to form a hybrid group of Afro-Portuguese. Commercial specialists, comfortable in two cultures, these people became important intermediaries in the waxing African-European commerce. These Afro-Portuguese and their descendants remained prominent in the Gambian commercial realm through most of the eighteenth century.

Following the Portuguese came English and French merchants, hopeful participants in the trade of slaves, gold, cowhides, bees-wax, and ivory. Unlike the Portuguese, the English and French set up trading posts on or near the Atlantic coast where they could store their trade goods, hold slaves, and generally marshal the trade of the surrounding area. From the mid-seventeenth century the English manned a post on James Island in the middle of the Gambia River off Niumi's sourthern river bank and they frequently had agents living in Juffure on Niumi soil near the island. Soon thereafter French merchants established a post at Albreda, near Juffure, in an attempt to stretch their influence, already firm in the Saloum River area and at several points along the Atlantic coast northward, to the Gambia. Notwithstanding periods of forced absence, the English and French maintained these posts and con-ducted a brisk trade in the region into the nineteenth century. In 1816 the British government built Bathurst (now Banjul) near the Gambia's mouth as an initial step to close off the river to other European merchants and to halt the slave trade. In 1856 the French ceded Albreda to the English as the latter's influence grew gradually along the Gambia until the official take over of the entire colony in the last decade of the nineteenth century.

The *mansakunda* of the Gambian states were long participants in the trade with Europeans, and while they prospered they grew dependent upon its revenues. Change in the nature of this trade and the subsequent loss of revenue for the *mansakunda* would account in part for the gradual decline of the states' influence and the institution of *mansaya*. Throughout most of the precolonial period the *mansakunda* had remained staunch upholders of their traditional, pre-Islamic animist faith, but they permitted Muslim clerical lineages to reside autonomously within the state, controlling a village and nearby agricultural land. The clerics practiced Islam and frequently used their Islamic magic to assist the *mansakunda*, particularly in warfare. By the early nineteenth century there were a number of these enclaves in the Gambian states. When the British halted the slave trade the *mansakunda* were deprived of an important source of revenue; when the British followed by encourag-ing the growth and sale of peanuts for cash after 1830 Muslims and other non-royal lineages of freemen found a new source for revenue for themselves; and as the British and French sold firearms to those with cash, who were increasingly the growers of peanuts, the potential for rebellion grew. A period of general disorder in mid-century made many residents of the states dissatisfied with their *mansa* and the traditional system of leadership. Rallying around select Muslim clerics, the dissatisfied elements revolted and fought a series of wars, the Soninke-*Marabout* Wars, which culminated in the 1860s in Niumi and Baddibu and somewhat later in other states. Although the British intervened to shore up some *mansa*, what *mansakunda* that remained in authority did so in name only. The last *mansa* of Niumi held his position into the twentieth century, but even before his death in 1911 the British had established colonial government in the form of a Chief for Niumi. Prior to this the French had supplanted traditional authority in the states of Siin and Saloum. By the beginning of the twentieth century the centuries-long authority of the traditional rulers in the states of the lower Gambia-Saloum River area was over.

By necessity, this is a brief, probably overly simplified, introduction into the complex history of this part of the Senegamiba. It should not serve to do more than acquaint readers with the main lines of historical development in the region so they can understand better the oral traditions that follow. For those who wish to pursue the subject further, I will include a relevant bibliographical essay at the end of the second volume.[18]

FOOTNOTES

[1] In *Oral Tradition: A Study in Historical Methodology* (Chicago, 1965), pp. 19-20, Jan Vansina defines oral traditions as follows:

> Oral traditions consist of all verbal testimonies which
> are reported statements concerning the past. This defi-
> nition implies that nothing but *oral* traditions--that is
> to say, statements either spoken or sung--enter into
> consideration. . . .It further indicates that not all
> oral sources are oral traditions, but only those which
> are reported statements--that is, sources which have
> been transmitted from one person to another through
> the medium of language. Eyewitness accounts, even
> when given orally, do not come within the sphere of
> tradition because they are not *reported* statements.
> Oral traditions exclusively consist of hearsay accounts,
> that is, testimonies that narrate an event which has not
> been witnessed and remembered by the informant himself,
> but which he has learnt about through hearsay.

[2] The word *griot* is generally thought to be a European corruption of *gewel*, which is the word Wolof speakers in Senegal use for the individuals in their society who are the traditional bards and professional oral historians.

[3] Donald R. Wright, "Niumi: The History of a Western Mandinka State Through the Eighteenth Century," Ph.D. dissertation, Indiana University, 1976.

[4] Jan Vansina, *De la tradition orale: Essai de méthode historique* (Tervuren, 1961); Colin Newbury, " A review of Vansina, *De la tradition orale*," *Journal of African History*, III (1962), pp. 513-514.

[5] Jan Vansina, *Kingdoms of the Savanna* (Madison, 1966); examples of such recent studies are Joseph C. Miller, *Kings and Kinsmen: Early Mbundu States in Angola* (Oxford, 1976); Steven Feierman, *The Shambaa Kingdom* (Madison, 1974); and John Lamphear, *The Traditional History of the Jie of Uganda* (Oxford, 1976).

[6] Members of the staff of Indiana's Archives of Traditional Music have published a catalogue of the Center's oral data holdings. See Ruth M. Stone and Frank J. Gillis, *African Music and Oral Data: A Catalog of Field Record-ings, 1902-1975* (Bloomington, Indiana, 1976).

[7] Philip D. Curtin, "Field Techniques for Collecting and Processing Oral Data," *Journal of African History*, IX (1968), pp. 367-385.

[8] We had to be careful, however, about references to downright famous *griot*s living in Banjul or even Dakar, the capital and major city in Senegal. *Griot*s of such fame invariably spoke on any subject with all of their authority but not with a great amount of knowledge.

[9]I do not mean to suggest that there is anything wrong with the more direct question-and-answer method. In fact, a good friend of mine, Tom Hunter, who was studying the transmission of Islamic learning among a group of people in The Gambia at the same time I was carrying out my field work, relied solely on this method, never using a tape recorder but simply writing down in his own kind of shorthand notes on the answers to his questions as his interpreter translated. Hunter got the data he was seeking just as I did. To use his method most effectively, he had to know a number of specific questions that would lead in the appropriate direction for his research. I did not always know such questions ahead of time and I never overcame my desire to get the narrator to say what he wished to say. Consequently. I never reached the point where I would interrupt an informant's talking so my interpreter could translate for me.

[10]This is not the place nor am I the person to write a lengthy discourse on the nature of African oral traditions. It is good that such writing has already been done. Those interested in reading more extensively on oral traditions and the methodology appropriate for using traditions for historical research should consult Vansina, and David Henige, *The Chronology of Oral Tradition: Quest for a Chimera* (Oxford, 1974). Chapter three of Daniel F. McCall, *Africa in Time Perspective* (Boston, 1964) is a concise treatment of the historical use of oral traditions.

[11]Those interested in reading an attempt I made to separate myth from history can examine my study of the Jammeh clan in *The Early History of Niumi: Settlement and Foundation of a Mandinka State on the Gambia River* (Papers in International Studies, Africa Series No. 32, Athens, Ohio, 1977), pp. 41-46. It might be instructive to read something of the Jammeh traditions of origin in the Unus Jata and Abdoulie Samba interviews that follow and then to read the above passage, which is my analysis of these traditions and discussion of the early history of the Jammeh clan.

[12]I discuss evidence of this change and why I believe it took place in "Koli Tengela in Sonko Traditions of Origin: An Example of the Process of Change in Mandinka Oral Tradition," *History in Africa*, V (1978), pp. 257-271.

[13]Though I have not been back to The Gambia since publication of Alex Haley's *Roots* in 1976, I would feel confident in gambling that there are persons all over the lower Gambia who are willing and able to recite the story of Kunta Kinte much as Haley wrote the story.

[14]The most thorough discussion of who the Fulbe are and how they came to inhabit such a wide area of the Western Sudan is in Philip D. Curtin, *Economic Change in Precolonial Africa: Senegambia in the Era of the Slave Trade* (Madison, 1975), pp. 13-22.

[15]Ibid., p. 30.

[16]From early in my study of the western Mandinka I was impressed by the general stability of their Senegambian states. Most of the states existed from at least as early as 1500 down through the nineteenth century. As I searched for keys to this stability, the one factor I continually found was mutual interest based upon marriage ties. The ruling lineages of Niumi, for example,

could rely upon the rulers of Baddibu to come to Niumi's aid in times of need because Niumi's ruling families had strategically married their sons and daughters into important families in Baddibu. In a sense, a threat to Baddibu was a threat to Niumi. and vice versa. And these marriage alliances spread far beyond these two contiguous states. A plot of all the marriage links among the lower Gambian states, if such were possible to construct, would look like a spider web and, indeed. the alliances served to bond the area together much as the links of a web hold together the longer strands. The area was truly a social and cultural unit, the individual states being autonomous parts of the large whole.

[17]The best general source of information on Ghana and Mali is Nehemiah Levtzion, *Ancient Ghana and Mali* (London, 1973).

[18]For those who do not have the second volume, good starting points for learning more of the precolonial history of the lower Senegambia are Curtin, *Economic Change*; my *Early History of Niumi*; or Jean Boulègue, "La Sénégambie du milieu du xve siècle au debut du xviie siècle," Ph.D. dissertation, third cycle, University of Paris, 1968.

UNUS JATA

THREE INTERVIEWS: September 7, 1974, January 7, 1975, January 14, 1975.

GENERAL SUBJECT MATTER:

1. Early settlement of Niumi (in a set narrative).
2. Questions and answers about political, social, and economic conditions in precolonial Niumi.
3. Same as 2.

LOCATION OF RECORDING: Indiana University Archives of Traditional Music, Access numbers 4357, 4381, and 4382.

The Informant. Seventy-eight years old, tall, stately, very black, Unus Jata is the only practicing member of a traditional Mandinka *jali* (*griot*) family with any primary association with the former Mandinka state of Niumi. For untold generations the Jata family provided *griot*s for the Sonko clan of Niumi. When Unus Jata became the family patriarch in 1951 he moved across the Gambia River to the village of Sanyang, where land for growing peanuts was better and more available than around their longtime residence in Berending. For twenty-three years Jata and some of his sons grew and sold peanuts, though Jata remained a practicing *griot* by making annual dry-season excursions around the lower Gambia, singing praises and telling stories for families requesting his services. The Sonko family of Berending always kept him there for several weeks or longer to provide various traditional services, to reacquaint family members with their history and folklore, and to entertain.

In early 1975, as he realized he was getting too old to be working actively in the peanut fields, Jata acquiesced to the wishes of the Sonko family and re-settled in Berending. He built a new compound on the very eastern edge of Berend-ing, somewhat separated from most of the Berending compounds as tradition dictated. From this new location he found himself better able to provide for himself and his family by performing the duties of a Mandinka *griot*.

The Interviews. The first interview--indeed, my first formal interview after my arrival in Africa--took place in Jata's compound in Sanyang, Kombo District, The Gambia on September 7, 1974. B. K. Sidibe and several others had told me about Jata; I went to seek him out.

The circumstances of this interview were unique, as it turned out would be the circumstances surrounding each interview I had with this man. Accompanied by Sidibe and Binta Jammeh, I entered the Jata compound in Sanyang and found Jata's eldest son there. He is a salesman of plastic sandals in Sanyang and sometimes in Banjul. This is indicative of what is happening to *griot*s' information and tales. Traditionally, the eldest son would be an apprentice to his father, learn-ing the entire repertoire so the traditions could be continued. However, in many parts of Africa today because of rapid and far-reaching social and economic change, the sons have different values and goals than their fathers and they go about reaching these goals in different ways. As a consequence, there are fewer and

fewer practicing *griot*s and oral traditions are becoming increasingly rare. Indeed, when Unus Jata dies, his traditions will not be passed on. The son said
his father was working in the fields and he agreed to take us there, about a mile
outside of town. In the heat of the morning, which must have been around ninety
degrees and very humid, we found Jata at work. Following introductions, Sidibe
told Jata what I wished to have him do, which was to tell me what he knew of the
early history of Niumi. Since a *griot* is normally compensated for his services,
Jata wanted to be paid. We eventually agreed upon a one and one-half hour recorded interview, for which I would pay twenty *dalasies*, or about twelve dollars.

In agreement, we returned to Jata's compound and began the interview. It con-
sisted of a narrative of the settling and foundation of Niumi, mostly folklore
with a thin core of historical truth, which Jata recited by rote. (Interestingly,
at Sidibe's prompting, a Gambian student had recorded Jata's narrative several
years earlier, and translations of the two turned out to be nearly identical.)
After forty-five minutes of Jata's narration I had to stop him momentarily to invert my cassette. I mentioned that we were roughly half done. To my surprise,
Jata refused to continue. He said he wanted to consult some of his written material
to jog his memory and would continue at another session later in the week. Sens-
ing Jata's displeasure about something, Sidibe suggested I give him the entire sum
of twenty *dalasies*. I did, and we left. Then, for the next four months, Jata refused to grant me another interview. It was not until January 1975, after I had
plied him with small gifts and gotten several friends of mine and several of his
patrons in Berending to intervene on my behalf, that he consented to a second interview and that I learned just why he refused to talk for so long a time. In the
initial interview, Jata, speaking rapidly as he normally does, narrated nearly his
entire set piece of information. This was something he was sure would take much
longer than forty-five minutes, though, in fact, it had not. When I stopped at the
half-way point to invert my cassette, Jata immediately sensed he was being tricked,
and he decided to halt the proceedings. Only after he was convinced that I was not
dishonest did he consent to another interview.

The first interview, then, consists of Jata's set narrative of Niumi's early history,
cut short by perhaps one-fourth. It took place in Jata's compound in a small, dark
room with five of us--Sidibe, Binta Jammeh, Jata, Jata's son, and myself--sitting close
together. The second and third interviews contain Jata's answers to my questions.
By the time of these latter interviews I had obtained quite a bit of information
from other sources, oral and written, and I wanted Jata to comment upon the things
I thought I knew. The second interview took place in the large compound of Imam
Ibrahimo Njie, the Muslim religious leader of Berending and one of Jata's patrons.
Several of the most important younger residents of Berending were in attendance,
listening and reacting to the things Jata said. The third interview, a week later,
was held in the open compound of the *Alkali* (village head) of Kanuma, a village
seven miles from Berending, where Jata was visiting. About twenty people of all
ages stood around and listened, seeming to approve of and enjoy what Jata was saying.

B. K. Sidibe served as social intermediary and interpreter for each of these interviews. Binta Jammeh translated each into English within a week of the interview.
Jata spoke in Mandinka.

Jata: I am seventy-eight years of age this year. I was born in Berending in Niumi. I came to settle in Kombo here twenty-three years
ago. My grandfather came from Kahon, in Senegal. He came to settle at Nioro Mamundaring. They left Nioro Mamundaring and moved
to Kular; then they left Kular and came to settle at Berending.
That was how they came to live with and become part-related to
the Sonko.[1] Our grandfather who came was called Wanige. Wanige
begot Yate, Yate begot Jokoi, Jokoi begot Karafa, and Karafa
begot Ass.

Q: Who was the *mansa* in Niumi when your grandfather came?

Jata: Koli Tengela was *mansa*. Our ancestors came with Koli Tengela.
Koli Tengela found our grandfather living in Senegal, and they
came with him to Niumi. When Koli Tengela came to Niumi, Bakindiki was the only town settled there. That Bakindiki was founded
by Sora Musa, but the Wolof were their overlords, collecting tribute from them. Kahon was the capital of the Wolof country. The
ruler of Saloum was Ndena Njie. The ruler of Kasing[2] was Wali
Jumung. Those were the two ruling in Siin and Saloum at the time.
They were overlords of Niumi because they were receiving tribute
from the *mansa* of Niumi.

Sora Musa was the first *soninke*[3] prince[4] to go to Mecca. He
spent three years there. This was before he settled in Niumi.
He went to Mecca[5] and when he arrived there they asked him,
"Are you a Muslim or a *soninke*?"

"I am a *soninke*," he said.

They asked, "Why have you come here?"

"I have come for my own business," he answered.

He spent three years there; then they released him and asked him
to return to his country, telling him that when he returned he
would not be defeated at war. He left Mecca and came to Mali
and found Sundiata Keita[6] ruling their.

In those days, when the women spoiled their sons,[7] the rulers
used to be able to predict what would happen in each period.
Whatever they predicted happened according to their predictions.
Sundiata said to Sora Musa, "My father's blacksmith, Susu
Sumanguru,[8] was entrusted this country when my father died. He
then refused to surrender the country to the sons of my father.
I want you to help us kill him and remove him. When he is gone
I shall take you to the house of all our fetishes. You can
wash yourself with all the fetish and secret waters there."[9]

30

They combined and fought against Susu Sumanguru until they killed him. Then Sundiata took Sora Musa to every fetish that belonged to him and washed him with all the secret waters. After that, Sora Musa was so powerful that whenever he took a single straw and planted it, it would grow into a fetish.

When Sora Musa left Mali and came west, it was Baddibu Iliassa[10] that he first built. When he had settled Iliassa, he left there and came to found Bakindiki. When he had built Bakindiki, he moved from there and founded the village of Juwala. It was he who built all of these. They all belong to Sora Musa.[11]

In Niumi the first *mansa* was Mama Adame. When she died Mansa Wame took over. When she died Mansa Kuru succeeded her. Then Karoko succeeded her; then Jeke; then Kabule; then Yaidi; then Kabulyadi Ngongirant; then Bakijuwana; then Kalamakoi; and then Musa Mama Ndang. They were all *mansa* of Bakindiki.[12]

Koli Tengela left Denya.[13] He came with a nine-cornered hat and a pair of trousers called *bibirikin*. The hat had nine different colors. They made it in the shape of a *mansa*'s hat, but it had nine corners and was made of cotton cloth. That was their symbol of leadership. When he left Denya he came to the land of the Wolof. He found a baobab tree there which had nine branches. It had no branch going straight up into the sky. It had a bat living in the hollow of its trunk, and the bat talked like a human being. There was also a pot at the tree which had just enough cooked food in it for every person, infant or adult. Everyone received food according to the size of his appetite. There was also a pot there which contained water, and that pot was equal to the first in that it had just enough water for every person, even an infant. Even if an adult wanted to wash his clothes, that pot would contain enough water for it.

When Koli Tengela arrived at the cotton tree, he declared, "I have come to my country."

The bat in the hollow of the tree poked his head out and said, "I do not deny your claim of having found a country, but whatever country you have found, it has an owner."

Koli Tengela asked, "How many rulers have been crowned here in your time?"

The bat replied, "Mansa Hun[14] was made ruler in my time here. He was a Wolof. Mansa Ha was appointed ruler of this country. He was a Wolof. Mansa Sintang was appointed ruler here in my time. He was a Wolof. Mansa Dondoli was appointed ruler here in my time. He was a Wolof. And also Mansa Monikandi Sumanyabali was appointed here in my time."

Koli got his men and they built a temporary shelter around the tree. Under the branches of the tree they cut out gates for each of their shelters. Under each branch of the baobab tree they made a door. But they built nine rooms in each of the shelters and they built nine beds in each of the rooms. On each of those beds nine adults slept.[15] Each had a horn with powder[16] in it and a bag containing shot, and the water container had a sword in it. That was how Koli Tengela came to this country.

Koli Tengela found a descendant of Sora Musa ruling called Mansa Wame. She was the first daughter of Sora Musa. She was living with her people. After spending three days there, Koli and his followers began to walk around to explore. They found the woman *mansa* and her people and said, "Behold, we have hosts in this country. We did not realize that we had hosts so we spent three nights living under the baobab tree."

The next day they returned to the woman *mansa* and her people. The following day they went again in the morning to greet her. The woman, therefore, decided that they should return their visit, saying,"Let us go and visit the Fula."[17]

When the woman and her followers arrived, they asked Koli's people what their surnames were. They replied, "We are called Bah."[18] They went to see them because they said the Sonko had spent three nights under the baobab tree and had visited them on three different occasions. They felt they should return the visit or else they would be impolite. After their coming, every morning they came to greet us. "Let us go and pay them a visit let us go and greet them," they said. That was how they left and went to meet their visitors under the baobab tree. That was Mama Andame and her followers. This was the daughter of Sora Musa.[19]

When they got there and saw how many they were, they were a little afraid, but they greeted them. They asked, "What are your surnames?"

They answered, "Our surname is Bah."

The queen said, "No, your surname is not Bah, it is 'Sonkalakore'--a group of quarrelsome people."

This remark of the Jammeh[20] that they were Sonkalakore was how their surname was changed from Bah to Sonko. But originally their surname was Bah.[21]

Koli Tengela was begot by Tengela, and Tengela was begot by Banna. Banna was begot by Yande. Yelda was the ancestor of all these people.

Q: Where did they come from?

Jata: They came from Denya.

Q: In what country is Denya today?

Jata: It is in Tilebo.[22]

Q: Would that be Mali or Guinea?

Jata: I do not know. In the book it says they came from Tilebo.
Mansa Wame said, "When you are settling in a land and another
comes there to live with you, you should tell him who you are
and what you are and how you came to live in that country, so
he will know how to fit into the situation. This is better
than inviting someone to live on the same land with you without explaining under what conditions they could be living.
These are large thoughts."[23]

For this reason, Mansa Wame's people returned to the Sonko
and said, "We have been living here; now we are your hosts;
but we must explain to you that the Wolof are collecting
tribute from us each year. It is a bundle of grass that we
take to them each year in the form of taxes."[24]

The Sonko replied, "We, too, can live in that condition. When
you go to a country and find them all hopping on one leg, you,
too, must hang up one of your legs. Whatever befalls them will
befall you, too. We agree to do what you do."

They did as the Jammeh for three years, and then they said to
them, "We came with our own leader, as rulers. We found you
with your own leader here. If you would agree to rotate leadership[25] with us--that is, if you would let us put on the shoe
that you take off--we would put an end to the yearly tribute
payment that you make to the Wolof."

The Jammeh agreed to this condition. They asked, "Can you truly
stop it?"

The Sonko replied in the affirmative.

Koli Tengela said to them, "When they come again to collect the
tax, tell them: 'It is a donkey that carries loads. We are
not donkeys. Humans do not carry loads.'"

They waited until the season for collecting tribute had come.
Then the Niuminka[26] did not collect grass to take to the Wolof
as was customary. The Wolof waited and waited and saw no sign
of them. They were surprised and they said, "Why have they not
come to pay their annual tribute? Have they forgotten that they
must bring grass?"

The Wolof sent a message to the *mansa* of Niumi. The *mansa* replied, "Tell them that it is the donkey that carries. Humans
do not carry loads."

The messenger returned and reported to the *bur*[27] of Saloum,
Ndena Njie, what had been said to him. Ndena Njie said to the
messenger, "You are lying. Are you so afraid of the strangers
who have joined them that you come back to us without even giving them our message?"

He sent another messenger. When the second messenger arrived,
the Niumi *mansa* told him, "Tell them that it is a donkey that
carries; people do not carry loads. We are tired of carrying
loads for them."

The second messenger returned and said, "The Mandinka have revolted and have refused. They said it is the donkey that carries loads; people do not carry loads."

The *bur* said, "You are lying also. You are afraid as well."

He sent a third messenger and this time Koli Tengela said to the Jammeh, "Wait! I must do something to this messenger so they will believe him. Once it was customary to send three messengers before anyone would believe it. Bring him here."

When the messenger came, he was asked to sit down. Koli Tengela took a knife from the sheath tied around his waist. He cut the messenger's ear from one side, cutting right under the chin, up to the second ear on the other side. He cut off the second ear, too, and also one of his fingers, and then he told him to return, because now they would believe that he would not do this to himself.

The messenger returned to the Wolof and said to them, "I need not tell you anything. You can see for yourself what they have done to me. If you send another messenger, they will kill him. Now you know that the Mandinka have revolted because no one would cut himself the way I am cut up--like this."

The Wolof said, "You are right."

They got ready to fight in this revolution. It was a very curious battle. Eventually they took the Wolof out of the country, across the river.

Q: Who was the ruler of the Wolof at this time? In which village in Saloum did he rule?[28]

Jata: In Siin.[29]

Q: Was he in Siin or Saloum?

Jata: He was living in Saloum. That is how it is written in the book.

Q: But they were two different states, weren't they, Siin and Saloum?

Jata: Yes, they were different countries, but they had a common border and they had much in common. Ndena Njie was the brother of Chukuma Njie. Chukuma Njie was his sister. Fatumang was also his sister. They were bordering with Kasing. Siin Saloum bordered with Kasing. It was Siin Saloum that fought against Koli Tengela. When they took them across the river my great grandfather said to him, "Fula, have peace. No man can be master of two *bantaba*.[30] The Wolof have escaped you."

He returned to Niumi and they made peace between them and the state of war between them ceased. He replied that he was willing for them to be friends again and to stop the war between them.[31]

The Wolof had a meeting among themselves and decided that they must pursue ways of dealing with this problem so that the position might return to what it was before the revolution. They wanted the Niuminka to remain as their subjects and continue to pay them tribute. They decided upon a plan which was to marry one of the *bur*'s sisters to the Chief of the Sonko, Koli Tengela. That would mark the end of hostility between them.[32] This was done, and when the formalities were over, the Wolof instructed the woman to observe her new husband's method of conducting war and to inform them as to how to fight them. When this was done they would prepare to fight them. They said to her, "This is the reason we are marrying you to him."

When the woman was given to Koli Tengela, he brought her to Bankere[33] and settled under the baobab tree. In those days all the men grew great big tufts of hair on their heads. It was not plaited. When the Wolof woman came to Bankere and observed this practice, she said to her husband, "You look like every one of your followers. You all have this great big tuft of hair. Let me plait your hair so that you will look different from them. When visitors come to your town they will know who is the leader. As it is, you all have the same hair style and you look alike. Nobody would know you unless you were pointed out to them."

Koli Tengela's men thought that was a good idea. They declared that on Friday they would plait their leader's hair so that he would look different. The plaiting was to take place under the baobab tree at the center of town. Koli's Wolof wife sent word to her brother, informing him that on Friday everyone would be gathered under the baobab tree for the plaiting of their leader's hair. She said, "You must wait until mid-morning and then come. When you come they will all have gathered under the tree and you can get into the village and fight them before they realize what is happening. You could thus overcome them."

The Wolof agreed to her plan and got ready.

That night, prior to the plaiting of the hair, Koli Tengela's wife got up, took a knife, and cut deeply into Koli Tengela's horse's bridle strap until very thin strings supported the bridle bit. She left a piece which was not strong enough to hold the bridle together. She also took the saddle and cut strips that tied the saddle to the horse. Then she went to Koli Tengela's trousers, which he would put on, and took the knife and cut deeply into the strings that he used to tie and hold them up. Only a small piece held the string together. Then she went to bed.

In the morning they went under the tree to plait Koli Tengela's hair. Everyone gathered there. She began by dividing his hair into three patches, one on each side with a tuft in the center. She plaited one side and completed it. She began plaiting the

other side. She heard no noise of a battle in the village.
There was no sign of her brother's approach, so she turned
the head to the side she had done. When she had loosened it
and started plaiting back again, her brother's army arrived
in the village and started fighting. Koli Tengela's Fula
slave came running and said, "Koli Tengela, you are lying
down but the Wolof have taken your town. They have arrived
with a large force."[34]

Koli Tengela shook his head from his wife's grasp, saying,
"Let loose of my head."

The woman said, "No, remain and let me finish plaiting your
hair." She held on to the tuft of his hair and would not let
go.[35]

He said, "Let go of my hair."

She said, "No, lie down and let me finish plaiting your hair."

Koli Tengela got angry and shook his head to free himself. Bees
flew out of his nose, ears, and mouth. They stung the woman and
killed her. Koli got up and ran into his house to put on his
trousers. When he had put one foot in the trousers he tried to
lift it up so as to put in the second foot, but the string broke,
so he pulled the trousers off. He tied two ends of a country
cloth[36] he had around him in the form of a trouser. He took his
juju belt[37] and tied it over the country cloth. He then leaped
forward and seized the bridle strap and put the bit into the
horse's mouth. When he tried to pull it off, the leather of
the bridle strap broke. He took the bridle strap off the
horse and threw it away. Then he went to get the saddle. As
he tried to tie the saddle onto the horse the strips broke
and he left that also. He jumped on his horse without bridle
or saddle and fell upon the enemy. He drove them away. Again
they drove them up to the river and crossed it. When he began
to pursue the Wolof across the river, our great grandfather said
to him, "Return, no man can be master of two *bantaba*. The Wolof
have escaped you."[38]

Koli was unable to bear it, so he took the saddle which he had
abandoned and threw it into the river and began to swim across.
When he was crossing his *griot* said to him, "Great Fula, please
return. No man can be master of two *bantaba*."

As he tried to swim back across the river, a great dragon snake
also began swimming in his direction. When the *griot* saw the
snake coming toward his master, he said, "Great Fula, return to
the shore. Allah only created humans. Here you are meeting
with a great snake. Return."[39]

Koli Tengela replied, "I will not." When he and the snake met
the snake lifted its head to bite. Koli Tengela got hold of
its neck and they dived into the water. Great bubbles began
to appear. They appeared on the surface again for a moment
and again they submerged and again bubbles began to appear.

They came up again to the surface and dived again, and this time when he appeared again he had left the snake. The snake also returned to where he left it. It did not continue its journey. It tried to go up on the shore, but as half of it was out on the bank of the river, it died. Koli Tengela swam back across the river, but when he reached his house he died there, unbeknownst to anyone. When he reentered his house, he never came out again alive.

Koli Tengela's first son was the one they called Mansa Demba Koto.[40] He lived with Mama Andame, but when she died Demba Koto demanded the hat.[41] The Jammeh said to him, "The agreement was that we would install two *mansa* to every one of yours."

Demba Koto said, "No, that was not the arrangement. We said that your *mansa* would be succeeded by one of ours."

The Jammeh wanted to refuse, saying, "This is easy. It is like sewing an old shoe. No great skill is necessary. You merely put the threads back in the same holes. We will fight with you as we did with the Wolof."

A battle ensued between the two families.[42] The Sonko were victorious, conquering the Jammeh. Bakindiki Koto was evacuated by the Jammeh.[43]

They continued to live together. Suki Manka Yari, Sonko Jaja, and Manka Fing Wali also came from Kabu, Tumana Sumakunda[44]-- they were sons of Janke Wali. They also came and said they were looking for a place to settle. Their hosts talked it over and agreed to let them settle. They said, "We, too, are looking for people to settle here." They explained the country's whole situation to them--how the kingdom was acquired, that it had been a Wolof country, and how they had fought and gained their independence.

The new migrants replied, "We also were the ruling people of Kabu. Janke Wali was our father. He asked us to leave Kabu, wanting us to be his successors and wanting us to continue his family tree. When we left he did not realize what was going on in Kabu."[45]

When Janke Wali was installed in Kabu he was asked to make a prediction. It was their custom that at an installation of a new ruler the ruler makes a prediction of what will happen during his reign. Janke Wali refused, however, saying, "I will not make a prediction. I will only predict if we return to the red sands which we have now abandoned. I have asked you to return to it and unless you do so I will not predict."

His people said to him, "Why would you not?"

He said, "If we do not go back to it, we will see the intermixing of Fula and Mandinka compounds in Kabu, one Fula compound here and one Mandinka compound there."

They asked a Fula in Kabu to do something and he refused to
do what was asked. He sent his four sons out of Kabu, saying
to them, "You go away. A great tragedy is about to happen in
Kabu and I do not want you to be here when it does."

Suki Manka Yari, Kubenbenke Yari, Manka Fing Wali, and Sonko
Jaja were the four sons he sent away. He wanted these to continue his family tree. They came to settle in Niumi. When
they arrived they found Mama Andame ruling with Koli Tengela.

When the Manneh[46] settled, they said, "We are the same as you
people; we are equal in everything you undertake. We have also
come as *mansa* in this country. That makes us the same as the
rest of you."

Their hosts agreed with these conditions and they settled with
them. They continued to settle thusly for a long time.

While Mansa Demba Koto was at war with the Jammeh, he saw the
island of Betenti and he wanted to settle there. At that time
they were living at Bankere, so he left Bankere and settled on
Betenti Island. When he spent one night on the island his
*marabout*s[47] said to him, "I know you can settle here, but from
my divination a place was pointed out which would be found along
the coast. You must follow the coast line until you hear people
reciting the Koran. You will find a bush near there which you
should cut down and turn into a village. You could settle there
and find your livelihood there, but this island is not suitable
for a bull."

Demba Koto agreed with the *marabout* and followed the coast until
he came abreast of the Jinak elephant grass. They heard people
there reciting the Koran, so they went into the village and
asked them. At Jinak Barra they found a great Muslim, Silamaba
Touray, and junior Muslims, Salamending Touray, Niama Sampatang,
and Karang Fofana.[48] Those were the founders of Jinak Barra.
They had moved there from Kombo Gunjur.[49] The big bush which
was near them was where they wanted to settle. At that time
Gunjar was built between Faraba and Basori in the bush. That
was where they were settling. Then they left there. They had
suffered a lot of hardship from the *soninke*s of Brikama. That
was why the four *marabout*s left the village to settle on the
island of Jinak. They found a place called Mansaringko.[50]
They built temporary sheds and commenced cutting down trees in
the forest.

After cutting the trees for three days the *marabout* said to
Mansa Demba Koto, "You declared that you wanted to visit the
men at work cutting the trees, but you left. You must give
one hundred cakes and three bowls of porridge for charity.
According to my divinations, if you do not do this, a lion
will kill off your men tomorrow. If it is not you, it will
be one of the most important men in your army."

Demba Koto gave out his charity and went to the forest the
next morning. He took his gun called *kabuso*[51] with him, but

his Fula slave carried along a double-barreled gun. When they
entered the forest and were walking, after some distance a lion
appeared and rushed at them. Mansa Demba Koto took out his
kabuso, but--Hah!--it was empty. The Fula slave fired, though,
and the full force of the bullet struck the lion in the chest
and killed it. People were called and came to the scene, saying, "The *mansa* has killed a lion. He killed it with a golden
knife and skinned it with a silver knife." Everyone gathered
there. The lion was white. They called the town they built
there Jatako. That is the Jatako of Jinak. Nobody mentioned
the slave. Everyone said it was the *mansa* who killed the lion.[52]

When he built the village there, he begot four sons: Dijang
Sonko, his eldest; Wakan Sonko, the second; Jenung Wuleng, the
third; and Bebe Sonko, the fourth. Between the time he took
mansaya and the time he died, 115 years passed.

While he was *mansa* the princes of the other families got together and declared that they were all dying off during the
reign of one *mansa*. They wondered, "Why should we die in the
reign of one man? Are we also not supposed to rule?" They
had all met in the swamp where they discussed the problem.
They agreed that a plan should be made to deal with the situation. The meeting was held at Jinak. If you ask today in
Jinak, you will be shown where *faile* is. People have not forgotten what happened at *faile*, even now.

The princes said it would be difficult to destroy the old man:
"If we shoot a gun he would kill us all. If we hit him with
sticks, Dijang Sonko will hear of it and he would kill us all.
We just wait. Every morning Dijang goes out to gather some
leaves for the old man at Mansaringko. He comes back and boils
them. When it is cool he gives it to the old man to drink so
his throat will be clear enough to speak. When he goes out in
the morning, before he returns we should tie a strip of cloth
around his father's neck and pull it and strangle him to death.
If we do this, he will not know how he died."

When the son left the next morning, they went into the father's
house. The Fula slave who was with him hid himself in the house
and none of the assassins saw him. They put the strip of cloth
around the old man's neck and pulled until he died. His tongue
came right out of his mouth and reached his chest. When Dijang
Sonko returned from getting the leaves he customarily boiled
for his father, he prepared and cooled them and came to greet
his father. He drew the net over the bed[53] and saw his father's
tongue hanging out. He declared, "Allah is great! He is the
slayer of *mansa*! Behold, he has killed my father!"

The Fula slave jumped up and said, "That may be so, but everything has a direct cause. The cause of your father's death
was the princes of the other families. They said that one
mansa had ruled for 115 years and they were all dying one by
one during a single reign. That was why they tied a cotton

cloth around his neck and killed him. Then they all left."

Dijang Sonko said, "Stop, do not say that again. If you repeat it, I shall kill you."

The Fula slave said, "You may do as you please, but your father was killed by the princes."

Q: Just a second, please. . . .

It was here that I stopped to invert my cassette and Jata refused to continue. It took him forty-five minutes to recite this much of his narrative.

FOOTNOTES TO THE FIRST INTERVIEW

[1]Jata is not speaking about his father's father when he mentions his grandfather. He uses the word grandfather or great grandfather to signify a remote ancestor. In this passage he is telling where his ancestors came from and, as best he can, suggesting how his family and the Sonko family of Berending developed a patron-client relationship.

[2]Residents of the lower Gambia refer to the former state of Siin as Kasing. Its residents are, therefore, Kasingkas. For information on Siin and its neighbor, Saloum, see Boulègue, "La Sénégambie"; Curtin, *Economic Change*; or a forthcoming article by Martin A. Klein.

[3]There has long been confusion surrounding the word *soninke*. Capitalized, it is one of several names for the ethnic group of Africans who founded and controlled the western Sudanic Empire of Ghana for several centuries of the first and early second millenia A.D. Along the Gambia River, however, *soninke*, lowercase, is a Mandinka word meaning, literally, "do drinking," which is used to identify non-Muslims. Because Muslims do not drink alcohol, those who traditionally "did drinking" were not Muslims. Hence, Sora Musa in this sentence was the first non-Muslim prince to go to Mecca.

[4]"Prince" may not be a good translation of the Mandinka word "*mansaring*," but I do not know of a better one. Translated literally, *mansaring* (or sometimes *mansading*) means "little *mansa*," but it usually refers to someone who will likely become *mansa* in his time or who is, at least, a prominent male member of a family that provides the *mansa* for a Mandinka state.

[5]Mecca is, of course, the holy city of Islam on the Arabian peninsula. Many fictionalized characters from Mandinka oral traditions and folklore are said to have been pilgrims to Mecca. I argue elsewhere that Sora Musa is a composite figure in lower Gambian Mandinka oral traditions. Part of the figure is based upon Mansa Musa, Emperor of Mali and noted Muslim pilgrim of the fourteenth century. See my *Early History of Niumi*, p. 45.

[6]Sundiata Keita, probably the most prominent figure in all Mandinka oral traditions, was the founder of the Mali Empire in the thirteenth century. For a fascinating account of Sundiata's life, taken from a *griot*'s account of the epic as recorded in eastern Guinea, see D. T. Niani, *Sundiata: An Epic of Old Mali* (London, 1965).

[7]According to B. K. Sidibe, this passage about women spoiling their sons actually refers to the loyalty and self-sacrifice of Mandinka wives for their husbands. It is a traditional Mandinka belief that a woman who devotes her life to

the service of her husband and accepts the subordination of her rights and privileges to his will gain prosperity for her son. Such action would gain her sons the blessings of Allah as well as her husband's gratitude. Women who accept this situation, arguing with their husbands and demanding their rights, ruined their sons' chances of becoming important persons in society. Those who did accept it "spoiled" their sons, but thereby made possible their social and often political success.

[8]Susu Sumanguru, or Sumanguru Kante, was ruler of a Susu state that was successor to ancient Ghana in a portion of the Western Sudan. Sumanguru is Sundiata's contemporary and adversary. Sundiata's forces supposedly defeated those of Sumanguru at the Battle of Krina. It was following this victory that Sundiata consolidated loyalties to him and formed the Mali Empire. For the oral account of the battle, see Niani, *Sundiata*.

[9]Mandinka are firm believers in protective amulets, charms, and waters. The more powerful, spiritually and magically, the person, the more powerful are deemed his fetishes. By letting Sora Musa wash himself in his fetish waters, it gave Sora Musa the protection of the most powerful man and greatest magician of all times among the Mandinka. It also supposedly made Sora Musa a successful fetishist in his own right.

[10]In The Gambia Mandinka give the name of the traditional Mandinka state before the name of the village. Here, Jata is referring to Iliassa, one of the primary villages of the former state of Baddibu, east of Niumi on the Gambia River.

[11]These villages "belong" to Sora Musa because he was the first one to settle them. According to Mandinka custom, the original settlers of an area and their descendants have special relationships with the *jinn*, or spirits, of the region. This accorded the original family usufruct rights to the land and water within some generally specified bounds. New settlers in the area had to receive permission from the original family to clear land for new villages and to use the surrounding land for farms. The best discussion of Mandinka land tenure and use I have encountered is R. G. Biddulph, "A Memorandum on Native Custom Regarding Land Tenure in the Kombo Districts of the South Bank Province," 1940, Gambia Public Record Office, Banjul, 76/20.

[12]Elsewhere I argue that these women *mansa* are fictitious figures that personify an undetermined number of generations of the pre-Mandinka existence in the coastal area between the Gambia and Saloum Rivers. The names of the women are not authentic Mandinka or Serer names. Instead, they seem to be what David Henige calls "spurinyms," or names formed that have meanings for those hearing them. In this case the names relate to the Atlantic-oriented life style of the people of the region before the arrival of the Mandinka. See Henige, *Chronology of Oral Tradition*, pp. 46-48, for a discussion of spurinyms. See my *Early History of Niumi*, pp. 45-46, for more complete treatment of the women *mansa*.

[13]The story of Koli Tengela that follows is an interesting combination of oral history and folklore from different parts of the westernmost Sudanic area. I discuss this story in detail in "Koli Tengela in Sonko Traditions of Origin," pp. 257-271.

[14]The names given the *mansa* are not real names. "Hun" and "Ha" are merely sounds indicating suspicion; *sintang* means legless; *dondoli* means wasp; and *sumany-abali* means "porridge that never gets cold."

[15]Certain numbers carry strong magical significance, particularly to Muslim diviners, healers, and protectors. Such numbers as nine, which is particularly powerful, three, and others can be found in much Senegambian folkore and oral traditions.

[16]The incongruity of an African several centuries ago carrying a horn with powder and shot bothers the *griot* not at all. It is merely part of his embellishment of the tale.

[17]The Sonko of Niumi claim to be Fula, or Fulbe, an ethnic group of lighter-skinned people who entered the lower Senegambia sometime after the Mandinka had settled there. It is interesting that Sonko living in other regions of The Gambia and elsewhere, who claim to be related to the Sonko of Niumi, say this is ridiculous. Nearly everyone else but the Sonko of Niumi believe all Sonko to be Mandinka. I suggest how this may have come about in my "Koli Tengela in Sonko Traditions of Origin."

[18]Bah is a prominent Fulbe patronymic throughout Senegal and The Gambia.

[19]Note the repetition in Jata's story. The accounts of *griots* are often very repetitive. I include such repetition in this interview with Jata to provide something of the "flavor" of the *griot*'s story.

[20]The women *mansa* are supposedly the ancestors of the Jammeh, the original ruling family of Niumi.

[21]Most Mandinka families have similar etymologies for their patronymics. Generally speaking, these can be overlooked in terms of historical of social significance.

[22]"Tilebo" means "the East." Many western Mandinka use the word to refer to the Mandinka homelands on the upper Niger River, though it often has a much more general meaning. The actual state of Denya was located on the middle Senegal River, more north than east of the Gambia.

[23]By saying, "These are large thoughts," Jata is putting his ideas into the dialogue of Mansa Wame.

[24]Oral traditions frequently speak of the payment of tribute in terms of one region providing another with a product for which the payer is noted. Niumi has considerable area of marsh and, hence, it has abundance of grasses used for thatching. Saloum, which is much less marshy, does not have similar grass in such supply.

[25]Most of the western Mandinka states that existed on or near the Gambia River in precolonial times rotated political leadership of the state among several lineages. The rotational pattern was supposedly fixed, though struggles over succession seem to have been frequent. Oral traditions from the region often speak

of such rotation in terms of "we will put on the shoe (or hat) that you take off."

[26]By placing the suffix -ka on the end of a name of a state, a speaker of Mandinka signifies a person from that state. When a town or district name ends in a vowel, then the suffix to designate a person from there is actually -nka; thus, Niuminka means "a person from Niumi." When the town or district ends in a consonant then only the suffix -ka is added.

[27]The *bur* was the political leader of the state of Saloum. The rough equivalent in a Mandinka state would be the *mansa*.

[28]I asked this question in an attempt to find out approximately when the events Jata is describing occurred, if indeed they did. For the state of Saloum there is a fairly accurate list of the *bur*, along with dates for their reigns. If Jata could have told me who was the *bur* when Niumi revolted, I might have been able to determine the approximate date for the event. For the list of the Saloum *bur* see Jean Boulègue, "Contribution à la chronologie du royaume du Saloum," *Bulletin de l'Institut Fondamental d'Afrique Noire*, Series B, XXVIII (1966), pp. 657-665.

[29]The questions here seem to confuse Jata. Typical of *griot*s, he does not admit there is something he does not know or that he is confused. Instead, he continues talking, mentioning a number of names and events, often repetitive, until he can regain command of his narrative.

[30]A *bantaba* is a village meeting place, usually a raised and covered platform in the center of the village.

[31]The previous questions so disturbed the sequence of the narrative that Jata here encapsulates much of the rest of the story in two sentences. He regains his place in the narrative soon hereafter, however, and then continues to tell the story in detail. I eventually learned to be more careful about asking questions during a *griot*'s narrative.

[32]Intermarriage was often used as a diplomatic tool, to seal an agreement or to mark the end of a period of warfare between two states. The state breaking an agreement with another where one or more of its families had marriage ties would, in theory, be acting against its own people.

[33]"*Bankere*" in Mandinka means "by force." It is supposed to be the place where Koli Tengela first settled in Niumi, somewhere in the northernmost part of the state. No village of Bankere exists today.

[34]Jata seems to emphasize continually the loyalty and usefulness of the slave to his master. See footnote 52, below.

[35]The struggle between Koli Tengela and his wife is something of a struggle between powerful magicians. Implied in Jata's tale is the fact that the Wolof woman is a sorceress. The Wolof believe that a woman plaiting someone else's (normally another woman's) hair has control over that person and can cause the person serious injury. Only a specific Wolof concoction can counteract these

effects, see J. K. McCallum, "Report of the Travelling Commissioner on the Jolluf People," 1907, Gambia Public Record Office, Banjul, 1/151, p. 61. Koli's wife tried to work her witchcraft on him in such a fashion, but Koli's own magic overcame his wife's Wolof magic and, as an intrepid fighter and leader of warriors on horseback, Koli was able to make shift without saddle, bridle, or trousers to rout the Wolof forces.

[36] In The Gambia, country cloth is called *pagne* (though pronounced pine, as in pine tree), which is a French word for loincloth or some type of indigenous cloth. Gambians probably got the word from neighboring Senegalese, who speak French, rather than from French traders visiting The Gambia to obtain such cloth several centuries ago. A country cloth is a piece of cloth of various colors and designs, locally woven on small, eight- or ten-inch looms. The strips are sewn together, perhaps half a dozen or more, to make a country cloth.

[37] A *juju* belt is a leather belt with amulets and charms, usually leather coated as well, affixed to it. These charms were worn for protection or to bring good fortune. They could be worn anywhere on the body.

[38] Note the traditional role of the *griot* as advisor to powerful men. It is supposedly Jata's ancestor, Koli Tengela's *griot*, giving this advice.

[39] The snake here seems to be a symbol of a local, animist religion. Allah did not create it, therefore its power is beyond the control of Allah and the humans he created.

[40] Demba Koto simply means "Old Demba."

[41] "Demanded the hat" refers to Demba Koto demanding to be *mansa* as promised.

[42] The Mandinka word translated here as "families" is *kabila*. The word is probably most accurately translated as "extended family," because it usually refers to several generations of one family living together in the same compound or several related compounds living in the same part of a village. Members of the same *kabila* have the same patronymic. B. G. Martin of Indiana University suggests that *kabila* is from the Arabic *gabīla*, meaning "tribe."

[43] Today, Bakindiki is a village in Niumi dominated by the Jammeh family. The Bakindiki Koto, "Old Bakindiki," to which most informants refer, seems to have been located a dozen or more miles north of the present Bakindiki, and nearer the Atlantic. In fact, there were likely several Bakindiki villages prior to the building of the present one.

[44] Kabu was almost certainly the most powerful of the western Mandinka states. Centered in what is now Guinea-Bissau, Kabu was regarded as the cultural center of the western Mandinka. Tumana was a region of Kabu, Sumakunda was the extended family that provided the important political officer of the state known as the *suma*. Among other duties, the *suma* had to coordinate activities in the state between the time of the death of one *mansa* and the investiture of another. For fascinating accounts of Kabu and its history see B. K. Sidibe's contributions to the Conference on Manding Studies, London University, School of Oriental and African Studies, 1972.

[45]Jata's chronology is off again. The events he refers to here and following as "going on in Kabu" were events that took place in the mid-nineteenth century. During this time the Fulbe of Kabu, long subjugated by the powerful Mandinka there, staged a social and religious revolution, ultimately gaining control of the once strong Mandinka state. The Manneh family was in Niumi long before this time. The Fulbe revolution was the last important event that happened in the former state of Kabu before the formal colonial period; it is likely for that reason that Jata remembers it and includes it in his narrative.

[46]The Manneh eventually came to share in political leadership of Niumi with the Jammeh and Sonko. Two extended families of Manneh fit into the rotational pattern of leadership.

[47]Whether Muslim or not, most *mansa* had one or more *marabout*--Muslim-magico-religious practitioners--living near them to divine future events, to make protective charms, and to provide other similar services. A good *marabout* was a welcome client for a *mansa*.

[48]From later investigations, I found these Muslims moved to Jinak late in the nineteenth century. Again, chronological problems appear in Jata's narrative.

[49]It is possible that Jata added this to his narrative during his twenty-three-year residence in Kombo, during which time he surely became familiar with the history of these Kombo families.

[50]*Mansaringko* means "home of the princes."

[51]Again, Jata brings in guns ahead of their time. Most Mandinka names for different types of guns are taken directly from the weapon's English or French name. They call one type of a shotgun a "fowling peeso."

[52]*Jatako* means "home of the lion." Note how the slave has to remain in the background. His glory is solely the reflection of his master's glory and, in theory he is content with this role.

[53]This could be a reference to a mosquito net, but it could also be a net behind which the *mansa* kept himself secluded. Mandinka *mansa* were not to be seen by common people on many occasions. Consequently, they often remained behind nets or curtains while eating, sleeping, and doing other things.

January 7, 1975

Q: Could you provide me with some basic information on *mansaya*?[1]
       For example, how did a state select a new *mansa* when an old
       mansa died?

Jata: When it was the turn of a family to provide a new *mansa*. . .
       in the past when the *mansa* died, they would select the eldest
       among them. But they used *jalang*.[2] If the *jalang* agreed, they
       would install him. If the *jalang* disagreed. . . .Some of the
       jalang were snakes; others were baobab trees where *jinn*[3] lived.
       They used these things. If the snake disagreed about their
       choice, they would not install him, or at least he would have
       to sit and wait for a long time before he would become *mansa*.
       Also, contending princes used *marabout*s to help them become
       mansa.

       When they were about to build here, Sora Musa. . . .Among the
       soninke princes he was the only one who went to Mecca.[4] He
       spent three years in Mecca. But when he arrived in Mecca they
       asked him, "Are you a Muslim or a *soninke*?"

       He replied, "I am a *soninke*."

       They said to him, "What have you come to find here?"

       He told them, "My business."

       He spent three years with them there and he left Mecca. They
       told him, "Go, and when you go, you will never be defeated in
       any battle."

Q: When the Jammeh first came here, what was their *jalang*?[5]

Jata: Their *jalang* was a *taba* tree and a silk cotton tree.[6] They
       used to give an uncircumcised girl to the snake, and a black
       cat.[7]

Q: Did the snake eat the girl, or what?

Jata: Yes, he could eat her. Do you know where Jerre is?[8] That was
       where they took her and the black cat. They would leave these
       for the snake. They would worship the *jalang* with the uncir-
       cumcised girl. If the *jalang* accepted her, this would mean it
       accepted the person they had selected to be *mansa*.

Q: How did they select the girl to be offered to the snake?

Jata: They would select her from one of the *mansakunda*.[9] She would not be a peasant or a slave; she would be a member of a *mansakunda*. If they would give a slave to the snake, it would not accept her.

Q: Who would own the *jalang* at that time?

Jata: The *mansa* who was ruling would have died, and the one to succeed him would be the owner of the *jalang*. That means he would be the one to wash the little girl and the black cat and take them to the snake. If they were in need of anything they would tell it to the *jalang* because they did not pray to Allah. They were *soninke*. They would sit and talk about their needs among themselves. The eldest princes sat and discussed this without the presence of a slave or a stranger. Whatever they thought proper, they would give the snake.

When they put something on the *jalang*, the next morning they would go there. If they did not see the little girl or the black cat, they would know the *jalang* had accepted them and agreed with their choice. But if they found them, they would know that the *jalang* had not accepted them.

Q: If the *jalang* refused someone, what would they do with her?

Jata: If the *jalang* refused someone, they would know that it had not refused that person, but the one they wanted to select to be *mansa*.

Q: What was the *jalang* of the Sonko?

Jata: The sajor baobab tree and *sitakulu sutu*, the baobab of Kobulu, the baobab with the navel, and *sita kilingoto*.[10] These were trees they worshipped.

Q: Why did they select baobab trees?

Jata: They just chose these trees.

Q: Do you know the things they put there to worship?

Jata: Yes, they put their own things, their *soninke* things. They would take wine[11] and rice cake and many other things, just like the Muslims do when they gather to pray to Allah. They would put rice cakes on the tree's roots and pour wine over the roots, asking the things they ought to do. That tree would then have a *jinn* that would be in charge of them.

Q: Did they take a black cat there?

Jata: No. They would take wine, a red fowl, and rice cake. They would kill the red fowl and throw it on the root of the tree.

They would then leave and go to another tree and do the same. But only at the first tree would they kill the red fowl; at the others they poured wine after the first one agreed.

Q: Once they had killed the red fowl, how would they know that the *jalang* accepted it and agreed with them?

Jata: If the things they asked for were accepted, the fowl would shake and die. If the *jalang* disagreed, the fowl would leave the place and go somewhere else and crow with his throat cut. Then it would fall dead.

Q: When it was time to select a *mansa*, for instance, when the *mansa* of the Sonko died, how did they know to which place *mansaya* should pass?[12]

Jata: They knew. If a *mansa* was from one *kabila*, it would go to another. If a *mansa* was from here, it would go to Bunyadu; from Bunyadu it would go to Bakindiki.[13]

Q: Did they turn over *mansaya* to the Manneh of Bunyadu willingly?

Jata: If you, he, and I discussed something and I said, "We all joined together; we came with ours and we found you with yours here; now we are in this business together and we will do it. If we should do this right, we should have the *mansaya* we came with. If this is part of our past, we shall take over."

They all agreed about that, and they settled with them. Bunyadu, Berending, Bakindiki.[14]

Q: Now let's talk about the administration of the state. Who were the administrators of Niumi's *mansa* when the *mansa* was from Berending?

Jata: He had people at Essau, Bunyadu, Sika, and Bakindiki. Those were selected men who helped the *mansa* in his administration. He appointed them just as government administrators are chosen today. They would be representatives of the *mansa* who would exercise the *mansa*'s authority.

Q: What was their primary function?

Jata: They carried out the wishes of the *mansa* within their area. For example, when the *mansa* wanted to go to war, he sent word to them to come to see him on a certain day. They sat down together and discussed the problems. They sent away with decisions and acted on the *mansa*'s instructions.

Q: When a Sonko was *mansa*, were his representatives all Sonko?

Jata: In those days all of Niumi was ruled by one *mansa* selected

by them all, so the *mansa*'s representatives were the representatives of the *mansakunda* in Niumi chosen by members of
the *kabila* they were from. When the *mansa* had something to
discuss, he talked about it with the Sonko, Manneh, and
Jammeh--his advisors.

Q: Who were the men who led Niumi's warriors in battle?

Jata: They were brave men whose courage and fighting skill made it
       so. The princes were all equal in that.[15] They all stood
       good chances to become *mansa*. In the meantime, those who
       showed courage and fighting skill were the hopes of the *mansa*
       in times of war. These were the military leaders, but they
       were not chosen by any other means than by merit.

Q: Was there not a warrior class or family, apart from the
       mansakunda that was recognized for its fighting?

Jata: Those were eliminated after a civil war. Those were the ones
       that Dijang Sonko drove away from the country. They were the
       Sanneh Manneh and Manka Kumato and Manka Fintong and Manka
       Taboro.

Q: Why did he drive them from the country?

Jata: They killed his father because he had ruled for a very long
       time--115 years. They feared he would rule longer than they
       would live so they killed him. He depended upon the *mansa-
       kunda* alone, the Jammeh and Manneh. "*Foronjayo*" was the term
       used for the ruling class, the *mansakunda*, the descendants of
       Koli Tengela, Sora Musa, and Kabu Sumakunda, the sons of Janke
       Wali.[16]

Q: Did you not have strong *kabila* here other than the *foronjayo*?

Jata: I tell you, those were the Sanneh Manneh, Manka Kumato,
       Manka Taboro, and Manka Fintong. When they left Niumi, none
       like them ever existed again. The *mansakunda* decided to live
       by themselves and so only the *foronjayo* lived in Niumi.

Q: In some areas *mansa* kept *mansajong*.[17] Did you have any in
       Niumi?

Jata: Yes, those were the captives of the *mansa*. They settled them
       all together and they were different from all the other *jong*.
       Their main use for the *mansa* was to be sold in times of short-
       age of food[18] or when he needed gunpowder in times of war.
       The *mansajong* were a collection of slaves who were brought to
       the *mansa*. If, for example, I went to fight in a war and
       captured ten slaves, on my return I would give five slaves
       to the *mansa* and keep five for myself. Such slaves kept by
       the *mansa* were called *mansajong*. These were the "children"

of the *mansa*. *Mansajong* are in Niumi to this day.[19] A *mansa* did not sell his slaves. *Mansa* did not trade. *Mansa* seized what they wanted, exercising their authority.[20]

Sometimes *mansajong* behaved like *griot*s. They got them to perform occasionally, though they still called them *mansajong*.[21] Other *mansajong* were like nephews.[22] These were not the ones they bought or captured or had given to them. That is quite different. A *barindingjong*[23] and a *mansajong* are quite different. The former works for his uncle's children. If a *mansa* had a sister who had sons, his sister's sons would be slaves to the *mansa*'s children. That was what they called "*barindingjong*."

Q: What sort of relationship was there between the Sonko of Niumi and their nephews?

Jata: Anywhere from here up to the Kasingka, they never disrespected their nephews. The Kasingkas treated their nephews quite differently from the Mandinka. If the Kasingka were in difficulty they would take their nephews and sell them.

Q: If a Sonko *mansa* had 300 *mansajong* and he died, and if *mansaya* then moved to another *kabila*, what would happen to those *mansajong*?

Jata: The one who became the eldest in the compound with his death would take responsibility for those *mansajong* until *mansaya* returned.

Q: Since they got *mansajong* in wars, if they did not have many wars for a period, then they couldn't have had too many *mansajong*, no?

Jata: In those days there were lots of wars. Many were brought about by men who wanted to show their own gallantry. They would leave their own villages on horses and raid another village within their own state, capture people, and sell them. They would be like children in this. This was called "*su-boro*."[24]

Q: How many major wars took place involving Niumi?

Jata: Three. It would be four, but they did not fight the fourth one here because they left here. Jali Kasa Manneh went to fight Kombo Faraba.[25]

Q: Whom did he go there to fight?

Jata: He went to fight Bana Sanyang. She was a woman. He sent a messenger there saying he wanted to marry her. She said, "If anyone sees me at the back of a prince of Niumi, it must be because there is a boil there which I would be operating on."

Jali Kasa Manneh prepared himself and told his people that he would go there. He went there and burned Faraba, Faraba Sutu, and Suwa Su.[26] He killed Bana Sanyang's father, cut off his head, and wrapped it in a *taba* leaf. He then took Bana Sanyang to Bunyadu and put her in the *mansa*'s harem.[27] Whenever he would hear Bana Sanyang's voice, he would call her and say, "Bana."

She would say, "Yes."

He would say to her, "Come here."

At this time he kept her father's dried head in a box. He would take it out and put it in front of him and then he would say, "I must greet you because people should not take long to greet their in-laws. If I want to marry a woman and I do not get her, I take her father's head to be my bundle of kola nuts."[28]

Q: When he was waging that war, did the whole of Nimui go to fight?

Jata: When he waged war, all of Niumi went to fight.

Q: What about the second war?

Jata: That was the battle between Koli Tengela and Jammeh when they first settled together.[29]

Q: And the third?

Jata: The third was when they killed Mansa Dembo Koto--when the princes killed him. The fourth was the battle that Mansa Demba Adama fought with Jokadu. Kelefa came to help him in that battle.[30]

Q: What brought about that fight?

Jata: A Fula woman brought that war, a Fula slave.

Q: How did it happen? Tell us a little about that.

Jata: The Fula slave woman? No, there are two stories about that and they are quite different. It would make me tired.

Q: Tell us then something about the *guelowar*. How did the *nyancho*[31] and *guelowar* come to Siin and Saloum?

Jata: *Guelowar* and *nyancho* are the same thing. *Nyanchoya*[32] came from Kabu. The Manneh were from Kabu. They are the *nyancho*. The way *nyanchoya* existed in Kabu--when they were coming from Manding[33] and they came to Kabu, the leader came with his *griot*. When they arrived it was night and they spent the night in a big hole. The *griot* was performing that night. You know what

some *timpo* holes are like.[34] As he performed, he disturbed
the old *jinn* who lived in the hole so he could not stay in
there. He came outside and sat down and faced them. They
were afraid of him. The *griot* played until morning. The
old *jinn* was the one who gave his daughter to the leader in
marriage. When they were married, if the woman gave birth
to a baby boy, it would become *mansa*. But if she should give
birth to a baby girl, it would be a *nyancho*. And that *nyancho*
would never get married.[35] If anyone did not tell you this
about the *nyancho*, then he did not tell it the right way.

Q: When the *nyancho* were growing strong in Kabu, what type of
people were in Siin?

Jata: At that time the people in Siin were Kasingka, not Wolof.
The people in Siin were Kasingka with Wolof mixed in them.
The *nyancho* came to them from Kabu.

Q: Did the Jammeh come here before the *guelowar* went to Siin?

Jata: The Manneh were the first to go to Siin. At that time there
was no village here. When the Jammeh came to settle here,
there were few villages. These villages were Samase, Kidika,
Kamanda, Balanta, Kokomarikunda, Sutoto, and Boararing.

Q: Where are those villages now?

Jata: They are all in ruins. Koli Tengela ruined all these villages
in battle.

Q: Who was settling there then?

Jata: I told you, it was the Jammeh. Jammeh built the villages here.
Sora Musa did it. When he was building here there were four
villages. Then they went to build Juwala and Iliassa.[36]

Q: Now Jammeh, Sonko, and Manneh--were they not related in Kabu
before they came here?

Jata: No, they were not from the same family.

Q: Where did the Jammeh live before coming here?

Jata: The Jammeh came from Tilebo.

Q: Did they pass through Kabu on their way?

Jata: No, they did not.

Q: I am interested in the Sonko because we have learned that the
Sonko in Sankola[37] came to that place very early. Even when
the first Portuguese came to this area, they found Sonko ruling.[38] There were Sonko in Wuropana, there were Sonko in Jarra,

also.   How do these differ from the Sonko here?[39]

Jata: They were all the same: Koli Tengla, Bubu Tengela, Ngaba Tengela, Taba Tengela, Tengela Banna. Koli Tengela was the one who came here.

Q: When he came, did he go to Kabu?

Jata: No, he did not go to Kabu.

Q: We know of a Koli Tengela who went to Futa Jalon.[40] Was he not the same one?

Jata: No, he was not the one. Koli Tengela, Saidy Bah, Saidy Lee, Saidy Faye, Saidy Bubu, Saidy Kahn, all were these same Bah-kunda people.[41] They got the Sonko surname here. The Jammeh gave them the name. The first surname of the Jammeh was Moko. Biran Njeme and Biran Mamadu fought a fierce war in a rice field, which they called Mokoya Faro. Biran Njeme followed Biran Mamadu and cut his head open. He said, "*Jimusali sara jimang. Kubire batama ning Tamba Nganinma, Jammeh Jammeh ngadi Aramisa sara Biran Njeme Chukuli ning yera.*"[42]

Q: On another subject, we have heard a lot about Kular. . .

Jata: Yes, Kular, that is behind Jokadu.[43]

Q: Was Kular a separate state? Tell us what you know about Kular from the past up to the present day.

Jata: When the people began to settle Kular, the power of Sora Musa was there. All the women in Iliassa came from Kular.[44]

Q: What people were living there?

Jata: The people of Siin were the ones settling there.

Q: Were they Mandinka or Wolof?

Jata: They were Wolof, but now they have mixed with Mandinka and both live there.

Q: Now tell us something about Islam and *mansaya*. In the past which Muslims came to this country with your people?

Jata: In those days all the people here were *soninke* unless they brought a *marabout* along.

Q: Who was their *marabout*?

Jata: His surname was Fati; I have forgotten his first name.

Q: Who were the Jammeh *marabout*s?

Jata: I did not hear that they had any.

Q: What about the Manneh?

Jata: They did not come with a *marabout*. They were *soninke*. However, during those times the *mansa* used to find war *marabout*s.
That does not mean that they would walk with their *marabout* on
the same road. They would settle, and only when they were ready
to wage a war would they go and seek a *marabout*. The *marabout*
would settle with them and prepare them for war.[45] But in those
days the *soninke* had lots of powers, too.

Q: Do you know who some of the *marabout*s were they called to work
for them.?

Jata: No, I don't know who they were.

Q: You know that when you have two governments there must be some
way of conducting relations between them. Who were those responsible for taking messages from one government to another
in the past?

Jata: There was no one responsible for that. Back then, if you
wanted to go to Bunyadu, you would be killed and eaten by the
vultures or you would become a slave if you did not wear your
protective *juju*.[46]

Q: Were there regular ties of marriage between Niumi's *mansa* and
mansa of other states?

Jata: Yes, they intermarried. The mother of Mansa Demba Adama was
from Brikama.[47] He was the last *mansa* of Berending.[48] She
was called Adama Bojang.[49] She was also from the *mansakunda*
in Brikama.

Q: Did the Sonko, Jammeh, and Manneh in Niumi intermarry?

Jata: Yes, they intermarried.

Q: Now if you were in difficulty here and you had a marriage
relationship with Brikama--say the *bur* of Siin was going to
attack and Brikama heard about it--would he send people to
come and help you?

Jata: He would send people if he was able. Because his daughter
was married here, if he could help, he would.

Q: Did they marry for this reason--to make supportive relationships?

Jata: No, they did not do that. If Allah decided two people must marry, they would marry. There were some who, when they went to war and saw someone they loved, would bring her back and marry her. Lots of this kind of thing happened.

Q: You mentioned earlier that one *kabila* alone cannot build a village. In an entire state, also, *mansakunda* alone could not build it. They had to join with other strong *kabila*. Who were these big *kabila* that came to Niumi to settle with the *soninke*?[50] Were they Muslim or *soninke*?

Jata: They could be either. Those that were strong had *kanda*. Any *mansa* must be sure that more than one *kabila* makes a country. Even one *kabila* wold not make a compound.[51]

Q: Tell us about *kandaya*.[52]

Jata: *Kandaya* was rare in those days. We had *kanda* during the colonial period. Before that, the reason there were few *kanda* was because there was only one voice, that of the *mansa*. Everyone followed him. Whatever he said, they had to do.

Q: Who became *kanda* during the colonial period?

Jata: Those were Janko Samateh. No child would abuse him and no adult would disobey him. Also Farafang Njie. Nobody would disobey him. He was our Imam here.[53] At that time there were many *kanda*. Sana Sonko was here. Nobody disobeyed him. Suku Samat was at Bakindiki.

Q: What makes someone a *kanda*?

Jata: If you are a *kanda*, whatever you say is done, just as if you were a *mansa*.

Q: Were people born *kanda*, or did they have to work to become a *kanda*?

Jata: They became *kanda*. They protected themselves[54] until everybody was afraid of them.

Q: If a fool went around and obtained many protective *juju*, would he be a *kanda*?

Jata: A fool would never seek *kandaya*. If someone was cursed, even when he got a new shoe the dogs would take it away. A person with a lot of people supporting him would say that if I am ashamed, many people will be ashamed as well. He would go and protect himself, finding a *marabout* to make *juju* for him. Then if anyone disobeyed him, the person would die. From then on, no one would dare disobey him. Even if he should tell a lie, people would do as he said. A *kanda* must have lots of people behind him. If he is ashamed, many people will be ashamed. Before all those people could be ashamed, he would work hard to prevent it.

From this point, though the interview was to continue for another fifteen minutes, most of the information Jata provided was repetitive of what he had said earlier. At the end of the interview Jata does discuss some events in the story of Kelefa Sanneh, the story that is probably Niumi's greatest and most widely recited folk story. However, the story is not part of Jata's memorized repertoire. For a complete version of the story of Kelefa by a *griot* who is noted for telling it, see the interview of Sherif Jabarteh, pp. 102-107.

FOOTNOTES TO THE SECOND INTERVIEW

[1]In Mandinka, -ya is more or less the equivalent of -ship or -hood in English. Thus, *mansaya* might best be translated as kingship.

[2]The *jalang* was the fetish or animist object the pre-Muslim Mandinka worshipped. The *jalang* looked over the family, made decisions for it, prophesied, and even caused evil when mistreated.

[3]A *jinn* is an animate spirit. Though not in this instance, a *jinn* is often a spirit that causes evil. Consequently, it often comes out as "devil" in translation.

[4]Here Jata is moving back toward his memorized narration that he provided in the first interview. He felt more comfortable with that than with answering questions.

[5]Our questioning returned to *jalang*, interrupting him, in fact, to prevent him from getting along in his narrative.

[6]A *taba* tree is a fruit-producing tree found in the lower Senegambia. The fruit, about the size of a small lemon, is a large seed with a soft, juicy covering. People eat the covering, throwing away the seed.

[7]An uncircumcised girl refers to a girl who has not yet gone through the bush school and rites of passage leading to adulthood. Thus, it would be a pre-adolescent.

[8]Jerre is a point of land of Niumi's river bank that juts into the Gambia's estuary next to a small island called Dog Island. It is about a dozen miles south of Barra Point by water.

[9]Liberally "the place of the *mansa*," *mansakunda* normally refers to one or more of the extended families that provided Niumi's *mansa*.

[10]These are all descriptions of specific trees. *Sita Kilingoto*, for example, was a very old *sita* tree, which stood apart from, and probably higher than, other trees.

[11]This refers to palm wine. For the *soninke* of precolonial times, and particularly for the *mansa* and their entourage, wine and imported spirits played important parts in their lives. Besides being offered to their spirits, these people drank alcohol frequently. It heightened their bravery in raids and battles and, as several informants suggested, it made them less predictable. If the *mansa* was indeed both loved and feared, then the wine, when consumed, added to his fearsome personality.

[12]This general questioning is an attempt to get Jata to speak about Niumi's rotation of *mansaya*, something I was surprised to find he knew little about.

[13]The order of rotation Jata gives is not the order cited by nearly every other informant questioned.

[14]This evasive answer is typical of Jata's comments when he did not know about something. He continued for nearly five minutes providing such answers to my questions about rotation of *mansaya*. These were omitted from the transcription.

[15]Jata's comment on the equality of courage and fighting skill among male members of Niumi's *mansakunda* is clearly a diplomatic one.

[16]These are the extended families that provided Niumi's *mansa*. He is describing them by mentioning their ancestors as narrated in the first interview.

[17]*Jong* is the Mandinka word that is most frequently translated as "slave," though as Jata and others describe the institution, it is something different from the form of chattel slavery with which we are most familiar. A *mansajong*, then, was a *mansa*'s slave.

[18]Selling or trading slaves was not normally done in western Mandinka society (outside of the commercial exchange of captives of war into the Atlantic slave trade, which is another matter), but there were exceptions to this general rule. One exception was in time of crisis, particularly when food was scarce. Mungo Park, on his journey up the Gambia at the end of the eighteenth century, encountered a Mandinka woman who had "sold" her child for enough provisions to keep the rest of her family alive. The selling of slaves at such times was considered a necessity. Otherwise, "house slaves," or slaves who had been living with a family for more than one generation, were not to be sold.

Food shortages were fairly frequent along the Gambia River; pre-colonial and colonial records make this clear. One of the critical sources of the power of a *mansa* of one of the Gambian Mandinka states was his ability to obtain food in times of need. Having *mansajong* or other things that could be exchanged for food in famine times was certainly part of the *mansa*'s basis of political, social, and economic influence. For more complete discussion of the role of food surplus in *mansaya* and general political influence in Mandinka states, see my "Niumi: The History of a Western Mandinka State," pp. 128ff., and 244ff., or Winifred Galloway, "A History of Wuli from the Thirteenth to the Nineteenth Century," Ph.D. dissertation, Indiana University, 1974, pp. 345-346. Ideas in these studies concur with Nehemia Levtzion's thoughts on agriculture as the basis of Mandinka civilization, expressed in *Ancient Ghana and Mali*, p. 117.

[19]Although legal slavery ended early in the twentieth century, not long after the British colonized The Gambia, long-time residents of various areas of the country still know which families were "slave" families and which were not. In some of the more remote areas individuals will discuss their family's "slave" status quite freely. In Niumi, however, no one would refer to another person or a specific family as *jong*--"slave."

[20]From other evidence, oral and written, it is clear that Jata's generalization about the behavior of *mansa* is not altogether accurate. Some *mansa* were astute traders; others much less so. Some *mansa* assumed they had license to take what they wanted from people in their state and others; others did not.

[21]Jata draws this distinction because he is a *jali*, the true *griot* in Mandinka society. Other performers did not enjoy the status of the *jali* in his art. For an interesting, informative study of Mandinka *griot*s in The Gambia, see Roderick Knight, "Mandinka *Jaliya*: Professional Music of The Gambia," Ph.D. dissertation, University of California at Los Angeles, 1973.

[22]There is a special relationship of mutual obligation between uncle and nephew in Mandinka society. A man is often more indulgent of his sister's son than of his own. Giving gifts and money on special occasions is part of this relationship; helping the uncle at special times, planting and harvest in particular, is also part of it. This is the only place where I heard the uncle-nephew relationship likened to the *mansa-mansajong* relationship.

[23]*Berindingjong* means "nephew's slave."

[24]Literally, "horse-running," these raids were occasions for the Mandinka warriors to show their courage and skill. Skillful riding and raiding were important parts of the Mandinka warrior's ethic, which was based on a sort of *machismo* spirit. For a brief discussion of this warrior ethic, see my *Early History of Niumi*, pp. 29-31; for a more detailed account see B. K. Sidibe, "The *Nyancho*s of Kaabu," unpublished paper, Indiana University, 1974, p. 10ff.

[25]Faraba is a village in the former Kombo state, located directly across the Gambia River from Niumi.

[26]Faraba Sutu is a village in Kombo. I have been unable to locate a village called Suwa Su or anything similar.

[27]The *mansa*'s wives resided (or were kept) inside a high-walled enclosure called a *sorongo*, sometimes referred to as "the *mansa*'s jail." The word translated here as harem is actually *sorongo*.

[28]This passage was accompanied by considerable laughter from those listening.

[29]See Jata's first interview.

[30]Kelefa refers to Kelefa Sanneh, the legendary western Mandinka warrior without peer. The legend of Kelefa, who came to help Mansa Demba Adama Sonko fight a war in Niumi, is probably the most popular ballad sung by western Mandinka *griot*s. For a translation of this ballad see the interview of Sherif Jabarteh, below, pp. 95-124.

[31]*Nyancho* is the name of an elite class of warriors who resided in Kabu and who dominated society and politics of that state for many years. Some *nyancho* left Kabu and went to other areas of the western Sudanic region. Outside of Kabu they sometimes go by different names. *Guelowar* is the name for *nyancho* in the

Wolof-speaking areas of Senegal that are the former states of Siin and Saloum.

[32]Again the -ya suffix, meaning "*nyancho*hood" or *nyancho*ness."

[33]"Manding" is the word many use to refer to the Mandinka homelands on the upper Niger River in what is today eastern Guinea and southern Mali.

[34]A *timpo* is a large animal, apparently something like a ground hog, that digs large holes in the ground.

[35]According to B. K. Sidibe, *nyancho* marriages were at best temporary and at worst non-existent.

[36]Again, Jata seems to contradict himself. He is not sure of the answer to this question that is based on his narrative in the first interview. Juwala is actually the town of Joal, the seacoast home of Senegal's President Leopold Senghor. It is located about fifty miles north of the Gambia's mouth, by water.

[37]Sankola was a Mandinka state located south of the Gambia in what is now the north-central part of Guinea-Bissau. An extended family of the larger Sonko clan provided *mansa* for Sankola.

[38]Evidence of this is in G. R. Crone, ed., *The Voyages of Cadamosto* (London, 1937), pp. 67, 92, and 95.

[39]Wuropana and Jarra were also Gambian Mandinka states in the precolonial period. Sonko families resided in both of these areas.

[40]There is sound evidence that a person named Kòli Tengela led a group of Fulbe out of Denya, across the Gambia River, into the upper Casamance region and, ultimately, into the Futa Jalon highlands of what is now Guinea in the late fifteenth and early sixteenth centuries. The latest information on this Koli Tengela is found in Yves Person, "Nyani Mansa Mamadu et la fin de l'empire du Mali," paper presented at the Conference on Manding Studies, London University, 1972, pp. 10-11.

[41]Jata has a tendency to recite memorized names, sometimes for other than clear purposes. Here, though, it seems he is saying that all of these people were of the same, Fulbe (Fula) ethnic group.

[42]This is but another etymology of a Mandinka patronymic, which likely lacks basis in fact.

[43]Kular is a village north and east of old Niumi. It seems not to have been part of the traditional Niumi state. Some eighteenth and nineteenth century maps show Kular as a separate state altogether, but I have found scant evidence besides these maps to suggest that it was. Jokadu is a portion of Gambian territory directly east of Niumi. It was once recognized as a part of the Niumi state, but over a period of several decades leading families there fought against Niumi and, ultimately, gained a degree of independence. Residents of Niumi do not accept the fact that Jokadu's revolution was at all successful. Conversely, Jokadu residents claim that they were never part of the state of Niumi. The truth, it appears, lies somewhere in between. The legend of Kelefa Sanneh (footnote 30, page 60) is a story based upon what was supposedly the last Niumi-Jokadu war.

[44]By this time I was beginning to get a good idea on the limits of Jata's repertoire. Obviously, he had little to say about Kular, and this surprised me because Jata said previously that his ancestors passed through--perhaps lived in--Kular as they were coming to Niumi. Unlike some other "generalists," Jata is very much the specialized *griot*. Ask him much beyond the history of Niumi and he has little to say. Interestingly, however, the "generalists"--the Gambian *griot*s who profess knowledge of many of the western Mandinka states and even wider areas--are the commercialized *griot*s, the performers who live entirely off their art. By contrast, Jata lives the humble life of a rural peasant. He performs for rural-dwelling, more traditional Africans who are, with few exceptions, poorer than the patrons of the other *griot*s.

[45]Preparing them for war meant divining, working magic, and manufacturing the important protective amulets and charms that were worn into battle by the combatants and their horses and were affixed to weapons. Successful *marabout*s were often thought to be the best at such preparations.

[46]I suspect here that Jata is tiring. The interview has been in process for about an hour. I suspect he could provide better answers than he is, in fact, providing.

[47]Brikama is a fairly large town in what was the former Kombo state, directly across the Gambia River from Niumi. This, again, attests to the important ties of marriage between powerful families of the different Mandinka states.

[48]Demba Adama Sonko was *mansa* of Niumi from February, 1834 to early in 1862.

[49]The Bojang family was an important family in the former state of Kombo. It is a patronymic frequently associated with the Jola ethnic group, traditionally located south of the Gambia, between that river and the Casamance. I have occasionally wondered, incidentally, if there is any connection between the Bojang patronymic in this area of Africa that was the home of the ancestors of some Black Americans and the nickname, "Mr. Bojangles," given to the famous dancer Bill Robinson. I have yet to investigate it.

[50]*Soninke* is sometimes used synonymously with *mansakunda* because political and social leadership of the former Mandinka states was based in large part upon the pre-Islamic religion of the people, connecting authority in an area with the spirits of the soil and trees.

[51]He means here that one *kabila* would not make a compound if it did not have other *kabila* to provide marriage partners and, hence, offspring.

[52]A *kanda* was a very important man who was a member of a family other than a *mansakunda*. Such a man could never aspire to *mansa*, but as Jata says, he could earn a great deal of power and authority.

[53]The Imam is the Muslim religious leader of a village.

[54]By "protected themselves," Jata is again referring to the common practice of obtaining many protective charms to ward off trouble and unfortunate incidents.

THIRD INTERVIEW

January 14, 1975

   The third interview with Unus Jata was probably the most frustrating session
with any informant during my ten months in West Africa. I went to the interview
naively expecting to obtain fairly detailed information about Niumi's *mansa*. I
returned with considerably less information than I desired, and I soon came to realize that some of what Jata had given me was blatantly spurious. By itself, the
episode was instructive.

   Many western Mandinka *griots* and some others in Mandinka society possess
lists of the *mansa* of the former western Mandinka states. Most of these lists are
written down, by now, in the Mandinka language with Arabic script. Possessors of
the lists tend to know only from whom they received them. They say, however, that
the lists were begun with the founding of the state and were handed down, generation
after generation, ever since. While I cannot vouch for the accuracy of most of the
extant lists, I can say that the overall accuracy of the basic list of Niumi's *mansa*
from late in the seventeenth century (when European records permit the first corroboration) leads me to believe that someone in the state kept reasonably careful records, written or oral, of the *mansa* of the state.

   Historians, who by nature are eager to find dates for the events they study,
have long collected such lists of reigning kings and monarchs, trying, once they
have the lists, to compute average lengths of reign and to employ other devices to
determine the age of the state concerned. (Such techniques, incidentally, have come
under fairly serious methodological criticism in recent years.[1]) Naturally, I wanted
to do the same, but I found that Niumi's *mansa* list--there being only one, albeit
with copies in many places--posed a special problem. Because in Niumi rotational
succession was in practice, wherein seven different families took turns providing
the state's *mansa*, in what everyone said was a set order, the *mansa* list is not one
long list of who succeeded whom in perfect order. Rather, the list is in sequence
by family, meaning it is really seven small lists instead of one large, integrated
one. The *mansa* of each family are supposedly in order, but because of the family
rotation of the office, one family member did not, at least in theory, succeed another. This made establishing dates for individual *mansa* and for the state itself
especially difficult.

   After my second interview with Jata I mentioned the research problems I was
having. Although I had the list of Niumi's *mansa*, hardly anywhere could I find
any specific information about the individual *mansa* on the list. Also, I was having a problem establishing any sort of reasonable chronology for basic events of
Niumi's history, as noted above, prior to about 1815. Jata said he could help.
He knew, he claimed, things about the individual *mansa* on the list. He said he
could tell me how long each *mansa* reigned, too. That is mainly why I returned

for the third interview.

My high hopes for the interview turned into disappointment, however. I spent the first fifteen minutes giving Jata the name of a *mansa* of Niumi and ask-- ing him to tell me what he knew about the individual and his reign. It turned out he knew little more than he had recited in his first interview--the set nar- rative on Niumi's history. The following sequence of questions and answers is typical.

Q: Some of the Niumi *mansa* I know a little about and others I know nothing about. When I name one of them, tell me anything you know about him, and also tell what he did during his reign. The first one I want to know about is Mansa Wali Jammeh.

A: Mansa Wali Jammeh was the *mansa* at Bakindiki.[2] Mansa Wali Jammeh and Koli Tengela were the ones who fought the Wolof. When they fought with the Wolof and defeated them, he told Koli Tengela that when he was no longer *mansa* Koli Tengela's people could take over.

Q: Besides this, what did he do during his reign?

A: I know that he fought this war with Koli Tengela and after that he did not fight again.

Q: O.K. What about Mansa Mamadi Sirra Manneh?

A: He was the *mansa* at Bunyadu.[3]

Q: What did he do during his reign?

A: He reigned for 17 years[4] and in the eighteenth year, during the dry season, he died. But he did not fight in any battle.

Q: Who succeeded him?

A: Mansa Jali Kasa succeeded him.[5]

This portion of the interview continued to progress very badly, so I de- cided to ask Jata about the lengths of reign of each *mansa*. Again, I would give him the name of one of the *mansa*; he would think momentarily and then tell me the number of years (actually, the number of rainy seasons) the individual reigned. We went through the entire list of seventy-two. He gave lengths of reign that ranged from a minimum of seven years to a maximum of forty-nine years, with the average being approximately twenty-four years. (I notice now that the number six does not appear in any number he provided.) By now I was suspicious of the infor- mation I was getting, so at the end of the interview I asked Jata to repeat the lengths of reign of about half of the *mansa*. He was happy to do so, but this time, almost to the individual, he gave me different numbers of years for their reigns. About the only similarity between the latter group of reign-lengths and the former was that neither contained the number six, a number often thought to have strong magical powers. It was clear, and sad: Jata had made up virtu- ally every number he had given me.

What follows, then, is the relatively small portion of the interview, edited quite a bit at that, dealing with topics other than Niumi's *mansa*. It is in this part of the interview, and this part alone, that material of reasonable cultural or historical value appears.

Q: What did they [the ruling families of Niumi, about whom we had been talking] eat?

Jata: They fed off of gunpowder and lead.

Q: How could they feed off these things?

Jata: They fought and captured people and brought them home. They would sell these people and obtain food and feed themselves. At that time they did not know anything about farming.

Q: To whom did they sell these people?

Jata: Not to only one person. Back then, they raided people. They would take their horses and go to a village in the afternoon. If they saw a small child, they would steal him and if they were killed in doing so, well, that was that, and if they escaped, that was that also.

Q: Did they do any farming?

Jata: They never farmed. If they did, their slaves were the ones who worked, not themselves. The Sonko never farmed.

Q: And the Jammeh?

Jata: No, they also did not farm. The *mansajong* worked the farms for them.

Q: What did their slaves grow on their farms?

Jata: They grew *coos*,[6] because there was not a lot of rice then.

Q: What kind of *coos* did they grow?

Jata: They grew this kind called *suna*.[7] In the fields some would be working while others would stand with their guns to guide them. If they did not do as they were supposed to, they would take some and sell them and thus feed themselves.[8]

Q: In the *mansa*'s compound who did the cooking and the other domestic work?

Jata: The *mansajong*.

Q: Did the wives and children of the *mansa* do anything?

Jata: No, nor did my great grandfathers. They did not know how to farm. They sometimes mixed the *mansajong* with the *jali* [*griots*] but they were quite different.

Q: When you *griots* were living with them, did they feed you?

Jata: Yes, we ate what they ate.

Q: If you wanted clothes, how did you go about getting them?

Jata: We went to them and told them what we wanted. Any day we
      wanted something we could go to them in their compounds. Any-
      thing we wanted, they would give to us whether they liked it
      or not.

Q: What did people wear back then?

Jata: There was not a lot of cloth then. People wore country cloth[9]
      that they wove from cotton.

Q: Who did the weaving?

Jata: The *mansajong*. They were the ones who worked in the cotton
      fields.

Q: It seems those who were not slaves did not do anything.

Jata: Yes.

Q: If a *mansa* had many slaves, he was in charge of them, and they
      worked for him, what did they get in return?

Jata: Whatever they wanted. All this would be the *mansa*'s responsi-
      bility. Their breakfast, lunch, and dinner were provided by
      the *mansa*. If a male slave wanted to marry, the *mansa* would
      give a female slave to him.[10]

Q: If a *mansa*'s son did something to a slave that should not be
      done, what would the *mansa* do?

Jata: He would not do anything, but the slaves would go to the *mansa*'s
      compound and do something. They would cause the *mansa* many
      troubles that day. They would go to the *mansa* as a *griot* would
      and expect things. They would fall upon his compound. On that
      day the *mansa*'s goats and sheep would end up on the slaves'
      compound. They would take them and their owners would not dare
      say anything.[11]

Q: Did the slaves live with the *mansa* in the same compound or in
      another?

Jata: They built separate compounds for them, but they still went
      to the *mansa* to get their food.

Q: If the *mansa* wanted to marry his daughter to another *mansa* of
      whom the *mansajong* did not approve, would they have anything
      to say about it?

Jata: They could not say anything. If a *mansa* were giving his daughter in marriage, he would take a slave woman and a slave boy and give them to his daughter to go with them. They would draw water and find firewood for her.

Q: When slavery was no longer in existence and those who were not slaves were still dependent upon them and refused to work, what happened to them?

Jata: Then everyone worked for himself. If someone had a big farm and needed many workers, he would send for people to work for him.

Q: What people?

Jata: Usually he would get members of the *kafo*.[12] He would just go to the village and say, "I am sending for the gentlemen of the village to come and work for me."

Q: What would the owner of the farm do for them in return?

Jata: He would kill a cow for them and also give them another cow. Nowadays, though, the people who worked would just tell him their working price. Nobody knows the exact amount. There is no fixed price.

Q: Did the *kafo*'s working on other farms help the village?

Jata: Yes, because they never really spent the money they got. They kept it. Then when the village had to have a celebration they would use that money. If they had strangers in the village who were having a naming ceremony, they would use that money to buy food for the strangers.[13] If something bad was going to happen, they would use that money to give out charity.[14] If another *mansa* captured a poor person from their village, they would use that money for the person's ransom.

Q: You know that in the past the *marabout*s were a bit like the *mansa*. They had people working for them. Is that still the case?

Jata: Yes. Some of the great *marabout*s, people worked for them.[15] After all, they sat inside most of the time, didn't they? If they did not have people working outside for them, do you think they would have been able to sit inside?[16]

Q: Do you still have these great *marabout*s?

Jata: Yes. Lamin Darbo died, but his sons are still here, Sedia Darbo and Tijan Darbo.[17] They were all here and there were more like that. They had up to 100 disciples. Without those disciples they would not have been able to sit indoors.

Q: How would a *marabout* with 100 disciples feed all those people?

Jata: All of those 100 had their own compounds with their own brothers, wives, and children. On Thursdays they would all go and work on their teacher's farm. After that, they would all go back to their own farms. They fed themselves while they were learning.

Q: When their crops came in, would they give some to their teacher

Jata: They would take some of their *coos* and give it to the teacher as charity.

Q: How many different types of *griot*s do you have here?

Jata: In Niumi the only *griot* we had was my grandfather. At that time there was no *kora griot* in this country.[18] Here we had the *mansajong* and our compound.

Q: How did people enjoy themselves?

Jata: We had *griot*s. I told you the *mansajong* beat drums. We also beat drums at first. They had one special drum they used when they had a big ceremony when they were going to install a *mansa* We, the people of our compound, had that drum. It was special. They never used it until they were ready to install the *mansa*, have a circumcision, or have a princess get married.[19] Those were the occasions when they showed off their culture, telling how they came to this country and so on.

Q: Did they have *kuran griot*s?

Jata: Yes, they had them. They lived at Tubab Kolong, but they all died.[20]

Q: Which *griot*s entertained for people--for fun?

Jata: If they just wanted to enjoy themselves, then the *mansajong* would play for them. They had a drum called *bulang kuno*. If it was not something for the *mansa* or something else important, we did not perform.

Q: We would like to know something about the Niuminka[21] and their fishing--was it their general custom, how did they go about it, how did they sell their fish, and so on.

Jata: They made *bandabo*.[22] They used to go to Jinak, Essau, Berending, Kanuma, and Bunyadu. They all assembled at Bakindiki and made a type of fishnet called *kaya*. They don't do *kaya* fishing any more. When they made the *kaya*, if they caught fish, they would all share them.[23]

Q: What did they do with the fish they caught: dry them? keep them?

Jata: Yes, they caught and dried fish and brought them here for the people to buy with *coos*. They would take some to the other regions of Jarra, Kiang, and Niamina.[24]

Q: Was trading dried fish an economic asset to them?

Jata: Yes, it fed them. They sold their fish for *coos* and then fed their families on the *coos*. They grew *coos* themselves, but at times the *coos* they grew would not be enough to feed the whole family.

Q: We have heard that during the wars the people of Niumi got horses. Where did they get them?

Jata: They got them from Saloum.[25]

Q: Who brought the horses here to sell?

Jata: Sometimes they would go themselves and get them. At times others would bring them here. If it was during times of war the people could go inside other countries and find horses and bring them out. Sometimes someone would want to sell his horse and would come here with it. If you wanted a horse and could not get one, you could go to someone who had protective *juju* to prevent guns from shooting you and he would help you get it.

Q: What did people exchange for horses if there was no money then?

Jata: I told you that. They gave them slaves instead of money. Back then slaves were their money.

Q: How many horses would they get for one slave?

Jata: You would get one horse for one slave. If you wanted you could give thirty-three *dalasies*, or you could give one slave, for they were the same price.[26] If someone went to another village to farm and he happened to buy a gun, when he came home he would fire his gun and all would know he had it. Those times were far more enjoyable than now.[27]

FOOTNOTES TO THE THIRD INTERVIEW

[1]See Henige, *Chronology of Oral Tradition*, and discussion of some of the points Henige raises in Ivor Wilks, "Do Africans Have a Sense of Time?" *International Journal of African Historical Studies*, VIII (1975), pp. 279-287, and David Henige, "Do African Historians Need to Fear the Slouching Beast of Skepticism?" *International Journal of African Historical Studies*, IX (1975), pp. 457-463.

[2]Niumi's list of *mansa* has Mansa Wali Jammeh as a member of the Jammeh family of Sitanunku, not Bakindiki. Both are Niumi villages. I asked about Mansa Wali first because I knew something about him and I wanted, in effect, to test Jata's knowledge. Jata failed. Mansa Wali was Niumi's next-to-last *mansa*, reigning from the mid-1870s to June 11, 1883, when he committed suicide in a British jail in Bathurst.

[3]Mamadi Sirra Manneh lived in Kanuma, not Bunyadu. He was Mansa Wali Jammeh's predecessor.

[4]He reigned for about eight years, from 1867 into the mid-1870s.

[5]Mansa Jali Kasa (or Jelali Kasa Manneh, as the list reads) reigned from 1751 to 1754. He was an active, anti-European monarch, so British and French records describe his activities more fully than others.

[6]*Coos* is what Gambians call millet.

[7]*Suna* is a type of millet with particularly small grains on the ear.

[8]Jata's description of slavery here makes one wonder if his ideas of the institution have not been corrupted by what he or others have read or heard about chattel slavery in other parts of the world.

[9]Here Jata used the words *dari fano*, which is a type of woven cotton cloth that English-speaking Gambians sometimes call "Kent material."

[10]This passage and some of those that follow show how different this type of "slavery" was from the American institution.

[11]Sidibe told me he had heard on several occasions that *mansajong*, when severely wronged, could practically pillage the *mansa*'s compound and cause him a considerable amount of trouble in general.

[12]A *kafo* is an age group, one of several unifying institutions of Mandinka populations. Each village would have several *kafo*; each *kafo* included men or women of the same approximate age. In parts of the Mandinka world this included all those who passed through initiation rites at the same time. Members of a *kafo*

in the same village provided intensive labor for individuals and provided for the general welfare of the village. In this passage, Jata is probably speaking of the youngest *kafo* in the village.

[13]"Strangers," as English-speaking Gambians call them, or *suruga*, as Mandinka-speakers know them, are simply persons from another village, usually a long way off, who have come to live elsewhere to improve their economic position, usually keeping the idea of returning to their native village when a certain amount of money or goods has been amassed. Saving is easier in a "strange" village where there will not be traditional, often financially burdensome, family responsibilities.

[14]When Mandinka sense misfortune coming, they will often go to a *marabout* or other magician/diviner, who will frequently prescribe the giving of charity to preclude the evil happening.

[15]Famous *marabout*s kept schools wherein they taught young Muslims progressively how to recite the Koran, how to read and write using the Arabic script, and, for a select few, the secrets of *moriya*, the Muslim arts of healing, divining, magic, and protection. It was these students, and perhaps some of their families, who worked for the *marabout*s as they were learning.

[16]There is a Mandinka saying about the length of time one should fight in a war. "Make peace early," it goes, "for if you kill everyone you will have to work for yourself. The head that rests in the shade is supported by those that are under the sun."

[17]The Darbo family is a strong Senegambian Mandinka family, with different branches of the family doing different things. The Darbo who are *marabout*s are some of the most widely respected Muslims in The Gambia. I have found evidence, too, suggesting they were a force behind some of the religious warfare of the mid-nineteenth century in the lower Senegambia. For more information on this family see my "Darbo Jula: The Role of the Mandinka Jula Clan in the Long-Distance Trade the the Gambia River and its Hinterland," *African Economic History*, 3 (1977), pp. 22-45.

[18]A *kora griot* is a *griot* who plays the *kora*, a twenty-one stringed harp-lute that produces a very full, melodius sound. See the interview below with Sherif Jabarteh, a *kora griot*.

[19]This special drum was called a *jung-jung*. Many of the western Mandinka states and some others in the Senegambia had *jung-jung* or similar instruments, used only on such special occasions.

[20]A *kuran griot* is one who plays the *kuran*, a small, four-stringed instrument roughly similar to a ukelele. See the interview below with Abdoulie Samba, a *kuran griot*. Tubab Kolong (translated, White Man's Well) is a village in southwestern Niumi, just a few miles up off the Gambia River.

[21]People from Niumi are often called Niuminka, but Niuminka has also come to be the name for the group of ocean-oriented people who are residents of the islands and coastal regions between the Gambia and Saloum Rivers. These Niuminkas are noted for their fishing and boating skills.

[22]*Bandabo* is a kind of net made of thin wood or bamboo.

[23]A *kaya* is a special kind of long fishnet. People used the *kaya* in a special way. When the tide was in, filling an inlet, the people would stretch a *kaya* across the mouth of the inlet. Then, when the tide went out, the fish that had been in the inlet would remain, either caught in the *kaya* or lying on the inlet's muddy bottom.

[24]These were Mandinka states along the middle Gambia River.

[25]Along the Gambia River, where there are tsetse flies, horses did not live long. To the north, however, Saloum was relatively tsetse free. Therefore, Saloum has always tended to have more horses than the Gambian states, and from time to time a reasonably lively exchange of horses for various products took place. Mandinka warriors were horsemen, and the horse was always a prized article in the Mandinka states. Some early Portuguese traders imported horses from northern regions into the Gambia River area.

[26]The *dalasi* is the basic unit of Gambian currency. In 1975 it was worth about sixty-five cents. Jata's mention of paying *dalasies* or a slave for horses shows his typical chronological ambiguity.

[27]In this part of Africa in precolonial times, guns were seldom used for fighting. Instead, they were used for celebration. People fired guns for ceremonies, mostly, it seems, when they were happy. When they fought, they used swords and spears, fighting upon horseback, if possible. Persons interested in the use of guns, horses, and fighting weapons in the western savannas should not miss reading Jack Goody's *Technology, Tradition, and the State in Africa* (London, 1971).

KEMO KUYATE

ONE INTERVIEW: September 15, 1974.

GENERAL SUBJECT MATTER: Early history and folklore of the principal families
                          of Niumi.

LOCATION OF RECORDING: Indiana University Archives of Traditional Music,
      Access numbers 4358 and 4359.

The Informant. The Kuyate patronymic is one of the most widely known and most
closely associated with traditional *griot*s in the entire Manding-speaking world.
Ancestors of the Kuyate are said to have been *griot*s of the legendary Sundiata
Keita, founder of the Mali Empire, and Kuyate *griot*s have played a major role in
maintaining the Manding *griot* tradition down through the centuries. The village
of Kaba (Kangaba) on the Niger River south of Bamako in Mali, the residence of
Kuyate *griot*s since the days of Mali's glory, has long been the center of Manding
oral history, folklore, music, and general *jaliya*--"*griot*ness." Even today,
*griot*s with the means to do so make something like a pilgrimmage to the Kuyate
in Kaba to study with the best and to hear the masters perform.

It is only in part because of his name that fifty-four-year-old Kemo Kuyate is
one of the half dozen or so best noted *griot*s in The Gambia. Kuyate was born
in the village of Saba located a few miles up off the Gambia River some thirty
miles east of Banjul. For many years Kuyate's extended family had been patronized by two influential families in Saba, the Singate and Makalo. Through his
early years Kuyate spent his time in and around Saba, learning the traditions of
these families and more. However, as happened frequently, Kuyate felt the lure
of the city and soon after reaching adulthood he moved to Banjul, where there
were more and wealthier patrons.

The contemporary *griot* in Banjul has become less of a specialist and more of a
generalist; Kuyate is no exception. To enable himself to perform for more families with wider interests than Saba or Baddibu history, Kuyate learned oral traditions of many of the former Mandinka states of the Gambia region of many prominent
Gambian families. He can speak at length on many different subjects. However,
Kuyate is something of a corrupted traditional source because he has learned to
read and, like many of us, he seems to place greater credence in the things he
has read than in the things he has heard. Fortunately, his ability to read ex-
tends only to Mandinka, in Arabic script, and the "books" he has are mostly lists
of rulers, genealogies, and the like.

Because he is a well-known, successful *griot*, Kuyate is reasonably wealthy and
quite well dressed. He is an extremely proud individual, carrying with him as
he strolls about Banjul an air of importance.

The Interview. I had been in Banjul just short of a month when I got the opportunity to interview Kuyate. I had met him once earlier, though we had not talked
"business" in any way, and I had heard of him from several people as I spoke to
them about reliable sources for the history of the lower Gambia. Intrigued by
the Kuyate reputation as well as the personal renown of this *griot*, I looked
forward to interviewing him.

Apparently, Kuyate had heard something more of my interests, for in mid-September he went to the office of B. K. Sidibe in the Gambia Cultural Archives to ask Sidibe if I might be interested in what he new about Niumi. Appreciating the opportunity and knowing my interest in Kuyate, Sidibe arranged for an interview the following day. Sidibe brought Kuyate to my room in a building on Wellington Street just past noon and we sat in straight chairs around a low table. Binta Jammeh, who would translate the interview, came with Sidibe.

Kuyate is a fairly large man, perhaps six feet tall and stockily built, and in his long orange robe, round white cap, white leather slippers with open heel, and sequined sun glasses he was an impressive sight. He brought with him some manuscripts, folded flat, to which he referred once or twice. They contained lists of the former *mansa* of various states along the Gambia.

We spoke briefly about topics of my interest, for Kuyate was already aware of my project involving the history of Niumi. Then he began to speak.

Sidibe was my interpreter for the first two-thirds of the interview. Binta Jammeh interpreted during the last third when Sidibe had to leave. Binta Jammeh translated the interview within three days of the recording. Kuyate spoke in Mandinka.

Kuyate: The Kuyate are the first Manding *griot*s. They began *griot* tradition. The reason Kuyate speak about Baddibu, Saba, and the Singateh is because our ancestors traveled and settled in Saba.

What I know about Niumi and The Gambia is what I am going to tell you here. There is nothing that matters in this world besides teaching each other what we know. One may know something; another may desire to know it; and the first would give it to him. But what I am going to give you now is not that which I have heard sitting down while it was told to me. I have seen it written on paper and I have become someone who can read something written on paper and who can write, too.[1] What I have seen on paper is what I took, and I very much want to make it known to you. I Alhaji Jali Kemo Kuyate.

What I know about Niumi is this: In the first place, it was originally called Niumi because the Kasingka were not able to say clearly the Mandinka phrase, "Let us stay here and mix," which is "*niani nioto.*" They said "*niomi*" instead.[2] The first town in Niumi was Bakindiki, but this Bakindiki was built by a woman. The reason why she built this town had to do with her quarreling with her brother over *mansaya* in Baddibu Iliassa.[3] When they told the woman that she should let her brother rule and also told the brother that he should let his sister rule, it was confusing, all the more since the sister was the elder and the brother was the younger. When both refused to yield, they decided to have what our elders called "*alkuo,*" or a kind of election. When it was over the brother won. This made the sister very ashamed. She said, "Insofar as he is my younger brother, this is bad, but also in all the remaining parts of The Gambia it is women who are ruling."

Q: In what states were women ruling?

Kuyate: That is what I am going to talk about. There were many of them. The names of the women *mansa* are all written here.[4] They ruled from Baddibu to Kombo, Jarra, Wuli, and Niani.[5]

The woman continued, "If my brother cannot wait but has undermined my authority, I declare that he has taken *mansaya* from me. That humbles me too much. I will go away into the world.

She fled. During this time Niumi was a mere forest; there were no towns there. When the woman left she went with two people, a woman and a man. When they came she saw Bakindiki and admired the place very much. This is different from the present Bakindiki. Old Bakindiki was in Senegal.[6] She told the man to make a tent for her. When the tent was made they settled there. Her father was ruling in Iliassa. People told him, "We have heard news about your daughter who ran away from you."

He asked them to tell him the place and they said, "Toward the west there is a big forest. That is where she is settling."

The father sent people after her. His name is not in the book I have brought to you today. It is in another book I am not able to bring at all. The people found her sitting in the tent. They greeted her, saying, "Mama," for that was her name. According to our elders, Mama meant Muhammad. They asked her why she left her father. She told them of the humiliation she had suffered through her brother taking *mansaya* while her contemporaries were ruling in other places. They told her that her father wanted her to come home so they could discuss the *mansaya* with her brother. She refused, saying, "Because the palm leaf has been tied around my brother's hand,[7] I do not think they will remove it and give it to me. I will not go."

They tried to persuade her, but she refused flatly, saying, "*Mbandunke*." This *Mbandunke* became Bakindiki because the Kasingka were not able to say it clearly.

At this time the town was full of elephants and lions. There were many more beasts than there were people. Because of this, they left and went to the present Bakindiki.

After the rule of her brother had ended the people of Iliassa went to call the woman so that she might rule there. She refused and told them that she had meant it from the beginning. They decided to give her her *mansaya* at Bakindiki. She agreed and became *mansa* there. That is why women ruled at that time.

Niumi had about twelve women *mansa*. They ruled consecutively. I do not know the number of years each one ruled; I did not bring that book.

When she was given *mansaya* and was settling there, people began to migrate from different towns in Baddibu to settle with her. People heard that a woman was ruling with men helpers. There was war then between them and Siin with Saloum. People left and came to fight. During Mama's reign there were wars with Saloum. They were taking advantage of a woman ruling in a town, saying, "Let us go and wage war against her and take her land and expand into it." Even then when you had wars between two *mansa* it was because one of them wanted to seize the other's land.

The Manneh came then from Kabu Sumakunda. These are the people of Kanuma. They came to settle in Berefet, Fogny.[8] The Jammeh[9] told them, "We want you to join us because there are many wars these days and we are not many. We do not want our enemies to take our land from us."

The Manneh said they were also rulers, but that they did not have *mansaya* in Kabu and they were migrating to find honor because *mansaya* is honor. If they arrived at a town where they were honored they said they would settle there.

The Jammeh told them, "Fogny is very near Niumi and you have already known that wars are taking place here. We have called upon you so you can help us and if we are not defeated what do you want as payment? We will give you lots of money."

The Manneh refused and said, "If we help you and you win, what you would give us would be *mansaya* so we could rule in turns."

The Jammeh agreed. The people of Kanuma became the first visitors of the people of Bakindiki and also their first warriors and helpers. They brought about the rotation of *mansaya* between Bakindiki and Kanuma.

After the war in which Saloum was unable to take the land from the woman *mansa*, the Manneh called the Jammeh and said, "The war is now over and your wish is granted."

The Jammeh then asked, "What should we do now, should we pay you with money?"

The Manneh refused, saying, "Money runs out, but since we have said from the start that we are rulers and we agreed upon it, what we want now is our payment of *mansaya*. We should rule in turns."

The Jammeh agreed and this brought about the rotation.

This Mama Andame Jammeh was succeeded by Mansa Wame. She was a woman. The reason they called her Mansa Wame was because of the time she ruled. During her reign there were

lots of fish in the sea. When there were a lot of fish the
women used to exclaim, "*Ba ye wamo le dung.*" This means
"The sea is rough today," because of the number of fish in
it. So they called her Mansa Wame. During her reign the
fish came out by themselves. She herself was very serious
and everything she did was attended to by her people and became something great.

When Mansa Wame had reigned for a long time and she died,
Mansa Furu began to rule.[10] She was a woman. They called
her Mansa Furu but she was a Jammeh. This Mansa Furu also
ruled for a long time. I have not brought the book with
the number of years they reigned in it.

When Mansa Furu died, Kabouyadi Jammeh succeeded her. Kabouyadi was succeeded by Mansa Nyunturanjang. This Mansa Nyunturanjang. . . .The long stick with which the people of Niumi
push their canoes into the sea from the mud is called "*nyunturanjang.*"[11] Her mother's children used to die soon after
birth and when Nyunturanjang was born and on the naming day[12]
they asked the mother what would she call her, she answered,
"When my husband is going to sea, the stick that he uses to
put his canoe is what I am going to name my child." Thus she
became Nyunturanjang Jammeh.

When Nyunturanjang Jammeh died, Mansa Kalamakoi began to rule.
She also was named after the calabash that they used to drink
wine from by her mother. The mother said she would name her
child after the white calabash they used to take wine from
their big wine pots.

When she died she was succeeded by Yayando Jammeh. Yayando's
sister used to tease Yayando's woman slave who came around
with little Yayando on her back. When people asked the woman
slave what the baby's name was, she used to say, "Her name is
Yayando--teasing--because I always put her on my back and roam
around with her, teasing her." This became her name: Yayando
Jammeh.

When Yayando died she was succeeded by Bakijuwana. The last
woman *mansa* was Musa Mama Nkemere. This Musa Mama Nkemere
was the cause of men gaining *mansaya* in Niumi. But during
the reign of these eleven women, when they were ruling the
men used to be behind them at night. In bed, the men did
not lie in front.

You can see, I do not want to get my words mixed up. I do
not want your writers or readers to get confused, so I must
be careful not to take things from different places. I want
to tell you now how *mansaya* of women was lost and the men in
the country got it. I must be careful, for I do not want to
confuse your translations.

This Musa Mama Nkemere was ruling in Bakindiki. Mansa Jasey
was at Bureng.[13] His sister was ruling at that time. The
*marabout*s used to tell his elder sister, "This, your younger

brother, he will spoil your *mansaya*."

She refused to listen and said she did not think Jasey would spoil it. They told her that he would. Jarra and Niumi are not in the same land. Jasey's elder sister in Jarra said she would use a hen in the compound as a pet. The name of the hen is in another book.[14] The brother also had a cock in the compound. When the cock was old enough he went and had sex with the sister's hen. The sister told the brother, "Your cock took my hen's virginity, so you must pay for it."

Jasey told her that this was an affair between fowls and he did not think he would pay anything for it. The sister told him, "If you do not pay for the loss of my hen's virginity, then I will call the people to judge."

The woman did this just to get rid of her brother because the *marabout*s had told her that he would take her *mansaya*. People in many places judged between Jasey and his sister, but it was Jasey who came out best because the people always told the sister that they found no fault in him, insofar as both the hen and the cock lived in the same compound and were not tied or kept in a house. They could not say the sister won because no one could keep fowls from chasing each other.

Musa Mama Nkemere of Bakindiki, the women rulers of Fogny, Kiang, and Jarra--they all sent their brothers away, the brothers that were to succeed them. Each one called her brother and told him, "Let me send you to Jarra to call on Jasey because you are all in the same category. You should wait until we die and then you should start to rule. We have heard that Jasey quarreled with his sister and if she is not there, then Jasey should rule. But go and tell Jasey to be in accordance with his sister, to respect her and not to allow any quarrels to occur between them."

When all these women sent their brothers away, the brothers joined together. Ndena Njie of Saloum was among them. Women were ruling there then, too. Ndena Njie was a man, but his sister sent him to Jarra to talk to Jasey. When they arrived in Jarra they told Jasey, "We are sent by our elders to tell you to bear with your sister and not to quarrel with her."

Jasey told them, "I think you are all very unambitious people and you have been so for many years. The women are ruling. We, the men, do not have *mansaya*. If my sister is angry with me and Allah has made her *mansa* without my being able to do anything about it, then what Allah has predestined for me she will not be able to do anything about. She is jealous of me and wants to spoil *mansaya* for me. We have quarreled about that and you, the princes of your states, should join me and take *mansaya* from the women, but instead you have come to coax me into being on good terms with my sister. I will not do that."

When he said that all the other princes got angry and asked

Jasey how he wanted things to be. He told them, "I want
you each to go back to your countries and come with one
person to Jarra and then let us join together."

At that time people sought *mansaya* in Manding.[15] For example, if a country wanted to gain independence, the leader
had to go to the country that colonized her, like we had to
go to London.[16] At that time the government of the black
people was at Manding. Anyone who wanted *mansaya* had to go
there. Mansa Jali Kasa was ruling in Manding at that time.

When Jasey said these things to the princes, all of them
got angry and assured him that they would go back, get ready,
and meet him in Jarra. They did so. Jasey told them the
one who was called Niumi Mansa Samake Jammeh--it is not
Samake Jammeh but Samake Demba, but I will make that clear
to you. . . .This Samake Demba left here, Bakindiki, and was
sent by Musa Mama Nkemere to go to Jarra to tell Jasey to
get along with his sister. Samake prepared and went to Jasey.
The rulers of Fogny, Jalla Wali, all of them went. When they
arrived, Jasey told them, "Let us go to Manding."

There were no cars or bicycles, those were not known to them.
He convinced them, "If you want to travel, you must go on foot.
One cannot use a horse from here to Manding. We must go to
Manding in secret--by magical means. If anyone cannot go in
that way, then he must not go. Let us go to Jambang Kunku."

When they arrived at Jambang Kunku, they took an axe and split
a lot of dry wood. Jasey set fire to the wood until it was
all burned. He asked the other princes to do likewise, so
that he would be able to know who to go with to Manding. All
of them threw their country cloths into the fire. They burned
into pieces. He then said he wanted each prince to take his
own country cloth from the fire. Jasey thrust his hand into
the ashes and took out his country cloth. Mansa Ndena Njie
did the same. Sankala Marong from Baddibu did the same.
Samake Demba also did the same. The ruler of Fogny wanted
to take out his country cloth, but he was unable to do so.
Jasey told him, "Brother, you cannot go. I will go with these
other ones."[17]

That was how Jasey went with them. I have cut it short for
you; maybe we can go back to it another time. I will now
tell you what happened during his reign and how Jarra and
Niumi had a *dankuto* in seeking their *mansaya*.[18]

When the princes went to Manding they were lodged by Jali
Kasa. When they arrived at Manding in those days, they
went and greeted the *mansa*, Jali Kasa, and said to him, "We
are soldiers of the West. Our sisters are ruling our countries and we have come so that you can help us have *mansaya*.
We want you to give us power to rule, because in every country
if you want *mansaya* and you do not go seek it from the proper
authority, you will not get it."[19]

Jali Kasa told Jasey, "We have a bird here which we have been unable to kill for a long time. My princes who came here were unable to kill this bird and it made us very worried."

This is why you hear people say: "Jasey fought with a bird and killed the bird." This is the history of Jarra, but it also concerned how the men got *mansaya*. During the fight, if Jasey swallowed the bird, he would defecate and it would come right back out. If it swallowed Jasey, he would come out in the same way. They did this and it continued for seven days. The other princes did not know anything about the fight so they did not help him.

Jasey's sister of the same mother and father was there. She had the same father, not mother, as the woman *mansa* of Jarra.[20] His real sister told him, "If you go to Manding, do not eat any food there before killing the bird, because if you do you will not be able to kill it. I will cook your meals for you here in Jarra and you will be coming to take them."[21]

There was a big hill between Sutung and Bureng.[22] It was called Tukoji. The woman took the food there and put it on a big stone. She then started beating a drum and singing, which went as follows:

> Sanku bel, Sanku bel
> Sanku bel, the kind-hearted,
> The princes who have gone to Manding,
> Jasey's food is furnished in Jarra.

When the song was over, Jasey could come and collect his food in secret and go with it. After five days the sister got angry and began to sing a new song:

> Sanku bel, Sanku bel
> Sanku bel, the kind-hearted,
> The princes have gone to Manding,
> Jasey's food is furnished in Jarra,
> The *mansa* who is nothing but a great eater.

This means that he went to Manding to seek food, but not to seek *mansaya*. So Jasey refused to collect his meals. After two days the sister was moved by their relationship. She worried that her brother was not eating anything while the one whom he was fighting always had food, making his enemy more powerful and able to kill her brother. She thus decided to go and help him. She left Jarra and went with an earthen pot that she had put into fire until it was bright red. She advised her brother to sit over the pot when he swallowed the bird. As soon as Jasey swallowed the bird, he went and sat over the pot. The bird stuck his head out and as soon as it touched the pot it died. When the bird died, Jasey took its head off and then he went back.

According to our elders, Manding was always dark, but when
this happened it became bright. People began to wonder if
the bird that brought darkness to them had died. Jali Kasa
sent people and they found the corpse of the bird. The *mansa*
then sent for the princes from the west and he asked them who
killed the bird. When Jasey had killed the bird, he took its
head and placed it in his shoe, and then he went home. The
mansa said to them, "The one who killed this bird left the
head in his shoe. Anyone who tries this shoe on and finds
it fitting will be the one who has killed the bird and also
the one who can lift it completely off the ground."

All the other princes tried their chances, but they failed to
make the shoe fit. Jasey's turn came and he said to the
mansa, "I will not tell you that I have killed the bird, but
you will know from your examination that I have done it."

He put his foot into the shoe and it fit perfectly. He then
lifted the head from the ground. The *mansa* agreed that he
had killed the bird. He was ready to let them go to their
respective countries.

Now Samake Demba was a very handsome man. The daughter of
Manding *mansa* fell in love with Samake. During their stay
this princess became pregnant and the *mansa* declared to the
princes that she had been made pregnant by Samake Demba. The
mansa said he would kill Samake.

When Jasey heard about this he begged them to allow him to
talk to Samake. Samake agreed that he had indeed made the
princess pregnant. Jasey told him, "Now what will we do?
The *mansa* said he will kill you."

Samake was willing that this happen, but he asked permission
of the *mansa* to return to Niumi and tell the people that he
had made the princess pregnant and therefore the *mansa* of
Manding was going to kill him. He wanted to do this because
he was sent to Manding by the people of Niumi and he felt
he must tell them of his whereabouts.

The *mansa* refused to let Samake Demba go because he believed
that if he went he would not come back. Jasey told the *mansa*,
"Mansa Samake Demba is a freeborn. I will take his place until he comes and if he does not come, you can kill me instead."

Samake was allowed to go. He was given six days and was to
return on the seventh. The people of Manding assured Jasey
that they would kill him on the afternoon of the seventh day
if they did not see Samake. Samake returned to Niumi and
told his people about the case that befell him at Manding
and why he must leave to return. They told him not to return,
but he said he had to, telling them about Jasey--that if he
did not return and Jasey was killed, then it would be great
shame for the people of Niumi and *griot*s and other people
would long talk about it. He was willing to die so he did

not want people to say he was afraid of death. So they let him go.

He arrived on the seventh day, but before he reached there it was already past the appointed time. All the people gathered and Jasey was taken into the bush to be killed. When Samake was tired of walking he took a long stick and wrapped his white country cloth around it and put it on his head, moving it about like a flag. When they were just about to kill Jasey, they saw the country cloth moving about and realized Samake was coming. When Samake arrived they released Jasey. The *mansa* of Manding said to him, "Samake, did you not know that I was going to kill you?"

Samake replied, "Yes, I knew."

The *mansa* said, "Then why did you come back?"

Samake answered, "Because of my honesty and purity, because I thought of myself and Jasey, and because if he was killed it would put great shame and scandal on me. That is why I have come back. I prefer death to shame in Niumi and Jarra."

Mansa Jali Kasa told him, "If one is seeking a son-in-law, one must look for someone who is as honest as oneself. Which one of you princes is freeborn? Both must be. If not, Jasey would not have risked taking your place until you came back, and Samake also would not have returned from Niumi. When you hear that someone is a Mandinka prince, that means he is honest, so I will give my daughter's hand to Samake. Allah has made him her husband."

They then decided to go and the *mansa* told them to leave the princess behind until he had consulted his relatives. He gave them each a sign and told each of them that whenever anyone saw that sign he should know that his *mansaya* was approaching. He said to Jasey, "You have come in secret. There is no road between here and your home, but I will give you three animals. They will show you the way. They will walk ahead of you, but do not disagree with them. Whichever way they take, you follow them."

Now be careful, for you know that as we, the *griot*s, say, "making a word too clear makes it unclear." These animals were monkeys. You know our elders say that monkeys are human beings. They are people of the prophet Musa. He gave them four monkeys, named Sema, Tako, Jakali, and Bubu. That is why we praise the people of Jarra with these words.[23]

The *mansa* told Samake, "When you arrive look for a dog and start hunting with your dog. Maybe your *mansaya* will derive from this."

Since your primary interest is in the history of Niumi, I need not tell you what is told of the other ones. I shall only tell of Jasey and Samake.

They left Manding and came home. Musa Mama Nkemere was ruling at Bakindiki. One part of the book says that there was another woman ruling at Bakindiki, but the other part says that it was this same Nkemere, who ruled for some time in Bakindiki and then went to Berending. She did not have a husband.

When Samake left Jokadu Bali[24] with his dogs he walked as far as Niumi. He hunted and when he killed his prey he roasted the meat and took it home. While going home each day he would go to the river at Berending called Nyanafara. He would take his bath there and give some of the river water to his dogs to drink. Then he would go back to Jokadu. He used to meet women at the river and when he had taken his bath and greeted them, they would all talk about how handsome he was. They went home and told the woman *mansa* and the elders about it.

The woman *mansa* sent word to Samake to go and see her. In the evening Samake went to the river. He found the women and they told him the woman's message. He said that he would be reluctant to go because the clothes he was wearing were not good enough and he did not want to go in dirty clothing. The women went and told the woman *mansa*, who immediately made a new shirt, pair of trousers, and shoes, and gave them to her women to give to Samake the next day in case he refused again. The next day he was given these clothes and told to go and see the woman *mansa*. He obeyed then and took the clothes. He had in mind what tokens the Manding *mansa* had told him to look for, and he thought his time for *mansaya* had come. He wore these clothes and went to meet the woman, who said to him, "I have sent for you, but it is not for bad intentions. I am the ruler here--Niumi and Jokadu. I have no husband and I want to give you my *mansaya* and marry you. You can take my *mansaya* because I see no reason why I should get married to you and still keep it myself. A wife should assist her husband."

Samake Demba agreed and asked her permission to go and tell his mother. He went to Bali and told his mother, "I am made *mansa* by the ruler of Niumi. Since I am your eldest son, I do not know if they want me to stay with you or with them. Because of that I have come to tell you before deciding anything, for you are my mother who looked after me until I became a grown man, prayed for me when I was going to Manding until I was promised *mansaya*. . . .Now I have it. I must come back to you so that you can pray for me and tell me your opinions about it."

The mother replied that wherever her son chose to settle, she would not disagree with him.

Samake got ready and left all the people of Jokadu. The woman *mansa* gave him *mansaya* and told the people of Niumi, "Allah has given me this man as a husband and I want to give him my *mansaya*."

He called her *griot*s and the *jung-jung* were sounded. The palm leaf was tied to his wrist and he was given wine to drink. In those days when a *mansa* was being installed, they would put wine in large gourds. The *griot*s would sit and wait with gunpowder and guns. Some of them would get up and tie the palm leaf to his hand. The *griot*s would then sound their *jung-jung*, while others would shoot with their guns. They would take a calabash full of wine to the new *mansa* to drink first before anyone else could drink it. The elders agreed with what the woman *mansa* was doing. They took a calabash full of wine, gave it to the woman, and said, "We have given you this because you are the one who should drink it, but since you do not want to drink it and want to give it to someone else, we will give it to you to give to that person, but we will not give it to him ourselves, because if someone tells you to give him his respect and he wants to give it to someone else before giving it to that person who is present, you should give it to him and let him give it to the person he prefers."

The woman *mansa* gave the wine to Samake. He drank it and left a little and gave it to her. She drank it and said that her *mansaya* was now ended. Samake said, "Since I am given this honor, I will stay for some time in Berending."

He went and told his mother that he was already the *mansa* but he did not know what to do for her because he was the one who should work for his mother but now he was living away from her. The mother said, "You should come visit me once every year. I do not say that you might not send people to see me sometimes, but you can come yourself once a year."

Samake returned to Berending and when he was going to visit his mother at the end of the year, they would prepare a lot of millet and they would catch fish and cook it. Samake would then choose a day and go to visit his mother. This is why you hear people say, "The people of Niumi paid tribute." Samake started it. So they made it a custom that every *mansa* of Niumi should take some millet to Jokadu. Some others wanted to use it as a sign of overlordship. If you conquered someone he would take some of his produce to you at the end of each year. This is how men obtained *mansaya* in Niumi.

Samake Demba had a son by the former woman *mansa*, but when she was seven months pregnant, Samake died. The people decided to wait until the wife delivered. Our elders used to name a son after his father when the father was dead before his birth. The woman give birth to a boy. The elders of Niumi said, "One should approach this thing carefully since male *mansaya* started with Samake, who was a native of Jokadu, not Niumi, and he was a Demba. If we do not make a plan, the Demba will own Niumi."

The child was called Samake Jammeh. That is why if you go
to Niumi they will say that their first *mansa* was Samake
Jammeh, and if you go to Jokadu they would say that their
first *mansa* was Samake Demba.[25]

Samake Jammeh was succeeded by Tenengwari Koto Jammeh, who
was succeeded by Mansa Musa Yabure. Yabure was his grandmother, who told the people to call him Musa Yabure because
she loved him so much. When he died, Mansa Musa Ndekelang
succeeded him. If a previously childless mother had a son,
she named him after her occupation. He was called Ndekelang
by his mother because she used to go to people begging for
bits of food. When he died, Sira Musa Koto succeeded him.
All this happened at Bakindiki. I will come to say how the
other towns in Niumi got *mansaya*.[26]

Sira Musa Koto was also a Jammeh. When he died he was succeeded by Sora Musa Ndebane. The one whom he was named after
was surnamed Ndebane, but they were all Jammeh. He was succeeded by Surankang Wali, and when he died he was succeeded
by Musa Wali Jammeh, who was succeeded by Bwang Jammeh. Some
Bwang Jammeh of Iliassa were named after this man. The last
mansa whom the Europeans found ruling was called Mansa Buntung Sanneh.[27] He was a Jammeh, but the one after whom he
was named was a Sanneh. During his reign he sometimes dreamed
at night. Banjul was like a forest in those days; people
cultivated rice there.[28] He called his sister and told her,
"I dream of this forest at night and sometimes I see a two-
footed thing. That makes me very worried."

His sister told him, "Tell the elders. Maybe they will know
the meaning of your dreams."

He called the elders and they told him that the Europeans
would settle at the forest he was dreaming about. The four-
footed thing was a car and the two-footed thing was a bicycle.

Mansaya passed from Bakindiki to Kanuma. The eldest at
Kanuma was made the next *mansa*.[29] It would then go to Sitanunku. The *mansa* at Sitanunku was a son of Musa Mama Nkemere.
If he went hunting and got tired he would rest under a baobab
tree and press his back against the tree and sleep. It was
one of these days when he heard an animal say, "If one builds
a town here, it will be prosperous and war will not destroy
it and all the people will be influential and wealthy."

When he heard this he woke up and went home to ask his
father's permission to build his own town at Sitanunku. That
is why *mansaya* rotated from Bakindiki to Kanuma and Sitanunku,
and then it went to Essau to a compound there called Njileng-
kunda. From there it went to Bunyadu and then to Essau
Manserringsu.[30] From Manserringsu it went to Berending and
from there to Bakindiki. This how they rotated *mansaya*.

The Sonko were Fula. If you hear *griots* call them "Sonko Desebake," it was because a Sonko's foot was very big and he used to hunt ducks from the river and it became his praise name: "Sonko Deseba *ning ji to kele la*." This means fighting in water.

Sonko was not their original name. A lot of them were coming and quarreling among themselves. The women who were getting water from the river heard them and became afraid. They ran and told the men that the people were quarreling. That brought about the Sonko surname.[31]

The Sonko settled at Berending when they came. That is why they called Berending the Sonko fence--the unfilled hole and the surpriser of strangers.

War happened with them only once. As I told you about the Manneh, so it happened with the Sonko. When they came both the Jammeh and Manneh were here. They joined the Jammeh to fight against Siin and Saloum. Siin and Saloum did not own Niumi. They wanted to take it and add it to their land, but they were unable to do so. The Manneh and Sonko joined the Jammeh to fight Siin and Saloum. The Jammeh won the war and they decided to make *mansaya* among themselves, the Sonko, and the Manneh. It was in the order of first come, first served. The Manneh came before the Sonko and thus had *mansaya* before them.

The Sonko came from Kabu in Berekolong. They were *manser-ring*[32] and they were traveling about the land seeking *man-saya*. They arrived in Niumi and found them at war with Siin and Saloum. They decided to help but asked for *mansaya* in return for their help. That is why they settled in Niumi and rotated *mansaya*.

The first Sonko *mansa* at Berending was Koli Bankere Sonko. We praise them with their Fula name: Koli Bankere. They were Fula whose surname was Bankere.

Jiffet was in Niumi. When the Sonko came they built Jiffet and settled there, but they did not rule there. They had *mansaya* in Essau and Berending. Koli Bankere died and was buried in Berending. They did not put names on graves then.

Among the Sonko who came--I have mentioned just the elder so far--but Bubu was there. Yoro and Pate were also there, but one cannot name the whole group. Tengela's sons were Bubu Tengela, Labo Tengela, Koli Tengela, and Burado Tengela. The Sonko were descended from Tengela from Kabu. Different generations came here.[33]

The last *mansa* of Niumi, Hamora, was named after Hamora Sonko. He was from Sika; he ruled there. He was a hunter and his brother was ruling at Essau, but they were not on good terms and people told the brother that Hamora was eager to kill his brother and usurp *mansaya*. The brother called

Hamora and told him. Hamora then got angry and left. He built his own town where he used to hunt. People told his brother, who ordered them to go and fetch him. They did, but he refused to leave, saying that he did not trust his brother. This led to the name of the town, "Sika."

The Sonko of Niumi are the same as those in Niamini and Wuropana. You know when generations increase they tend to migrate to different places.[34]

Here Kuyate ceased his narrative and I began to ask him specific questions.

Q: Did the *mansaya* of Niumi collect tribute from the people living in Niumi?

Kuyate: Before one paid tribute to another he would have been conquered and a subject. Since men did not work on the *mansa*'s farm but on their own, he would pay a certain percentage of his produce to the *mansaya* each year. We would call that a head tax.[35]

Q: Was the prominence of the Sonko family in any way tied to Europeans?

Kuyate: Sonko prominence in Niumi did not originate with the Europeans. It did not come from their attachment to the Europeans who then helped them gain prominence. Europeans came at the time of the ruler I mentioned earlier. They came to the *mansa* and said, "We want you to give us this island."[36] It was a difficult decision for the *mansa* to make because of disagreements among the people themselves. When the *mansa* decided to dispose of the island to the Europeans his sister said to him, "We must not sell the island to the Europeans. If you sell the island that we so often dream about, all the fugitives and escaped slaves will go and hide there."[37]

"I realize that," he said, "but the time has come to dispose of the island."

Some informants say the island was sold for five baskets full of two-shilling pieces.

The Europeans said to him, "We just want the area covered by this animal hide."

He agreed to their condition, but then they cut the hide into long, thin strips, which they joined together into a long rope and they measured the area of their occupation that way. Thus, a large area was taken. They stretched the leather rope on the ground several times and when he saw the extent of the area, he wanted to take back his agreement, but his elders would not agree.[38] This is one of the reasons why the Europeans helped the Sonko in all their undertakings until they became powerful.

Q: How did people in Niumi participate in the trading of slaves?

Kuyate: In Niumi during the slave trade those who had slaves sold them when they ran short of food. Also, in times of war when they ran short of gunpowder they sold slaves and got gunpowder. At James Island[39]--many slaves were sold there. The people who sold the slaves bought beads of various sizes and colors. Europeans brought these here for sale and Africans sold their captives to them. Formerly, women wore these beads as head ornaments. Some were yellow.

The Sonko, Manneh, and Jammeh sold their slaves on James Island. It was the Africans who captured the slaves and sold them to the Europeans. Domestic slaves were used on farms or for collecting firewood for wives of their masters. They would cultivate the land; they would become messengers. This is how the slaves were used. They were mainly captured within Niumi. If invaders came and lost a war, many of the young people were seized and sold into slavery. Some villages that were destroyed had their young girls and boys captured and sold. The old people were killed. If you capture an older man who knows the country, he will return to his village as soon as he is able. The young would not know the way back to their villages. These were the ones they made into ideal slaves.

Q: Did people of Niumi travel far upriver to trade?

Kuyate: Niuminka did not travel in canoes up the river. People were afraid to travel far because every state had its own ruler and there was not much friendship between them. There was often warfare between them. One did not often see a person leaving Niumi and going to Jarra, Kiang, or Fogny to trade.

Q: Was salt trading an important part of the Niumi economy?

Kuyate: The people of Niumi still make salt, though you know a person does not make salt, but Allah makes it. People take the salty water and put it in a cooking pot over a fire. Condensation takes place and salt is produced. Toward the end they realized that the sun takes away all the water and the salt remained. It was this salt that they collected. There are two types of salt: *kusudo*, which is salt mixed with sand and is brown in color; and pure salt, which is white and made by Allah from the sun. The one the Niuminka make for themselves is the one they condense. They started trading in salt a long time ago. In those days people found life very difficult. They knew salt was very important and

only Niumi was suitable for collecting salt. Other lands
like Jarra, Baddibu, Kiang, and Kombo did not have land
suitable enough to make salt. They sold salt in Kiang,
Jarra, Baddibu, and Fogny. But now from here up into Senegal they all buy their salt. They put salt into sacks in
Jokadu and put it on the road. Some people think it is
rice in the sacks, but it is salt.[40]

Q: How important was fishing to the economy of Niumi?

Kuyate: At first it was the Niuminka who fished along the river.
         They were living near the seaside, catching fish for their
         own use. Then they said, "The fish that we catch and cook
         for ourselves, let us see whether other people will like
         it."

         That is how they began to catch fish and sell it to differ-
         ent towns. When they saw that many people wanted fish very
         much, they caught fish and dried it and sold it together
         with fresh fish. They put fish in boats and sold them clear
         to Dakar, Kaolack, and Guinea-Bissau. On my last trip to
         Guinea-Bissau I saw people selling dried fish there from
         Niumi. This made the people of Niumi very influential and
         wealthy. If anyone gets something from fishing, then that
         is clear profit.

Q: What crops did the Niuminka grow?

Kuyate: They grew every kind of *coos*. They also grew rice and ground-
         nuts.[41] Cultivable land was not great in Niumi Bato; there
         were many small valleys. In Niumi Banta they farmed much
         more. They also fished, but they did not derive as much
         benefit from fishing as Niumi Bato. Niuminka also grew
         cotton seed and they carved wood with an iron rod for re-
         moving the seed from the fiber. If they had a lot of cotton
         for their families and if they had plenty of food, they would
         sell their extra cotton to people who had been too busy to
         grow their own.

     The remainder of the interview is almost totally repetitious of earlier
portions of the interview. By this time Kuyate had said much of what he knew
about the former Niumi state, its people, and the way they lived.

FOOTNOTES TO KEMO KUYATE INTERVIEW

[1]Compare Kuyate's pride in knowing how to read and write and his reverence for the written, as opposed to the spoken, word with the attitude of a more traditional *griot* with the same patronymic, Mamadou Kouyate, a Mandinka from the village of Djeliba Koro in eastern Guinea. In Niani's *Sundiata*, p. 41, Mamadou Kouyate says,

> Other peoples use writing to record the past, but this invention has killed the faculty of memory among them. They do not feel the past any more, for writing lacks the warmth of the human voice. With them everybody thinks he knows, whereas learning should be a secret. The prophets did not write and their words have been all the more vivid as a result. What paltry learning is that which is congealed in dumb books!

[2]In nearly every former Mandinka state I encountered a story similar to this one about how the state got its name. The stories usually involve someone mispronouncing a word or phrase. To the best of my knowledge, the name Niumi comes from a word, *niumi*, meaning "seacoast" in some of the dialects of Mandinka spoken southeast of the Gambia in parts of Guinea-Bissau and Guinea. Niumi was the only spot where the traditionally savanna-oriented Mandinka controlled land that bordered the ocean. See A. Teixeira da Mota, *Mar, Alem Mar* (London, 1972), pp. 91 and 139-140, where he cites information provided by Antonio Carreira, a man with long experience among the Mandinka of Guinea-Bissau.

[3]*Mansaya* is the equivalent of "rulership" or "kingship." Iliassa is a major town on the lower north bank of the Gambia River in the area that was the former state of Baddibu. The Jammeh family of Iliassa was one of five extended families that provided *mansa* for Baddibu.

[4]Kuyate here is referring to the stack of manuscripts he brought along.

[5]These are all Mandinka states that occupied land bordering a section of the Gambia River.

[6]Today Bakindiki is a village in The Gambia across the river, directly east of Banjul. Old Bakindiki was supposedly in the Niumi Bato area around or north of Jinak Creek near the present Senegal-Gambia border.

[7]In several of the western Mandinka states tying a palm leaf on the wrist was part of the installation procedure for a new *mansa*. The man with the palm leaf tied to his wrist was the *mansa*.

[8]The Manneh family was one of the families that would eventually provide the *mansa* of Niumi. Kabu was perhaps the major western Mandinka state in most of the precolonial period. Its center was in what is today Guinea-Bissau.

Sumakunda is the family from which comes the official, the *suma*. The *suma* in a western Mandinka state coordinated activities between the time of the death of one *mansa* and the investiture of another and had other administrative duties. Ordinarily, a *suma* could not become *mansa*--at least in the state where he was *suma*. Berefet is a village across the Gambia River from Niumi. It was located in the former state of Fogny, a state that seems to have been ruled by members of the Jola ethnic group.

[9]Kuyate now uses the surname Jammeh when he refers to the family of the woman *mansa* of Niumi.

[10]Kuyate is referring to a piece of paper as he gives the names of these women *mansa*. The names of the individuals only were on the paper.

[11]The names of the women *mansa* may be what David Henige calls "spurinyms," or names formed from words that have some meaning to the people living in the area. These names may indeed relate to the Atlantic-oriented life style the people of Niumi Bato led before the arrival in large numbers of Mandinka. See Henige, *Chronology of Oral Tradition*, pp. 46-48.

[12]Mandinka children are not given a name until they are about one week old. Then a ceremony is held and the child is named. The delay in naming the child reflects the high rate of infant mortality in the society. A baby who does not live beyond one week has no name and does not actually become accepted as a member of society. His or her death, then, is less difficult for the society to accept.

[13]Bureng is a village off the south bank of the Gambia about seventy-five miles upriver from Banjul. It was one of the "royal" villages of the former state of Jarra.

[14]Relying upon his "books" for his knowledge is handy for Kuyate. Whenever there is something he feels he should know but does not, he can say that he has the information in a book, but the book is not with him. From what he has to say, it would sound as if Kuyate has quite a library.

[15]Manding refers to Mali, the Mandinka Empire on the upper Niger River, or the Mandinka heartland in general, which is in the same area as the center of the Mali Empire.

[16]Obviously, Kuyate knows a certain amount about colonial government.

[17]The story of the princes going to Manding to seek *mansaya* is a popular one in almost all of the former Mandinka states of the lower Gambia. However, in each of the stories I heard the ruler of Fogny never accompanies the other princes. This is undoubtedly because Fogny was not controlled by Mandinka rulers and its system of government was different from the other states that surrounded it. Fogny was primarily a Jola state, though intermixture in Fogny among several ethnic groups was heavy. Considerable research will have to be done before we can know more about this anomalous Gambian state.

[18]See my interview with Abdoulie Samba, below--footnote 57. A *dankuto* is a special relationship among two parties that entails reciprocal obligations.

[19]In my "Niumi: The History of a Western Mandinka State," pp. 209ff.,
I describe some of the things a Mandinka member of a *mansakunda*--a ruling
family--would do to perpare himself to become *mansa* of his state. One of the
most imporant things he would do was to travel to the proper places--usually
to the courts of noted *mansa* to learn from the *mansa* himself and his followers,
*griot*s, magicians, *marabout*s, and others the secrets of obtaining the high
office. The phrase in the text, "if. . .you do not seek it from the proper
authority, you will not get it," reflects a widely held maxim among Mandinka
experts on *mansaya*. "Going to Manding," as these young men do, was the best
place to learn about *mansaya*.

[20]In a polygynous society, as Mandinka society is, a person can frequently have a number of sisters, only a few of whom share a common mother as
well as a common father. The others are half-sisters. A person's half-sister
can have a mother of a different ethnic group. Jasey's sister, the woman *mansa*
with whom he has quarreled, is his half-sister; only their father is the same.
The sister who is cooking for him is his full sister--Kuyate calls her his
"real" sister--who has both mother and father in common with Jasey. Somewhat
naturally, full siblings are often closer to one another than are half-siblings.

When speaking of siblings, Mandinka often designate those who share
both parents in common. The phrase used is "*ba keleng, fa keleng*," meaning
"same mother, same father."

[21]Practically speaking, this would be impossible because Jarra is
hundreds of miles west of the Mandinka homelands on the upper Niger.

[22]Sutung and Bureng are two villages in Jarra.

[23]When *griot*s sing the praises of groups of people, they usually have a
set of names that they use. Most large families have their own "praise names"
that *griot*s use; they use certain names, too, to praise people who live in the
former Mandinka states. People living in Jarra are praised with the names of
these four monkeys, among other things.

[24]Jokadu is the eastern portion of the former Mandinka state of Niumi.
Residents of Jokadu rebelled against Niumi's overlordship in the nineteenth
century and gained a degree of independence with that revolution.

Bali is one of the major villages in Jokadu.

[25]Nearly everyone who recited oral traditions about Niumi says that
Samake was the state's first male *mansa*. However, some--mostly members of
Niumi's strong families--say that Samake was a native of Niumi and was named
Samake Jammeh while others--mostly members of Jokadu's strong families--say that
he was a native of Jokadu and was named Samake Demba. Here Kuyate offers his own
version of the story, which explains how the confusion arose in the first place.
It is his own embellishment; I did not hear this version from anyone else.

[26]The names of *mansa* that Kuyate has provided in this paragraph are
names that Niumi's "official" list of *mansa* gives to women rulers. Kuyate
uses the names but calls them men.

[27]Mansa Buntung Sanneh Sonko Jammeh was not the *mansa* the English found ruling in Niumi when they added all of Niumi to their Gambian protectorate in the 1890s. Mansa Maranta Sonko was the last *mansa* of Niumi. Mansa Buntung Sanneh Sonko Jammeh reigned from 1862 until January 27, 1867. He was the last *mansa* of Niumi to come from the Jammeh family of Bakindiki.

[28]Actually, in the days of Mansa Buntung Sanneh Sonko Jammeh all of Banjul was not a forest. Bathurst, the major English settlement in the Gambia River area, had been established on Banjul Island since 1815, half a century before Buntung was *mansa*.

[29]Kuyate certainly means the eldest member of the "royal" family--the Manneh--in Kanuma. There were a number of families living in Kanuma, but only the Manneh family provided Niumi's *mansa* from that village.

[30]There were two families of Sonko in Essau that provided *mansa* for Niumi. One was called Njilengkunda--"Njileng's place"--and the other was called Manserringsu--"the home of the princes."

[31]This story about the Sonko surname is similar to that told by Unus Jata in my first interview with him.

[32]Binta Jammeh translated "*manserring*" as "prince." A *manserring* was a young male member of a Mandinka *mansakunda*--an extended family that was of the social class that provided the *mansa* for a Mandinka state. There were, of course, many young men in these extended families, and all of them, or even most, could not be the state's *mansa*. Therefore, some *manserring*, from time to time, would gather about them their close relatives and followers and strike out to seek their fortunes and, hopefully, to find *mansaya* in another Mandinka area. It is to this activity that Kuyate refers in this sentence.

[33]The story of Sonko traditions or origin is a complex one. I have attempted to sort out some of the complexities in my, "Koli Tengela in Sonko Traditions of Origin."

[34]There are Sonko families living in the areas of the former Mandinka states of Wuropana and Niamina on the south bank of the Gambia over one hundred miles upriver from Niumi. Kuyate is saying they are all related.

[35]British colonial authorities in The Gambia levied a tax on each head-- each individual--living in a district. Family heads usually had to pay the tax for their families. Kuyate is likening the former tax paid to the *mansa* of Niumi to the British head tax.

[36]"This island" refers to Banjul, upon which the British built Bathurst. Residents of Niumi claim that Banjul was once part of that former Mandinka state. The fact that a *mansa* of Niumi ceded rights to the island to the British remains a sore point for many Gambians to this day. Incidentally, the *mansa* who sold Banjul to the English was not the one Kuyate mentioned; it was Kolimanka Manneh, who reigned from 1814, or possibly before, to 1823.

[37]Once Gambia became a British colony and slavery was abolished, fugitives and escaped slaves did indeed go to Banjul--then called Bathurst--to seek the protection of British law. Naturally, Africans who sought the fugitives or owned the slaves resented this intrusion.

[38]Though this story of how the Europeans deceived the people of Niumi in regard to how much of Banjul Island they wanted almost surely did not happen as Kuyate tells it, his mention of the *mansa*'s wanting to take back his agreement but not being allowed to by the elders is instructive of the amount of authority the Mandinka *mansa* held. For all major decisions the *mansa* had to consult a council of elders (called a *beng*) representing the major lineages in the state. The councils overruled the *mansa* with some frequency.

[39]James Island is a small island in the middle of the Gambia River off Albreda, which was formerly one of the major trading centers in the state of Niumi. From 1661 until the foundation of Bathurst in 1815, with occasional hiatuses, English merchants occupied a fort on James Island from which they conducted trading activities up the river. The principal items of English commercial interest were slaves, ivory, gold, cowhides, and beeswax. In exchange they brought iron, cloth, alcohol, horses, firearms, and metalware.

[40]I disucss the manufacturing of salt and its importance to the early history of Niumi in my, "Niumi: The History of a Western Mandinka State," pp. 31-34.

[41]Gambians grew groundnuts--or peanuts--for export only since 1829. How much earlier they grew them for their own use is not clear. The Portuguese introduced the peanut, which is indigenous to South America, to Africa in the sixteenth century, but Gambians and others on the Upper Guinea Coast seem to have made negligible use of the legume before the nineteenth century. See George E. Brooks, Jr., "Peanuts and Colonialism: Consequences of the Commercialization of Peanuts in West Africa, 1830-70," *Journal of African History*, XVI (1975), pp. 29-54.

SHERIF JABARTEH

TWO INTERVIEWS: January 1, 1975 and some time in the early 1970s.

GENERAL SUBJECT MATTER:

  1. Relations between the Mandinka states of Niumi and Jokadu, including
     narration of the legend of Kelefa Sanneh; questions and answers on
     Jokadu and specific families living in the Niumi-Jokadu area.
  2. Narrative history of the Kinte family of the lower Gambia.

LOCATION OF RECORDINGS:

  1. Indiana University Archives of Traditional Music, Access numbers
     4378 and 4379.
  2. Gambia Cultural Archives, Banjul.

The Informant. Sherif Jabarteh,[1] a traditional *griot* in his mid-forties, is almost certainly the person best suited to recite the various histories of many of
the non-royal families living in the former Mandinka states of the Gambia's lower
north bank: Niumi, Jokadu, and Baddibu. His grandfather lived in Sika and
Jurunku, two villages in old Niumi, and in Bareto, a village no longer in existence but once located near Kassewa in Jokadu, where he was patronized by families
living in both former states. His father was the *griot* of one Janko Kinte, an
influential man who lived in the village of Kintekunda Janeah in the former state
of Baddibu. Jabarteh himself is the *griot* of the Konte family of Bani in old
Baddibu, but he lived three years in Sika (Niumi), being patronized by the Chief[2]
residing there, and he learned the stories of his father and grandfather relating
to Niumi and Jokadu and to the Kinte family. Thus, on these two recordings he is
narrating the stories he knows best.

Besides being a highly regarded traditionalist, Jabarteh is a noted player of the
kora, a twenty-one-stringed Mandinka harp-lute regularly associated with Mandinka
*griot*s. He recites his narratives to the music of the *kora*, but seldom does he do
the playing himself. Nearly always in his company is an apprentice who is learning to play the *kora* and learning *jaliya*--the art of the *griot*--from one of considerable repute.

The Interviews. I had been conducting interviews some four months before I came
to interview Jabarteh. By that time I had considerable information on Niumi's
history from *griot*s and non-professional traditionalists. One particular point
confused me and one particular legend fascinated me. I had heard of Jabarteh and
wanted him to attempt to help me out of my confusion and to recite his noted version of the legend. I was not clear about the history of the state of Jokadu and
its relationship to Niumi. Many claimed Jokadu was a part, some saying a tribute-
paying part, of Niumi; others said Jokadu was and always had been in independent
Mandinka state. Some old maps showed the Jokadu state; others showed only Niumi
controlling the area of Jokadu. Since this area was Jabarteh's specialty, I
thought his version of relevant traditions might enlighten me about Niumi's relationship with Jokadu. Also, I had heard several times, and recorded in brief

version, the legend of Kelefa Sanneh, which is probably the most popular oral tradition sung in the lower Gambia. Kelefa symbolizes the last true Mandinka warrior, the last remnant of the waning *nyancho*[3] surclass among the western Mandinka, whose lot in life it was to ride horses, raid others, and fight for the glory and honor of Mandinka rulers. As the legend goes, Kelefa came to Niumi from Kabu, the Mandinka state centered in what is today Guinea-Bissau, to help Niumi's *mansa* overcome a rebellion in Jokadu. With his traditional spear, on horseback, Kelefa fought valiantly, but he was killed by a Jokadu sniper, who shot Kelefa from a long distance. The story is beautiful when sung and, I think, meaningful in its symbolic portrayal of the decline of an entire way of life that upper class Mandinka led for several centuries. Jabarteh was purportedly the best player and reciter of the legend. I wanted him to perform.

Through Sidibe, who seemed to know (and know the whereabouts of) every Gambian *griot*, I arranged to have Jabarteh come to my room on Wellington Street in Banjul on January 1, 1975. He arrived dressed in a long off-white gown, a white cap, and open-heeled shoes. He was accompanied by an apprentice, who carried Jabarteh's cumbersome *kora*. After discussing my interests and what I wanted him to talk about, Jabarteh decided, to my pleasant surprise, to play the *kora* himself as he narrated. Therefore, we sat on the floor to aid his playing. I turned the tape recorder on and sat the microphone in front of him about three feet from the rounded calabash-resonator of his instrument. When he began to play the room literally filled with music. He eventually spoke an introduction and then proceeded to narrate about relations between Jokadu and Niumi, bringing into his narrative the legend of Kelefa Sanneh. This is the first interview that appears below.

Sidibe was my interpreter for this interview, though through the first two-thirds of the recording no one besides Jabarteh said a word. Binta Jammeh translated the interview within about ten days of its recording.

The second interview is one the Gambia Cultural Archives has graciously allowed me to print in this volume. It was recorded some years ago--my best guess is in the early 1970s. Sidibe and Winifred Galloway recorded the interview with Jabarteh, having been asked to do so by Alex Haley, whom Americans know today as the author of *Roots*. Haley had interviewed Keba Kanyi Fofanna[4] in Juffure, a village near the Gambia's north bank in the former state of Niumi, in the mid-1960s and had gotten information he wanted about Kunta Kinte, the individual he believed to be his ancestor because of oral traditions he had heard from members of his family in the United States. Intent upon writing *Roots*, Haley asked Sidibe to attempt to find more oral traditions about the Kinte family. Naturally, Sidibe went to Sherif Jabarteh, whose father was *griot* of a prominent member of the Kinte family, and asked him to recite his story of Kinte history. It is this story that appears in the second interview. I include this interview because it deals with a Mandinka family familiar to some Americans and because it is an oral tradition representative of many of the family histories that *griot*s recite throughout the Senegambia.

Sidibe translated this interview orally; Galloway typed the words as he spoke. Sidibe and Galloway edited the interview slightly. It is reproduced below as typed in final copy by the staff of the Gambia Cultural Archives.

FIRST INTERVIEW

January 1, 1975

Jabarteh: It is I, Sherif Jabarteh, narrating on the topic of Jokadu and Niumi conflict. Jokadu and Niumi are the same lands. The reason why Jokadu left Niumi and settled separately is what I am going to disucss with Bakary Sidibe and this white American.

Jokadu and Niumi became separated because of Samake Demba. Samake Demba was born in Jokadu Bali.[5] Samake Demba had *mansaya*,[6] but before he had it, he went to Manding Mansa.[7] Several of them left The Gambia: Samake Demba of Bali, Jarra Mansa Jasey Banna, Fogny Mansa, and Kungtala Wally, they were the ones who left. Whenever people wanted *mansaya* then, they went to Manding to seek it there.

During this trip many things happened. It was during this that Jarra and Niumi got their *dankuto*.[8] When they all reached Manding they explained their reason for their journey to Manding Mansa. They told him they came to seek *mansaya*. He said to them, "I shall tell all of you how to get *mansaya*."

Now Manding Mansa had a daughter who was very beautiful. This daughter became interested in Samake Demba of Bali. Samake discussed this with her but told her, "Do not enter my house because I have come to seek *mansaya*." But during the nights the woman always jumped over the fence to meet him in his house. Nature compelled Samake and they had intercourse and she became pregnant.

Manding Mansa then inquired, "Who is responsible for making my daughter pregnant?" Samake Demba declared, "I am the one, but I was forced by your daughter to do so. I tried all I could but your daughter always jumped over the fence to meet me."

"Is it so?" he asked.

"Yes," Samake Demba said, "because she followed me temptation compelled me. I was unable to ignore her so I made her pregnant."

Manding Mansa said to him, "So I am going to kill you."

Samake replied, "Yes, you can kill me, but before killing me I would like to be permitted to go back home to Jokadu Bali to tell them"

97

So the Mansa gave him a certain length of time. He then asked him, "Who will guarantee you to act in your place if you do not return on time?"

Jarra Mansa then said, "I will act for him, and if he does not come back you can kill me."

Samake started his journey and it took him one month to reach home. By then there were no cars and one could only travel on foot or on horseback. He reached Jokadu Bali and he said to his people, "I have gone to Manding Mansa to seek *mansaya*, but something befell me there caused by Manding Mansa's child. Manding Mansa says he is going to kill me, so I have made the necessary arrangements to come and bid you farewell. I have Jarra Mansa Jasey Banna acting as guarantee for me. If I do not go back they will kill him."

The people asked him, "Is it so?"

He said, "Yes, they permitted me to go."

Samake Demba then started his journey back, but before his arrival the actual day came nearer. Then Jarra Mansa Jasey Banna said, "This man has not come back yet and the time has come so you kill me in his place."

They dressed Jasey Banna in the dress of the man to be executed. They took him to be killed at the usual place. Coincidentally, Samake Demba was coming with a long bamboo stick upon which he had tied a white flag. He waved his flag to show his arrival so they would not kill Jarra Mansa. When they saw it they said, "Let us wait because someone is coming waving a white flag."

Samake met Jasey dressed in the execution dress. Samake said to them, "The reason I tied my flag to the stick is that I do not want him to be killed. I have come so you undress him and dress me up."

Jarra Mansa Jasey Banna was taken up and Samake Demba was dressed and laid down. Jarra Mansa then came and said, "Kill both of us together."

Manding Mansa then came and said, "If one should make these people *mansa*, whenever they make promises they will never fail to keep them." Then the Manding Mansa said, "Leave them, do not kill them. Raise them up."

They raised them up and Samake Demba shook hands with Jarra Mansa Jasey Banna, who said, "There is a *dankuto* between us and if a Niumi person ever makes a Jarra person cry, then he will suffer the consequences, and vice-versa." So Jarra and Niumi's *dankuto* started from that day.

Later on, Manding Mansa said to them, "Samake Demba, you must now become *mansa*, but you will obtain your *mansaya* by taking care of dogs. Jarra Mansa Jasey Banna, you will also become *mansa* when you reach home even if you do not do anything, just because of your righteousness.

When Samake Demba returned to Jokadu, he used to follow the dogs and say to his people, "I have come and I will not get *mansaya*." He kept dogs for hunting. By then there was a woman *mansa* in Niumi Berneding called Mamang Kibili Sonko. She had no husband. Samake Demba used to go hunting in Niani Fara.[9] The water level never goes down there in either the rainy or the dry seasons and it was there that the woman *mansa*'s servants used to go to wash their clothes. Whenever Samake came near there he always took his dogs there to drink. Whenever these servants returned to Niumi they always said to Mamang Kibili Sonko, "But one very handsome man always comes to the lake for his dogs to drink. He is very handsome."

Then she would reply, "If you should go, you tell this man to come so I can see him."

Samake came there without fail and one day they said to him, "Samake, we want to go with you to Berending."

When Samake arrived at Mamang Kibili Sonko's house, she came out with her royal paraphernalia on and stood at the door. When she saw Samake Demba she caught hold of him and they went inside the house. She asked him, "Where do you come from?"

He said, "From Jokadu Bali."

She took off her things and gave them to Samake Demba and said to him, "I am a woman *mansa* but I have no husband and I am seeking one. I hear that you come to Niani Fara and I know that you will also become *mansa* and I will be your woman."

This was how Samake became *mansa*. She called all their elders and said to them, "I have got a husband and he will be the *mansa* and I will be his woman."

He then sent a message to his relatives in Jokadu Bali, saying, "I have become a *mansa* and I have done so as I was told in Manding." The people used to collect bundles of millet as taxes and they collected unpounded rice, because then there was not enough money.

The *mansaya* was normal and as time went on, Mamang Kibili Sonko died and Samake Demba was left as ruler of the land. The Niumi people refused to let Samake Demba return to Jokadu. He said, "I must go home," and they said, "You are not going to go. You were made *mansa* here and since Mamang Kibili died you must stay here."

Then the people of Sitanunku[10] said, "They have caused us trouble because Samake Demba left *here* to seek *mansaya* in Manding." They called him Samake Jammeh. The Jokadu people said also that Samake was a citizen of that place. Samake himself said that he was a citizen of Jokadu. This is what caused the conflict, but he was a citizen of Jokadu Bali. This is how he got two names, Samake Demba and Samake Jammeh.[11]

When Samake Demba left he went to Jokadu Bali. The Niumi people let him go and collect taxes because when he was in Niumi all the collected taxes used to go there. The Jokadu people refused being taxed by the Niumi people. This was what caused the partition of the land.

The Niumi people had conflicts with the Jokadu people because of Samake Demba's departure to Jokadu Bali.[12] It was the Berending people who went to get him. By then the Berending people were settled at Sangako Madina.[13] The Jokadu people refused to be taxed, so they decided on Niumi and Jokadu becoming separate lands. This caused the partition of Jokadu and Niumi.

Mansa Demba[14] was the first to be crowned, but he tried all he could and could not get at Jokadu and he did not know how to do so. Then there came one Fula man from Jokadu with whom he met at the boundary between the two lands. There was then a valley seen after passing Kassewa where the cattle used to drink.[15] The Jokadu cattle and the Niumi cattle fought. After the fight they fought again on the reconciliation day. They fought among themselves. The Jokadu people then remembered their old quarrel.[16] But Mansa Demba was still interested in getting at Jokadu.

Now whenever the Niumi people needed messengers, they used the people of Juffure. They were also the *falifo*.[17] There happened to be one man living in Juffure then and he was the one they sent to take their message to Jokadu. This man was Alhaji Darbo. Naturally, everyone would like his country to become wealthy; Alhaji Darbo was like this. Mansa Demba called upon him to go to Jokadu. He said to him, "Tell them not to have differences with us because it is not good for two neighboring villages to be on bad terms."

But there were some people then who wanted Jokadu and Niumi to fight. Alhaji Darbo of Juffure went to Jokadu and said to them, "The Niumi people have asked me to tell you to agree to their demands and if you refuse them you will never be on good terms with them again, and if they should fight you they will conquer you." Then when he was leaving Jokadu to return to Niumi, just before he reached Niumi he took off his shirt and tore it all up with thorns. When he arrived he took off his shirt and said to Mansa Demba, "You have sent me to the Jokadu people to seek reconciliation, but they do not want it. They have beaten me and torn my shirt."

We should always fear hypocrites because they are always
responsible for the bitterness between two lands and two
families and breaks in the tranquility of a village.

After reporting the false story of his first journey, he
was asked again by Mansa Demba to return to Jokadu and
tell them that only two adjacent rice swamps have their
waters overflowing into one another. But when he came
back this time he said to Mansa Demba, "The Jokadu people
said that though you have strong feelings that you have
more people than they do, they will conquer you."

The Niumi people became annoyed and made the concrete decision that they were going to fight. There were then
very good hunters in Jokadu. There was one influential
man, Hamadadu Segani, who was feared. He was a gun
shooter and he learned it from the *jinn*.[18] When Hamadadu
Segani was young he had no babysitter and so his mother
took him to the rice swamps with her.[19] She placed him
under the tree and always glanced at him while working.
Then a female *jinn* came and took away Hamadadu Segani
from the tree and placed another baby there. The baby
was not a human being but a *jinn*. When the woman came
to suckle the baby she said, "This is not my baby because
my own baby had his head shaved and this baby's head is
not shaved." Then she held the baby and got him to suckle.

The *jinn* took Hamadadu Segani Demba until he became grown.
She had her husband teach him about hunting until he became an able hunter. He gave him a gun and lead. His
gun was called *dudumbulu*. He then left and went to his
people, but they were afraid of him at first sight and
he said to them, "I was brought up by the *jinn* but I think
I was born in Jokadu Tambana here.[20] I think I was exchanged in the bush." The people declared it to be the
truth.

There were then some very influential people in Tambana:
Manbanding Segani Demba, Thielly Kumba Segani Demba, Kali
Metta Burko, Jumbu Metta Burko, Nuhung Jaja Segani Demba.
Hamadadu Segani became their leader. All these men were
hunters and they were very good ones. They were the ones
who made people fear Jokadu. Mosambu Manneh was from Bunyadu. He was also a very good hunter. Jarra Banna was
also a very good hunder residing in Kassewa near Bereto.
It was at Bereto that our ancestor Karunga settled.[21]

The people of Niumi knew there would be a great conflict
between themselves and the Jokadu people. There were
some *marabouts*[22] residing at Jokadu Dasalami. Jokadu
Mansa was at Bali and the influential people were at
Tambana. The *marabouts* residing at Dasalami were the
Fofanna Kanyi.[23]

It was then that Mansa Demba wrote a letter to Kelefa Sanneh in Badora for help.[24] Kelefa looked at the letter and said, "I do not know anything but wine."[25] He took the letter to the street and found a Futa Toranka[26] whom he asked to look at the letter. When he examined it he said, "This letter is from Niumi Berending from Mansa Demba. He said that he has a fight and would like you to help him."

Kelefa then took the letter to his parents, Dala Ngaling and Mariama Nanki. They said to him, "Kelefa, we do not want war because war is not good for a single child."

Kelefa said, "I must go because everyone will die when his time comes."

At that time there were four families in Badora and each one had one thousand warriors, which they gave to Kelefa for his assistance. When Kelefa was coming from Badora, he had four thousand warriors. When he was coming he was accompanied by his family for part of the way. His mother took out a *juju* horn[27] from under the plaiting of her hair and said to him, "Take this because if you should die it will announce your death, and if you do not die, bring it back with you."

When Kelefa reached Fula Mansa Falicon Banna's place and explained the subject of his journey, Falicon Banna said to him, "I have given you one hundred male cows and one hundred female cows."

Kelefa said, "I want you to help me with gunpowder and bullets."

Falicon replied, "Proceed, because I have no war between me and the other people."

It was that day that Kelefa consulted the fetishes and they said, "Before you to to Niumi, go first to Fogny, to a village called Berefet, where there is a silk-cotton tree near the river. The tree is called *jombong bantang*, and if the fetish responds to your call, then you can proceed."[28]

Kelefa proceeded with his people to Fogny Berefet and he bought a black male cow for the sacrifice to the fetish. From there he went to Fogny Mansa Kungtala Wali, who asked him where he was going and he replied, "I am going to answer Mansa Demba's call."

Fogny Mansa said to him, "I will give you one hundred male cows and one hundred female cows."

Kelefa answered, "Give me gunpowder and bullets instead of that."

Wali replied, "I have no war between me and any other people."

So Kelefa then proceeded to Kiang Mansa, who also said
to him, "I will give you one hundred male sheep and one
hundred female sheep."

Kelefa said, "I prefer bullets and gunpowder to that to
go to war."

Kiang Mansa replied, "Proceed on, then, because there is
no war between me and other people."

Kelefa next went to Jarra Mansa and was asked where he
was going. "I am going to answer Mansa Demba's call,"
he said.

Jarra Mansa then said to him, "I will give you one hundred
male and one hundred female cows."

Kelefa replied, "Before giving me that would you give me
gunpowder and bullets for the war?"

Jarra Mansa then said to him, "Proceed, for no war exists
between me and the other people."

From there he proceeded to Baddibu Mansa Sankala Marong
of India.[29] Sankala asked him where he was going and he
said, "I am going to answer Mansa Demba's call."

Sankala Marong said, "I will give you one hundred boys
and one hundred girls."

Kelefa replied, "I prefer gunpowder and bullets to that
because I am going to war."

Sankala Marong then said, "Proceed, because I have no war
with those other people."

From there Kelefa crossed over to Jokadu Dasalami, where
he was asked by Arafang Bully the same question and he
replied that he was going to help Mansa Demba. Arafang
then agreed to give him one hundred male and one hundred
female goats. Kelefa told him, "I prefer gunpowder and
bullets to that because I am going to war."

Arafang told him, "Proceed, then, because no war exists
between me and the other people.

At last he reached Mansa Demba's in Berending. Mansa
Demba said to him, "I am the one calling you for a war
in Jokadu."

Niumi used to collect taxes from Banjul then.[30] The
Portuguese were the first ones taxed and Niumi once had
troubles with one Portuguese called Sang Dimingu.[31] He
was the first Portuguese to come here and he found the
women working on the island. The women used to take
canoes from Barra Point to Banjul to work and they always
went back in the evenings.[32] When the women saw the

Europeans they wanted to run away, but his interpreter told them not to run. The interpreter, known as James Island, asked them, "Who is the island's owner?"

They replied, "Mansa Demba of Berending."

They then crossed over to meet Mansa Demba in Berending and they said to him, "Give us an area to settle on Banjul."

"Would you pay me a tax?" Mansa Demba asked.

"Yes," he replied.

From there he went up to Jarra and said, "I want you to give me an area here."

Jarra Mansa told him, "You can build one house but I must tax you." The European agreed. From there he went to the area between Sika and Juffure and he built a shop there. He then went to Albreda and built a house there, so the Mandinka called the place Sang Dimingu. It has a reason why it had a second name. Sang made many trips, one with a sailor who became ill there and died and was buried there. The Europeans bought and called that James Island.[33]

Mansa Demba sent to the *marabout* for soothsaying and he was told thus, "Your stranger who has come to help you for war will be recognized more than you if you go to war." So Mansa Demba told Kelefa that he was going to send him to Banjul to collect the taxes.

The Jokadu people also had a *marabout*. He was from Niamina Sotokoi and was called Alhaji Mariama Daffeh of Surokunda.[34] Hamadadu Segani Demba got him to work for the people of Jokadu. While this *marabout* was being lodged at Jokadu Bali he wrote a *dumbukafundo*[35] and they buried it at Bali. He wrote on a horse's skull and they buried it at Meme.[36] He wrote on a donkey's skull and they buried it at Tambana. He wrote on seven sticks used by the blind men and on an iron slate and they buried those in the water of Tankonding Lake situated between Niumi and Jokadu. He then said to them, "If Jokadu happens to be conquered, you can take me and all my abilities and throw me into the Miniminiyang Creek." Then he went back home.

Mansa Demba, having heard of all this, sent a person with money to go and see the *marabout*. When he reached his house he said to him, "I have already committed myself in Jokadu." But Niumi sent a woman messenger, who got the *marabout* to change his mind. He wrote on a special slate and gave it to Mansa Demba's messenger. It was to be thrown into the river when the Jokadu people were expected. He said, "There will be a great noise in the river and the Jokadu people will think the Niumi people are coming by sea. Those who then get into their boats and embark will have their boat wrecked and will not be able to take part in the fight."[37]

When Kelefa came, he met the Niumi people ready for the
war. He collected the taxation money from the European
and was taking it to Mansa Demba in Berending. He crossed the river in a canoe. At Barra Point he met an old
woman, who begged for some snuff from him saying, "I have
no snuff." He gave her the snuff and she said, "I am just
from Niumi Berending and all the people have gathered to
go to war in Jokadu."

Kelefa then rode his horse to Berending, where he met
Mansa Demba's wife. He said to her, "Keep this money for
me." When he reached the Meme bridge he found the Niumi
people arguing about which way to go. Some said Tambana,
some said Dasalami, and some said Bali. Kelefa then said,
"Mansa Demba, why did you call me for a war and then leave
without telling me?"

Mansa Demba replied, "The reason is because I was foretold
by the soothsayer that you would die on the battlefield."

Kelefa said, "Everyone will die when his time comes."

So Mansa Demba apologized and suggested that they should
go to Tambana. Kelefa rejected the suggestion, saying that
the people of Tambana were blacksmiths. They then suggested they go to Dasalami, but Kelefa rejected that, saying, "Those people are Muslims." They next suggested they
go to start the fighting at Bali, but still Kelefa rejected
it, saying, "That is not a good place. Wherever we start
it should be impossible to get from there to Niumi. Is
there not a village called Baringyakoto?" When the people
replied that there was Kelefa said, "Then let us go there."[38]

On approaching Kuntair[39] one can see a valley, and it was
through there that Kelefa Sanneh and the people of Niumi
passed. They went to Madina Jikoyi, Patoko Fenyoto, then
to Kularikoto, and crossed to Baringyakoto.[40] The foot-
steps of their horses are still there because it got dried
up.

When they were ready for the battle Kelefa and the Niumi
people stood behind their war fences.[41] Hamadadu Segani
Demba and the Jokadu people also stood over their war fence
on a Monday. Those who joined the boat to come got their
boat wrecked and they all died. They started the war on a
Monday at about nine o'clock. Whenever they fired at Kelefa
he would catch the bullet. He was resistant to bullets.
But whenever he fired he always killed about ten people
with one bullet.[42] Whenever Hamadadu Segani fired his gun
he killed about twelve people. Whenever he fired the *jinn*
woman took back the bullet and placed it inside his gun
again. His great grandson, Kekoto Segani, is a hunter
and a *marabout* also.[43]

When they were all ready they fought until evening of
that Monday. Then on Wednesday the *jinn* said to Hamadadu,

"This Jola[44] cannot be killed by bullets, but only by a
deer's horn put inside a gun." He did what the *jinn*
told him, but it was futile because it could not kill
Kelefa. On Thursday she advised him to take a pure Fula's
waist beads, so they went to one village called Hamadi
Faleya in Jokadu. There was a Fula woman there whose
waist beads they cut from her. She was called "*Wurinding*."
He placed the beads in the gun and fired at Kelefa. It
was futile again because it could not harm him. Then on
Saturday the *jinn* said, "This Jola is not so easily killed.
Go and get a one-year-old cock."

Kelefa was then killing people like birds. The battle was
at its climax because Hamadadu was killing even more people
than Kelefa. The Niumi people outnumbered the Jokadu people
but the Jokadu people were being helped by the *jinn*. This was
the reason for the graveness of the war for the people of
Niumi. By then all the influential people and good hunters
were in Jokadu. Many people died at this battle from both
Niumi and Jokadu.

The *jinn* told the people of Jokadu, "If we want to conquer
Niumi we must kill this Jola." He was their hope. So they
then got a one-year-old cock, killed it, and took off the
spur and placed it in poison. The *jinn* still advised them,
"Whenever you want to kill him a leper must go up a tree and
you must load the gun and give it to him." The leper climbed
into a baobab tree, one of a group of four you can still see
coming from Baringyakoto going to Kular, on the road near
the river. They said to him, "Stoop down three times before shooting Kelefa and it must be on a Monday."

When he stooped three times, on the fourth he fired and
this time Kelefa was shot under the armpit. When it touched
him the gun he was holding dropped from his hand. The
people asked him about it and he said, "I shall not resist
this shot, I will die."

Kelefa's horses neighed as the time approached. They
lifted Kelefa but he was not yet dead. They searched for
his horn but they could not see it. Kelefa then said,
"Mansa Demba, I want you to tell me those who really worry
you in this war. Tell me so I can kill them before I die
myself." The people he killed were all from Jokadu, but
he could not kill the influential people. As he killed
them, he fell. By that time Mansa Demba was standing behind the fence. Kelefa was lifted and carried to a rubber
tree and placed beneath it. He asked them, "What kind of
a tree is this?"

They replied, "A rubber tree."

He said, "A rubber tree is transparent and I have cried
whenever I was beaten by my peers."

From there he was taken underneath a *santang* tree.[45]
When he asked and was told it was a *santang* tree he said,
"An adult who is likened to a *santang* tree in quality must
retain that character."

From there he was taken underneath a mango tree and he said,
"It is this tree that children learn to climb. I was never
beaten by my peers until I cried and it was not on me that
my peers learned how to fight."

He was then taken to a *sinjang* tree.[46] When he was told
where he was he asked, "How do the seeds taste, and the
roots?"

The people replied, "It tastes bitter."

He said, "Then if I should die, bury me here. There will
be anthills at the foot and head of my grave. No grass
will grow on my grave forever in this world."

His prediction came true because his grave is still without grasses. The last time I went there I only saw three
small plants growing. Even now there is a flat anthill
there.

The war was interrupted. The Niumi people could fight no
longer and those who wanted to run ran away. One Fula man
in Niumi wanted to replace Kelefa, but he could not do it.
He was shot by Hamadadu Segani, and he took his spear and
crossed the river in Kular and went into French territory.[47]

This was the reason for conflict between Niumi and Jokadu.
This is why the elders always feared when Jokadu and Niumi
had differences, because many important people always die
during this conflict. The Niumi people ran away because
the Jokadu people had already conquered them. The Niumi
people are still filled with regret over this. Whenever
you narrate this story the Niumi people always become in-
furitated.

After it was over they took Kelefa's spear to Niumi Juffure.
They took it there because his grandfather, Nuhung Tall,
lived there. After the war they almost gave it to the
Europeans in trade, because by then there was starvation.

Here Jabarteh stopped his narrative and invited me to ask specific questions
over what he had said or other matters. I had some other topics upon which I wanted
him to comment, so I proceeded.

Q: How did the people of Bali originally obtain *mansaya*? I
          had heard that traditionally they were blacksmiths.[48]

Jabarteh: The people of Bali were not blacksmiths. The Tambana
          people were the blacksmiths and they were the Segani.[49]

          The ruling family of Niumi is that of the Sonko. When

the people of Bali came the Sonko were ruling. When they came here the place was flat. They were the first settlers here so that is why they are said to be the *chosan* of the area.[50] When you go to an area and you do not meet anyone there and you clear that area and stay there, then you must become the *chosan*. They all came from Pakau, but they were former settlers of Kabu. Before their people became *mansa* they had to go to Manding to seek it.

According to what I have heard, there was another *mansa* in Bali before Samake Demba. When Samake left as *mansa* in Bali there was not another *mansa* there because of fetish practices.[51] Samake Demba did not witness the war against Mansa Demba because he became ill and died before it broke out. From Bali *mansaya* passed to Dasalami and the war happened in the time of Arafang Bully of Jokadu Dasalami.[52] He ruled in precolonial days. They say there was one other *mansa* there before Arafang Bully, but I do not know his name. Jokadu Tambana had one *mansa* also and his surname was Jammeh.[53] It was from these people that the Toranka took over.[53] When they lost *mansaya* they were sabotaged and they did not get it any more because of fetish practices.

Q: Of what ethnic group was the woman *mansa* whom Samake Demba married?

Jabarteh: She was Mamang Kibili Sonko. She came from Siin to Berending. She was not a Mandinka but a Serer. The area around Berending had their *mansa* installed by Siin Mansa. They even took their collected taxes to Siin, and all this was stopped by Mansa Demba. The taxes then were rice and millet, but he refused to send any, instead sending gunpowder and bullets. When Siin Mansa received these he said, "The bearer of these things will never again bring in his taxes."[54]

Q: In which particular village in Manding did people go to seek *mansaya*?

Jabarteh: They went to Kaba.[55] When you want to go there you must go to Mali and from there you can go directly to Kaba by car. Everyone came from Manding. But the Jammeh of Baddibu are Serer.

Q: What relationship did the Jammeh have with Kabu?

Jabarteh: It was through traveling and mixed settlement. The Jammeh of Bakindiki, Kabu, and Baddibu are the same. The Jammeh of Baddibu Iliassa always go to Nioro or Siin to take wives. For example, Kebba Jammeh. . . .Presently he has a wife in Mbour, who has not even come to live with him.[56]

Q: How did people become influential?[57]

Jabarteh: Through bravery. An influential person is one who is very brave. He is never afraid to talk of something or do something, nor is he asked to do things.

Hamadi Kura was a great *marabout* and he had contacts with the *jinn*. His Koranic books are still there. His grandson Kekoto Segani, is still there. In fact, even he has contacts with the *jinn*, because he once shot one *jinn* and killed him. People could not see it but they could hear cries in the forest saying, "Kekoto has killed him." He said that he went to hunt and he lighted his torch and the *jinn* also lighted his torch. Then Kekoto said to him, "Don't put your torch light on me." When the *jinn* stopped Kekoto shot him and killed him. People even came from Senegal to get protective *juju* from him. He is not a very active hunter as he once was. He says that he still has Hamadadu's bullet. Hamadadu was a Muslim but his father was not.

Q: Were there *soninke* as well as Muslims in Jokadu?

Jabarteh: There were some *soninke* in Jokadu, but there were Muslims as well. Their last *mansa* was a Muslim. The greater part of the Tambana population was Muslim then.

FOOTNOTES TO THE FIRST INTERVIEW

[1]Sherif is the Mandinka version of the Arabic *Sharīf*, which supposedly refers to persons who are descendants of the Prophet Muhammad.

[2]A Chief is a political leader in The Gambian governmental structure who has authority over an area called a district. One of the first colonial officials established by the British as they instituted their control over The Gambian colony, the office of Chief was continued by The Gambian government after independence in 1965. The Chief in Sika was the Chief of Upper Niumi District. A few years back the Chief residing in Sika was defeated in an election and the present Chief of Upper Niumi resides in the village of Lamin about fifteen miles downriver from Sika.

[3]As noted earlier, *nyancho* were the founders of the Mandinka state (or empire) of Kabu. They were a surclass of rulers and warriors who lived by a code of *machismo* that glorified bravery and heroism in battle and included a strongly-held animist faith.

[4]For my interview with Fofanna, in which he speaks very briefly about Kunta Kinte, see the second volume of "Oral Traditions from the Gambia, Volume II, Non-Professional Informants."

[5]Bali is a village in the eastern part of Jokadu District of The Gambia lying near the Senegal border. It is presently a thriving town because of its thriving seasonal peanut trade. The story of Samake Demba that follows is Jabarteh's version of the tradition narrated by Kemo Kuyate, above. I include it for the sake of comparison. Each *griot* includes his own embellishments, but the basic stories are quite similar.

[6]Again, *mansaya* is best translated as "kingship."

[7]Manding Mansa is the ruler of Mali, the Mandinka Empire centered on the upper Niger River, the area of the Mandinka homelands.

[8]A *dankuto* is a special, close relationship between two persons, families, or states.

[9]Niani is the name of the former Mandinka state directly east of Baddibu.

[10]Sitanunku is a village in the former state of Niumi near the Gambia River, just a few miles inland from Jerre Point. The predominant extended family living in Sitanunku is the Jammeh family. Traditionally, the Jammeh family of Sitanunku was one of the seven families that provided the *mansa* of Niumi in rotation.

[11]There is a long-standing dispute between members of the Jammeh family of Niumi and those of the Demba family of Jokadu over whether Samake was a Jammeh or a Demba. Naturally, each claims Samake as an ancestor. I had hopes that Jabarteh would enlighten me on this dispute, but he simply states the way it was because "Samake himself said that he was a citizen of Jokadu." This is dubious evidence, of course, since Samake is almost surely a mythical figure. But what is interesting is that the people of Jokadu will go about claiming Samake as one of their own, citing Sherif Jabarteh as evidence. If he says it is so, that is good backing, which can only be refuted, in part, by the word of another *griot* of equal repute.

[12]Jabarteh begins to repeat himself and the narrative is not so organized as before because he is between stories, that of Samake Demba and that of Kelefa Sanneh. His repitition and disorganization is indicative of the rough transition from one to another. Eventually, as he gets into the Kelefa Sanneh story, the narrative will smooth out.

[13]Sangako Madina is a village located on the Atlantic coast just a few miles north of the Senegal-Gambia border. Traditionally, this was part of the state of Niumi. The legends of the Sonko family, who are "the Berending people" Jabarteh mentions, say the Sonko first lived in this northern area of Niumi before moving further south to the villages of Berending and Essau, their homes for several centuries down to the present. This means that Jabarteh is speaking about events that happened a long time ago--back when the Sonko were living in their original villages in northern Niumi.

[14]Mansa Demba refers to Niumi's Mansa Demba Adama Sonko, who was *mansa* from 1834 to 1862. Note the transition in time from the preceding paragraph. I believe Jabarteh recognizes the general difference in time, but it does not bother him greatly because both events occurred a long time ago--in the "distant past." In his mind I would guess he is thinking that Niumi and Jokadu had been quarreling for a long time over tax and such matters. The warfare between Niumi and Jokadu, into which the Kelefa Sanneh story fits, took place in the mid-nineteenth century. European records mention this fighting from time to time in the 1830s and 1840s and it may have been part of the widespread social revolution taking place in the area that culminated in the so-called Soninke-*Marabout* Wars of the early 1860s.

[15]In precolonial days borders were not always clearly delineated. Between Niumi and Jokadu, however, a valley seems to have marked the boundary. The fighting of the cattle, even on reconciliation day, seems to suggest that the fighting was widespread and practically never-ending.

[16]Here Jabarteh makes reference to the quarrel mentioned in the paragraph above that happened back when the Sonko were living in the north of Niumi.

[17]In most western Mandinka areas a *falifo* was simply a resident foreigner, but in Niumi a *falifo* seems more specifically to have been a man from another state who had married a woman of one of the "royal" families. *Falifo* were particularly useful as less biased administrative officials. They divided things that had to be divided equitably and they carried messages without adding

their views to the content. As the story continues it will become obvious that Alhaji Darbo of Juffure is not a good *falifo*.

Juffure is a village next to Albreda, just off Niumi's southern river-bank opposite James Island. It was a point of commercial and social contact between Niumi's residents and foreign traders, African, Eurafrican, and European. The Darbo family came to Juffure as *jula*, or traders. Through their successful trading operations involving slaves and other commodities, the Darbo family grew prosperous and indeed married family members into important families along the lower river. Members of the Darbo family seem to have served as intermediaries between Europeans and Africans in Niumi and beyond. For more on this family and its precolonial commercial operations, see my, "Darbo Jula."

[18]*Jinn* are devils. This is an interesting piece on Hamadadu Segani, sometimes called Hamadadu Sekan or Hamadadu Sekan Demba, and his learning to shoot from the devils. Until roughly the early part of the nineteenth century Mandinka in the lower Gambia used guns almost solely for celebration--they made noise. Sometime in the early decades of the nineteenth century, however, there developed some sharpshooters who did not have the traditional Mandinka qualms about fighting with guns. (Mandinka had thought it cowardly to fight from long distance; their traditional way of fighting was close-in, with swords and knives.) These individuals, using their new fighting methods with some success, seem to have altered drastically methods of conducting warfare in the region. The Soninke-*Marabout* Wars of the early 1860s may be explained in part as the outgrowth of this new type of warfare, where previously dominated groups of people, led by the *marabout*s, using the equalizing weapons of firearms, overthrew the *soninke*, the families that had for so long provided rulers for the Mandinka states and had been the elite class in western Mandinka society. The legend of Kelefa Sanneh is particularly meaningful to the Mandinka who hear it because it symbolizes the demise of this elite group of Mandinka rulers. It is no coincidence that Kelefa goes into battle on horseback with his spear, only to be shot from his horse by a devil-assisted sniper in a tree. For information on the background of the Soninke-*Marabout* Wars and the wars themselves see, Charlotte Quinn, *Mandingo Kingdoms of the Senegambia: Traditionalism, Islam, and European Expansion* (Evanston, Ill., 1972), Chapters 2-8, and Martin A. Klein, "The Moslem Revolution in Nineteenth Century Senegambia," in *Western African History*, Vol. 4 of *Boston University Papers on Africa*, edited by Daniel F. McCall, Norman R. Bennett, and Jeffrey Butler (New York, 1969), pp. 69-101.

[19]In Mandinka society there is a division of agricultural labor between the sexes. Men grow millet and peanuts; women grow wet rice.

[20]Tambana is a village roughly in the center of what is now Jokadu District of The Gambia. According to tradition, the village was founded by the Jammeh family before members of that family moved on further west and founded two villages in Niumi, Bakindiki, and Sitanunku.

[21]Bunyadu is a village in Niumi about seven miles from Barra Point. The Manneh family founded Bunyadu; the Manneh of Bunyadu was one of Niumi's seven "royal" families. Kassewa and Bereto are villages near the traditional demarcation line, the valley, between Niumi and Jokadu.

[22]A *marabout* is a Muslim teacher, healer, diviner, and magical practitioner. When Mandinka fought wars one aspect of the preparation for fighting was to get *marabout*s to make protective amulets and charms and to work magical practice on the enemy to insure victory. *Marabout*s who were successful at this sort of thing were highly respected and sought after.

[23]The Fofanna Kanyi family is a family of Muslim holy men who serve as *marabout*s and religious leaders in several communities in Niumi and Jokadu. Alex Haley's primary informant, the late Keba Kanyi Fofanna, was a member of this family.

Dasalami (from the Arabic *dar as salaam*, the land of peace) is a village in eastern Jokadu District not far from the Miniminiyang Creek, which separates Jokadu from Baddibu. There are several villages with this name, or one similar, throughout The Gambia.

[24]Kelefa was from the former Mandinka state of Kabu, which was centered in Guinea-Bissau. Badora was a section of Kabu located near the head of the Gêba River estuary just south of the present-day city of Bafata.

[25]Kelefa was a *nyancho*. He drank palm wine, rode horses, fought, and raided people; he did not read.

[26]A Futa Toranka is a person from Futa Toro, a region in northern Senegal inside the bend of the Senegal River. Many Fulbe from Futa Toro are learned Muslims who can read and write using the Arabic script. This is undoubtedly why Jabarteh places a person from Futa Toro in the position of being the reader in Badora.

[27]A *juju* horn is a magical piece made of cow's or goat's horn filled with secret things. It is the type of device that a *marabout* would make for someone going off to fight.

[28]Mandinka warriors consulted their fetishes before going into battle. The fetish was to give the warrior some idea of his prospects for success and to relate to him any special instructions or ways of fighting that would lead to successful combat. In this instance Kelefa is told that if the fetish does not respond to his sacrifice, then he will not be successful and should return home.

[29]The Marong family of India, a village in Central Baddibu District, was one of five families that provided *mansa* for the former Mandinka state of Baddibu.

[30]Jabarteh launches into a long digression here on Banjul Island and the Portuguese. He does so to set the scene for Mansa Demba sending Kelefa to collect taxes at Banjul, discussed below.

[31]Sang Dimingu is a form of Santo Domingo, which was the name of the first Portuguese, or Afro-Portuguese, settlement on Niumi's Gambian banks. Jabarteh uses the name symbolically for the first Portuguese in The Gambia. Similarly, immediately below Jabarteh calls the interpreter in the narrative "James Island," which was the name of the first permanent English settlement in the area. Symbolically, the name stands for the English in The Gambia before the colonial period.

[32]Before the English erected dikes and drainage ditches there, Banjul Island was a low, swampy area where rice could be grown. Jabarteh is referring to Niumi women, who took canoes over to Banjul Island to work in rice fields.

[33]There actually was a Portuguese sailor who died in the Gambia River on the second voyage of Alvise da Cadamosto in 1456. His name was Andrew and he was buried on the island the English would call James Island. Cadamosto called it St. Andrew's Island. See John M. Gray, *History of the Gambia* (London, 1940), p. 6.

[34]Niamina is the name of the former Mandinka state just upriver from Jarra on the river's south bank. Sotokoi is a village in Niamina. The Daffeh family is a noted Mandinka *marabout* family.

[35]*Dumbukafundo* is a type of protective charm that a *marabout* made. Burying these charms in specific places served to protect the people from harm during warfare.

[36]Meme is a village in Jokadu located on the Niumi-Jokadu border.

[37]Such portrayal of wars as competition between magical practitioners is a common motif in Mandinka traditions about warfare.

[38]Baringyakoto is a village located north of Bali across the present Senegal-Gambia boundary. This implies that Kelefa had a vision about where the fight should take place.

[39]Kuntair is the seat of Gambian government in Jokadu District. It is on the main east-west road passing through Jokadu.

[40]These are all villages in northern Jokadu or across the border into Senegal. By going as Jabarteh says, the people of Niumi went around the creek upon which Baringyakoto lies and came upon it from the north.

[41]In reading British reports of the Soninke-*Marabout* Wars in the region one finds Mandinka fighting from behind stockades. It seems to have been the popular tactic of the time to build a stockade and then shoot from behind it—a change in tactics brought about by the increasing use of firearms in fighting.

[42]Kelefa here uses a gun. This does not fit with other versions of the story I heard. And people say that Kelefa's spear is still in existence (though no one was ever able to show it to me).

[43]I assume Kekoto Segani is a person living today. I did meet several people who said they were descendants of Hamadadu Segani Demba.

[44]It is interesting that Jabarteh refers to Kelefa as a Jola. Kabu was a Mandinka state, though it did contain people of several ethnic groups, Jola being one. The patronymic Sanneh is sometimes considered a Mandinka surname, sometimes Jola. Perhaps Kelefa had some Jola in his ancestry, perhaps not.

[45]I do not know what kind of a tree a *santang* tree is.

[46]I believe a *singjang* tree is a large tree bearing round green fruit, which, when chewed, gives off a sour juice.

[47]Of course, this was not French territory in the mid-nineteenth century, but today both Kular and Baringyakoto (now called Baria) are in Senegal, which is what Jabarteh means by "French territory." Senegal was a former French colony.

[48]An informant in Niumi had mentioned to me that the people of Bali were blacksmiths. In Mandinka society blacksmiths were respected and feared, being workers with fire and elements from the earth where spirits dwelled. Along with leather workers and *griots*, they formed a separate group, sometimes likened to a caste, but certainly not in its Indian manifestation, which usually lived separately from others and married only within the group. Members of this group could become very influential people, but they would never become *mansa*. *Mansaya* was set aside for a special elite group of freeborn Mandinka.

[49]If the Segani were blacksmiths, it explains in part why Hamadadu Segani was associated with *jinn* and had such magical powers. See footnote 48, above.

[50]*Chosan* means "traditional people" or "original settlers" of an area. The *chosan* of an area had a special relationship with the spirits of the soil there and they were usually accorded the rights to *mansaya* there.

[51]It was possible to usurp *mansaya* through use of fetishes and certain magical means. This was fairly common practice in places where *mansaya* was not so clearly established as it was in the larger Mandinka states.

[52]Jabarteh compresses a great deal of time here, from Samake Demba, the original *mansa*, to Arafang Bully, a nineteenth-century leader in Jokadu.

[53]A Toranka is a person from Futa Toro, usually a member of the Fulbe ethnic group. When colonial rule came to The Gambia a Fulbe family, relatively latecomers to Jokadu, living in the village of Kuntair, obtained Chiefship and became the colonial authority in Jokadu. Many of the Mandinka in Jokadu believe the traditional Mandinka families living there should provide the Chief of the district. Thus, they believe the "Toranka took over" unjustly.

[54]This discussion may pertain to the villages lying along the Atlantic coast north of the present Senegal-Gambia border--the villages of Missera, Sangako Madina, Bakadaji, and others. I have seen reports of English officials in The Gambia in the 1850s telling of Mansa Demba Sonko's efforts to "liberate" these villages, long considered part of Niumi, from dominance by other states, Saloum or Siin.

[55]Kaba, or Kangaba, is usually regarded as the traditional center of the Manding world. Supposedly, the best *griots* still perform there. It is located about eighty miles south of Bamako in Mali, on the Niger River, about forty miles from the Guinea border.

[56] Intermarriage among ethnic groups is an important factor in Senegambian ethnicity and history. The Jammeh seem to be products of intermarriage
and general intermixture of Serer and Mandinka. While they tend to speak Mandinka
and accept Mandinka traditions as their own, many consider them to be Serer. This
is a frequent phenomenon, which may account for why Jabarteh calls Kelefa Sanneh
a Jola (see footnote 44, above). I discuss intermarriage and Senegambian ethnicity
in my *Early History of Niumi*, pp. 91-92.

[57] The word for an influential person that Jabarteh uses is *kanda*. *Kanda*
were important people other than members of the families that traditionally provided the *mansa* of the state. The status of the members of the *mansakunda* families was in part ascribed; the status of the *kanda* was totally earned.

Jabarteh: There is nothing like time--my father's time, my mother's time. There is nothing like one's own time. And if you do something for a *griot*, he will mention it.

I, Sherif Jabarteh, shall recite the tale of Jane Kinte.[1] Yancouba Saho will play the *kora*. We shall talk of how Jane Kinte left Sahel[2] to settle in The Gambia, and of his life and of his family begotten there.

People now call the Kinte "*jula*,"[3] but this was not always so. Jane Kinte was a Muslim when he came, a successful *marabout* from Mauritania. When he came to Baddibu Sankala Marong was ruling there.[4] It was Sankala Marong who brought him. Mansa Sankala used to hear the people say, "There is a *marabout* in Sahel who is, we hear, a good one." So Sankala Marong sent for Jane Kinte, and when he came Mansa Sankala lodged him with his brother, Bakari Marong, at Marongkunda.[5] The Mansa did not want the *marabout* to live at his own town, India. Sankala Marong brought the *marabout* to do *marabout* work for him, to prepare his wars and battles. Every king in those days had a *marabout* who worked for him.[6] So Jane Kinte worked for Sankala Marong and stayed at Marongkunda.

Now Bakari Marong had a daughter affected by a great ulcer. So Bakari Marong said to Jane Kinte, "When you finish working for my brother, will you help me cure my daughter's ulcer? Will you ask God to help us cure it?"

The *marabout* answered, "When I am finished with your brother's work, you can bring your daughter to me."

When the *marabout* was ready, Bakari Marong brought the girl for him to see. Jane Kinte declared that the sore was badly infected, but he found a remedy and put it on the ulcer, and the girl was healed. Then the father said, "Since you have healed my daughter, would you like to marry her?"[7]

He gave the child to Jane Kinte in marriage. After a while people began to rumor that she suffered from another ailment. "Now she seems to be pregnant," they said. The rumor was true.

When she had born a son for Jane Kinte, he sent word to her family that Jane Kinte's wife had delivered. And the *soninke*s of Baddibu began to be afraid. Their fetishes had foretold the coming of a stranger who had kingship in his mind. If he did not reign himself, then his son or grandson would.

So great was Jane Kinte's fame at Marongkunda, great numbers came to see him from various places. Even kings like Jarra Jasey Banna had heard news of him, and they all wanted him to be *their* court *marabout*. Jane's coming to The Gambia became a national event. It was known by every important person that Jane Kinte had come to Baddibu.

The Marongs began to fear his fame, and the news of his son's birth made them more afraid. But Jane Kinte showed them his gratitude. At the baptism of his son they asked him what he would name the child. "In Sahel," he said, "I would name the boy for one of my own family. But when you come to live with people who show you kindness and hospitality and who give you their daughter in marriage, one must return such honor with equal honor. I would like you to name this child after one of your own people."

The Marongs thanked him for this consideration and said, "There is an old man here called Lang Marong. We shall give your child his name, and we shall call him 'Lang Kinte'."[8]

As Lang Kinte was growing up his father left Marongkunda to visit other places in The Gambia. But he left Lang with his maternal uncles in Marongkunda. The Marongs transferred their suspicion from the father to the son as he grew in fame and following. They said that Lang was growing too influential. So they devised a plan to make him leave Baddibu. The uncles sought a quarrel with their nephew. Lang Kinte moved from Marongkunda, but he did not go far. He built his own village close by and called it "Kintekunda." The two villages were very close together and later they grew into one, so people called it "Kintekunda-Marongkunda."[9]

When Jane Kinte left Marongkunda, he and many followers went to Jarra Sankuya,[10] where he stayed for a long time. Jarra Mansa Jasey Banna heard that he had come.

> Koli's father, Jumulung,
> Jumulung's father, Jumulung.
> Dembang's father, Dembang.
> Land of three queens.
> And seven renowned *kanda*.
> Jasey have right in Jarra.[11]

Mansa Jasey paid the *marabout* a visit. "I would like to commission you," he said, "to do some work for me. I heard of your fame in Baddibu and have wished to get to know you."

So Jane Kinte consented to work for Jarra Mansa, and he
steadily grew more popular. Attracted by Jane Kinte's
fame, a Sankuya man offered him his daughter. Jane Kinte
married her and she bore him a son. Said the *marabout*,
"I have been most fortunate in coming to this country.
They gave me a wife at Marongkunda; she bore me a son.
Here too I have a wife and look, she also bore a son for
me. This is indeed good fortune." He named the child
Muhammadou and said that each of his wives' first-born
son should be called Muhammadou. His wife's parents left
Sankuya and went to live in Pakalanding.[12] Jane Kinte
followed and went to live with them there. In Jarra, too,
it was predicted that the Kintes would one day rule.
People began to be cautious of him, but he was still very
popular. Jane spent a long time in Jarra Pakalanding,
and his wife bore him a girl, Jabu Kinte. All first
daughters of the Kintes are called Jabu. Names the Kintes
had in the past are still repeated in their children. If
you go to Kintekunda Janeah you will still find someone
there named for Bala Kinte. You would find another named
for Ansu Kinte and still another named for Janko Kinte.

Then the *marabout* moved on to Kiang Jiffarong,[13] taking
his wife and Jabu with him, but leaving Muhammadou behind
with his uncles in Pakalanding. Muhammadou grew up in
Jarra and had a son called Lan Kinte, who became the Chief
of Jarra West District at Pakalanding. Lan begot Bua
Kinte, who succeeded his father as Chief of Jarra West.[14]

Jane spent eight years in Kiang Jiffarong. There, too,
they gave him another wife, for his fame preceded him
wherever he went. He was a distinguished scholar and
marabout. He had another son by this woman and he named
him Lang Kinte. Lang Kinte remained in Jiffarong with
his mother when Jane Kinte moved. The *marabout* did not
wish to settle yet and moved from area to area where they
invited him to go. One of Jane's descendants at Kiang
Jiffarong was also called Lan Kinte. He became senior
court member in Kiang West District and, therefore, became
Acting Chief every time the Chief's post fell vacant.

From Kiang, Jane crossed to Niumi at a place called
Makalung, just behind the C.F.A.O. buildings and very close
to Albreda.[15] His wife from Jarra still accompanied him
with their daughter Jabu. People came to meet and welcome him and he went to live in Juffure, an old town in
Niumi.[16] There were only a few towns then. There was
a village called Kassewa and when you left this town you
saw no village till Sami, and when you left Sami you saw
no village till Juffure. There was nothing between Juffure
and Sitanunku nor between Sitanunku and Bakindiki. And
when you left Bakindiki you saw no village till Kanuma.
Those were the towns in Niumi in those days.[17]

When the *marabout* reached Juffure the people gathered
to pray for him that he might settle permanently with
them. This has become a custom in Juffure. They in-
vite *marabout* visitors to live with them. Jane agreed
to stay a while but warned them that he was a traveler.
They gave him a wife there, his fourth wife in The
Gambia. She bore three children for him. The first
was a girl, whom he called Jabu Kinte. The second was
a boy, who died young. And the third was another boy,
whom his mother named Bamba Kinte. Then Jane left
Juffure to travel again, leaving Bamba behind in Juffure.
One of his descendants was Bamba Kinte, who begot several
children, among them Bamade Kinte and Kusufa Kinte, who
still live at Juffure. Bamba's wife, Julanding Darbo,
also had children by him and these too live at Juffure.

Kunta Kinte was the grandson of Bamba Kinte.[18] He was
the one who got lost and became the ancestor of the American Kintes. In those days, when Europeans visited The
Gambia, their first landing place was Albreda. They
went on shore and captured people.[19] That was how Kunta
Kinte was captured. But if these descendants of Kunta
Kinte should visit The Gambia, European though they may
be, if you compare them with the other Kintes of Juffure,
Kintekunda Janeah, and Kintekunda-Marongkunda, of Pakalanding and of Jiffarong, you would see a strong resemblance
between them and they would all be men of consequence.[20]

When Jane Kinte left Juffure he left his wife behind and
stayed a while at Niumi Sami. Next he went to Kasai, but
he stayed only two months and then he returned to Baddibu
and lodged at Saba, until he saw the people grow unfriendly.
Then he asked them to show him a place where he might build
his own village. They were anxious to get rid of him, so
they took him out in the evening and showed him a place
to the west of Saba, which they said was a dwelling place
of the *jinn*. But the Kintes were *marabout*s and they were
successful at it. Jane Kinte built his village there.
He said, "Though I have long lived in Gambia, I have no
place to call my own. Only my sons have built their own
compounds.[21] This then is my own village, which I shall
call Kintekunda Janeah."[22]

While Jane was living there, his eldest son, called Bala
Kinte, left Mauritania and came to live with him. Bala's
mother was not a Gambian, but he looked like the other
Kintes. Even now, when you see the Kintes' faces, you
see a strong resemblance between them. From wherever
they may come, they are all descendants of Jane Kinte.

The *marabout* dwelt in his town for some time and then
fell ill from an ailment hereditary with the Kintes, a
kind of lumbago which affects their backs down to their
waists. He called his people together and gave thanks

to his host and to God for his good fortune in Gambia. He counted his children and thanked God again that they were all in easy reach of one another. Then he died, just as all great men must die. If I now call on Jane Kinte, he will fail to answer, for he will not rise until the day of judgment.

Messengers were sent throughout the land to inform them of Jane's death and the people assembled at Janeah. He left his family well provided for, and many were scholars in their own right. As eldest son, Bala Kinte became lineage head.

That chieftaincy had been predicted for Jane Kinte's family was common knowledge with the elders. It came to Kintekunda Janeah this way:[23]

There was no Chief at Saba then; chieftaincy was lodged at Salikenya.[24] But sometime later they decided to sub-divide the district of Salikenya. Many applied and began campaigning. There was Burama Janke Singate and Ansu Jelema Singate, a court member, and both great *kanda* in the district. But the Kintes were very popular and they were also very wealthy. If Bala had wanted chieftaincy for himself, he could have had it then. But he was mar-ried to the daughter of Ansu Jelema Singate. So when the vacancy appeared he chose to help the father of his wife.

When Ansu Jelema died there was another struggle for chief-taincy. This time, Bala Kinte's grandson, Janko Kinte, contested for the office. Janko Kinte was the son of M'Fali Kinte and M'Fali Kinte was the son of Bala Kinte. They called M'Fali Kinte "M'Fali Nansa" for his mother, Nansa Jaite, who came from Baddibu N'Jabakunda.

Now Janko Kinte was a great trader, for after Jane Kinte died they noticed that anyone who became a *marabout* died soon after, so the Kintes changed their profession from scholarship to trade. They were still educated in Arabic, but they left the clerical pursuit alone because of their belief that it brought death to them. Henceforth they called them "Kinte Jula."

Janko Kinte was a scholar when he left Kintekunda to go and trade at Fogny Kantonku.[25] He settled there and traded and soon was known as "Jula Janko." When he left Fogny Kantonku he moved to Fogny Vintang,[26] where he spent one year. Then he came to Albreda and spent two years there. He left and went to Kesjenkens[27] to Sherif Momodou Futi, Ibn Adam's father at Kesjenkens. One day Sherif Momodou Futi grew very excited and said, "Janko, let me show you what is written in our Mafuj ancestral document."

But he had a son called Ibn Adam Lee who overheard the conversation and said, "Father, you are talking to Janko Kinte, not to Adam Lee." If it were not for this timely intervention, the father would have rewarded more handsomely than necessary Janko's loyalty and hard work.[28]

After studying with Sherif Momodou Futi he went to Sherif Sadibu in Sahel. When he graduated from Sherif Sadibu's school he called himself "Sherif Janko Kinte."

Janko left Sahel and continued to trade, moving to Suarekunda in Baddibu, where he became very prosperous. Then there came a lean year. There was a shortage of food throughout the land, and Janko Kinte made many loans to people. During this period of hardship the chieftaincy fell vacant. The Commissioner visited the district and told the elders that he would entrust the district to Janko Kinte. Then he passed on and went up river. In those days Commissioners came to us from Sierra Leone. They traveled up and down the Gambia once a year and then returned to Sierra Leone.[29]

Meanwhile Janko asked no one to repay his loan, for he knew that the chieftaincy would be contested. When the time for choice came the Commissioner gathered the elders and said, "You have no Chief in this district and I wish to install one. Who do you wish to become your Chief?"

Replied the elders, "We thought that Janko Kinte was already our Chief."

"No," said the Commissioner, "he is only Acting-Chief."

"Then we want you to install him as Chief," they said. "We want no one else but him." Everyone was indebted to Janko because of the hardship in the land.

When they gave Janko the staff of office at Missera in Saurekunda, he told the people there that he must spend the night at Kintekunda Janeah, for he was descended from Jane Kinte, for whom chieftaincy had been predicted. These predictions were now fulfilled in Janko Kinte. Before he became Chief they called him "The great Jula Janko"; then they called him "Sherif Janko" and "Arafang Janko." Now they called him "Sefu Janko Kinte."[30]

Janko Kinte had four wives. The first was Nembali Jabarteh and second came Jaite Jawara. He married a third at Suarekunda and her name was Mbikinding. She became the mother of Lan Kinte Mbikinding. Lan Kinte Mbikinding begot Sambujang Kinte, a shopkeeper in Banjul today, and Saim Kinte, a lecturer at Yundum College,[31] and Tuss Kinte, who is in Manchester, England. He is an accountant there. Janko Kinte's fourth wife was Bute Baro from Baddibu Gunjur. It was she who bore him Sherif Kinte, the Chief of the district today at Kintekunda Janeah.

Since Jane Kinte came to Gambia all predictions about him have come true. He had chieftaincy at Kintekunda Janeah and at Pakalanding in Jarra.   God blessed his family besides with a profound intelligence. Even the last Kinte descendants, like Saim and Tuss Kinte, are scholars in their own right in the field of Western education. At home those not so fortunate as to take up Western education are learned Arabic scholars. So learning is a tradition of the Kinte. You can hardly find a Jane who is not a scholar and fairly well off. Even in the United States when you go there and meet the descendants of this Kinte, you will find them in possession of scholarship or great wealth or both.[32]   I have never seen these people; I have never been to the States either, but where you find a Kinte you find education.

This is I, Sherif Jabarteh, giving the account, and Yancouba Saho playing the *kora*.

FOOTNOTES TO THE SECOND INTERVIEW

[1]The name is pronounced as if it were Jon-nay Kin-tay.

[2]The sahel (the Arabic meaning "shore," speaking here as if the northern limits of the Western Sudan were like the shore of the Sahara Desert) is the relatively dry land stretching east-west across the northern portion of the Western Sudan. Part of the sahel passes through Mauritania. Jabarteh speaks of it as if it were a country.

[3]*Jula* is the Mandinka word for merchant, or trader. Many today consider members of the larger Kinte clan to be traders.

[4]The Marong family is one of five extended families that traditionally provided the *mansa* for the former Mandinka state of Baddibu. Sankala Marong was supposedly the first Marong to become Baddibu Mansa.

[5]Morongkunda is a village in western Baddibu (now called Lower Baddibu District).

[6]B. K. Sidibe adds this note here to the text in the Gambia Cultural Archives:

> Even *soninke* (pagan) rulers, such as Sankalang Marong appears to have been, kept Muslim holy men near them and consulted them as well as their own fetishes in time of need. The prayers of a *marabout* on behalf of anyone employing him were considered to be very effective. Not all *marabout*s got equally good results, so when rulers heard of one whose work was supposed to be good, he went to a lot of trouble to consult him and, if possible, to get him to come and settle near him. They were consulted frequently, well-paid for their work, and left alone to practice their religion undisturbed because of the fear their special prayers inspired.

> Since he was surrounded by his *soninke* family and court, Sankalang Marong may have considered that his own town was not a suitable place for a prominent *marabout*, who had his own family and followers to think about. The *marabout* himself would have undoubtedly disapproved of the drinking, drumming, and other noisy activities which went on in a king's town and would have felt it a bad influence on his family.

> Also, a ruler's *marabout* was not always known to the general public. He preferred to keep his connection with this source of strength well hidden. He lodged him with a trusted attendant who kept a close eye on the *marabout*'s clients and visitors in order to make sure that the king's enemies were not employing him, perhaps to work against the king. Sometimes even grand *marabout*s were not above that sort of double dealing.

[7]The curing of a woman, usually of a bad sore, by a healer and magical practitioner before being allowed to marry her is a common motif in Mandinka epics.

[8]Lang is a version of the name Lamin, which is itself a version of or nickname for the name Muhammad.

[9]Marongkunda is indeed today part of a large village called Kintekunda-Marongkunda.

[10]I can find on no map a village in Jarra called Sankuya.

[11]Here Sidibe adds the following note:

This is a typical Mandinka praise: cryptic and elusive, designed to evoke in the listener's mind ideas or emotions associated with the persons or places named. The listener is assumed to know the stories alluded to, just as a person from a Christian culture knows what is meant when someone is referred to as a "prodigal son," or when someone refuses to join a blanket condemnation of someone else by "refusing to cast the first stone." The first three lines are names of illustrious Jasey ancestors. It is difficult to guess the meaning of lines four and five without more detailed knowledge of Jarra history. In some lower river states before Mandinkas gained firm control, women sometimes ruled. "*Kandas*" are great, wealthy, influential men, but not necessarily of the traditional ruling houses. The last line means that the Jaseys claimed the right of rulership in Jarra. Praise songs sometimes yield valuable clues to the affairs and developments in the history of an area.

[12]Pakalanding is a village in what was the former Mandinka state of Jarra. It is about fifteen miles upriver from Elephant Island, which marks the big north-ward bend of the Gambia, and about three miles inland from the river.

[13]Jiffarong is a village in the former Mandinka state of Kiang, across from Baddibu. It is in the southeast portion of that state about two miles up off the north bank of Vintang Creek.

[14]If Jane Kinte's grandson, Lan, became Chief of Jarra West, then Jane Kinte must have lived around the early decades of the nineteenth century.

[15]C.F.A.O. is the French commercial organization *Compagnie Française de l'Afrique Occidentale*, which maintained a trading concern in Albreda for many years. It was one of the two large French companies that monopolized the import-export trade in French-speaking West Africa. The operation of Albreda was a branch of C.F.A.O.'s network in Senegal. Albreda is in old Niumi on the Gambia's north bank, in sight of James Island.

[16]Juffure had several locations in the past, but all were in reasonable proximity of Albreda. During the years of the slave trade it was a busy com-mercial center, where Africans, Eurafricans, and Europeans met to conduct

business. The *mansa* of Niumi had special persons living in Juffure and Albreda
to oversee the trade. If Albreda was long a French trading post, Juffure conducted more dealings with the English and the Eurafricans in the river.

[17]All these towns are in Niumi. See Map 6 (p. xii) of Niumi and Jokadu
for their location.

[18]Obviously, this is a discrepancy with the version of the Kinte tradition that Haley received while tracing his roots, for if Jabarteh's genealogy is
correct throughout the story, then Kunta Kinte could not have lived more than
a few generations ago.

[19]Despite what many people think, few Europeans went on shore in the
Gambia River and captured Africans to send them into the Atlantic slave trade.
The African states were too powerful and the Europeans often too sickly or too
few in number to allow or enable this to happen. Slaves coming out of the
Gambia were exchanged by Africans for European commodities.

[20]I would guess that Jabarteh is aware of Haley's trip to Juffure and
is referring to him in this passage.

[21]Mandinka extended families live in compounds, which are groups of dwellings, all around a common courtyard and surrounded by a fence or other type of
enclosure.

[22]Sidibe adds this note in the text:

*Jinn*s are supposed to be invisible devils, immortal, some good and
some bad. They have their own dwelling places. Each compound and
every person is said to "have a good *jinn*," a protector. But it
is extremely dangerous to settle in a place already inhabited by
"bad" *jinn*s, who are antipathetic to humans. This is why, when
people were thinking of settling a particular site, they sent seers
or *marabout*s in first to check whether or not the site was truly
uninhabited. Otherwise, if they should unwittingly build their
houses across a pathway of *jinn*s, they ran the risk of numerous
deaths or illnesses, houses falling down, fires, or other disasters.

Not only did the *jinn*s have their own places to live, they had their
own favorite times of day: the gray before dawn, dusk just before
dark, two o'clock in the afternoon, the hottest part of the day, and
midnight.   These were the "witching hours," when *jinn*s were most
likely to be out and about and when it was dangerous for ordinary
people to be abroad--though *marabout*s, sorcerers, seers, fetishers,
and so on liked to conduct much of their own business at these effective times. Therefore, to take a noted *marabout* to a known *jinn*
habitation, in the evening, and to tell him that this was the only
available place where he could live, would seem to be as good a way
as any to get rid of him, since they probably thought he would refuse to live there after he found out what it was. *Marabout*s were
dangerous people to offend by outright refusal. So the Saba people
went through the forms of hospitality and offered what he had

requested: a place to live. If he chose not to live there that was his own affair. Unfortunately for them, Jane Kinte was a very able *marabout* and was therefore able to clear the area of its dangerous inhabitants and to build a town where he lived peacefully.

[23]The following story of the division of Salikenya District is about events that occurred during British colonial rule in The Gambia, during the first half of the twentieth century.

[24]Salikenya is a village in western Baddibu about six miles south of Kintekunda-Marongkunda.

[25]There is a village of Kantonkunda across Vintang Creek from the former state of Fogny. It is in Kiang. I know of no Kantoku in Fogny, though the region has many small villages and it is certainly possible that such a village exists.

[26]Vintang (or Bintang) is located in old Fogny on the south bank of Vintang Creek, just a few miles from where that creek enters into the Gambia River. It was one of several lower-river commercial centers.

[27]Sidibe includes a note saying Kesjenkens is in Mauritania. I cannot find it on any of my maps.

[28]Here Sidibe adds the following note:

*Marabout*s had their own secret prayers, sacred passages, and so on which they have found to be very effective and which they hand down to their children as a legacy. Ibn Adam Lee was moving to save his inheritance, preventing it from being given to a stranger.

[29]Between 1866 and 1888 the British administered the parts of The Gambia they considered their colony--actually only Bathurst and the Cape St. Mary's area on the river's south bank and the river bank along the opposite side--from Sierra Leone. Each year the colonial governor was to come to The Gambia and oversee the colony. However, after 1888 the Gambia was made a separate colony. Jabarteh seems to have this confused. In the colonial administrative structure "Native Chiefs" had authority over the various districts and districts were grouped together in larger provinces. In charge of provinces were Traveling Commissioners who, because of the nature of the territory and the lack of sound communications therein, spent much of their time traveling from district to district overseeing the work of the Chiefs. It must be to this Commissioner that Jabarteh is referring, though no Commissioner came from Sierra Leone during the colonial period in Baddibu.

[30]Arafang is a title meaning "learned man" or "scholar." *Sefu* is the Mandinka version of the word Chief.

[31]Yundum College is The Gambia's teacher-training institution, which is located about twenty miles southwest of Banjul near the country's airport.

[32]Here, again, Jabarteh is showing he is aware of Alex Haley.

ABDOULIE SAMBA

ONE INTERVIEW: November 12, 1974.

GENERAL SUBJECT MATTER: Early history of western Senegal and the north bank
                          of the Gambia River, with particular emphasis on the
                          precolonial states of Jolof, Saloum, and Baddibu.

LOCATION OF RECORDING: Indiana University Archives of Traditional Music,
      Access numbers 4371 and 4372.

The Informant.   Abdoulie Samba was born in the village of Sarakunda in a region
of The Gambia called Sanjal, near where the Gambia River makes its first big
northward bend about one hundred miles upriver from Banjul, around 1928. "That
was where I was born," he emphasizes, "and that was where I learned to play the
konting," the four-stringed chordophone upon which he accompanies himself throughout all interviews and performances. In 1952, when he was twenty-four years old,
Samba made his first trip to Banjul, then called Bathurst, the seat of British
colonial government in The Gambia, and he must have liked what he saw, for six
years later he moved permanently to the colony's capital. By that time he had
heard and learned much of the oral tradition extant in the former Mandinka state
of Baddibu, of which Sanjal was generally considered a part, and having traveled,
listened, and learned in a fairly wide region of Senegal to the north of his home,
he possessed a repertoire of oral history and folklore from the old Wolof and
Serer states of Jolof and Saloum and from a few neighboring areas.

Once settled in Banjul, Samba became one of the city's most popular traditional
musicians and entertainers. Playing his *konting*, he performs at weddings, naming
ceremonies, and similar traditional festivities. He also sings and recites oral
history and folklore for particularly interested parties, on demand, and accompanied
by his wife, Kani Sumano, who is reputed to have the most powerful voice in Banjul,
he performs the still popular, traditional Mandinka music of the lower Gambia before large groups. Samba presently resides at 1 Peel Street in Banjul.

The Interview.   My interview with Abdoulie Samba was arranged for me by B. K.
Sidibe, who, as Research Officer in charge of the Gambia's Cultural Archives,
knew Samba to be one of the most knowledgeable *griot*s in the lower Gambia. I had
been wanting to collect oral material covering an increasingly wide region of the
Senegambia, so when I mentioned to Sidibe my interest in Baddibu and Saloum, he
offered to arrange an interview with Samba. We met about mid-morning in Sidibe's
office, which then was in a group of Gambian government buildings called The
Quadrangle, just behind McCarthy Square in Banjul. Samba came dressed in an
ankle-length black gown trimmed in silver--the popular style in urban portions
of much of the Senegambia--having wide, billowy sleeves that can be folded back
onto the shoulders. He wore also a small, black cap and a pair of white shoes,
pointed at the toe and open at the heel--also a popular style among the urban
middle class in the Senegambia. Once inside, we sat at a small wooden table,

128

upon which was placed my tape recorder. Besides Sidibe, Samba, and myself, Binta Jammeh was also present. Since she was going to translate the interview, we thought it advantageous that she be present. About half way through the interview Samba's wife, Kani Sumano, entered and quietly took a seat. She was dressed colorfully, with a head-tie to match her dress and large, gold earrings. Though she never uttered a word, she would occasionally raise one hand and loudly make a single snap of her fingers, this apparently occurring when Samba made a particularly noteworthy point in his narrative. Following the interview Sumano told Sidibe that she would have liked to sing and was a little "put out" that no one had asked her to do so.

To begin the interview, we told Samba of my work with the history of Niumi and of my general interest in the history of regions along the Gambia's north bank and beyond. I asked him to tell me the things he thought were important in the history of that area. He began by playing his *konting* for several minutes without saying anything. Then, when he settled upon a refrain he liked particularly, he began reciting, alternately saying a phrase or a sentence and playing the refrain, with embellishments. He played through the entire interview, which lasted nearly two hours.

Sidibe acted as interpreter and Binta Jammeh translated the interview within a week of its recording. Samba spoke in Mandinka.

Samba: My name is Abdoulie Samba. I live at number one Peel Street in Banjul, but I am actually a Baddibunka of Sanjal Sarakunda.[1] That was where I was born and that was where I learned to play the *konting*. I was twenty-four years old when I first came here, but I was thirty when I settled here. My knowledge of history begins with the history of Manding and continues with Jolof, Baddibu, Sanjal, Saba, Siin, Kajor, and Saloum.[2]

Saloum originated from Jolof. It did so because of Chukuli Njagilani, Njagilani Sarr, Sarr Njajan, Njajan Njie, Abodj Njie. . . .[3] Chukuli Njagilani begot Biran Njeme Kumba, the ancestor of the *bur*[4] of Saloum and those of Kahon and Kanyi-morijang and Iliassa.[5] They were his grandchildren and great grandchildren. When Biran Njeme Kumba lived in Jolof, the number of years between then and now would come to about six hundred.[6]

When Sora Musa was coming from Manding,[7] it was Biran Njeme Kumba he found ruling in Jolof. Sora Musa's surname was Keita; Biran Njeme Kumba was named Njie. He ruled Jolof, the gateway to the west. When you left the Sudan coming west in those days, first you went to Mauritania. When you left there you came to Futa.[8] When you left Futa you came to Jolof; then you came to Kajor, and then to Walo. From Walo you came to Siin and from there to Saloum. Jolof, Siin, Saloum, Kajor, Baddibu--all these states were the same.

In those days when you wanted a wife and you were of a
noble family, they would advise you to go to a certain
town and to a certain family in that town. The family
you belonged to had already been used to taking a wife
from a certain family and that was where you would be
advised to go. That was why they were all closely inter-
related. People in those days did not marry any woman
or man they saw. They always married according to their
rank and their family relationships.[9]

Biran Njeme Kumba was the ruler of all Tiligi.[10] All the
western states paid tribute to Biran Njeme Kumba. Whatever was the major produce of the state was what they paid
as tribute to the ruler. The state of Kajor took sand to
Jolof. Even now you can go to Jolof to the household of
the Linguer[11] and you will find heaps of sand that were
taken to Biran Njeme Kumba. After Kajor, Walo Barob took
fish as their tribute. In those days there were plenty of
fish in Walo Barob.[12] Next was Siin. In those days there
were mats in existence which are not made now. They called
them *tagar*. They were straw mats that people sat on. Saloum
made winnowing fans. That was what they paid as tribute to
their ruler. In Baddibu they cut grasses. That was what
they paid as tribute. The ruler would build his houses with
those grasses. When you left Baddibu you came to Saba.
They took palm wine as tribute. Sanjal made mats and took
them as tribute. Niumi Bato took palm oil as tribute to
their ruler. When you left Niumi Bato and went to Jarra,
they took palm leaves as tribute. The palm leaves were
made into rope. When you went to Niani. . . .[13]

At that time Biran Njeme Kumba Njie was the ruler of
Kelidibi,[14] but during his reign he appointed people to be
rulers in every area. In Siin you would find Mansa Wali
Jammeh; in Kajor you would find Damel Birema Faal; in Saloum
you would find Njejan Ndure; in Baddibu you would find Mansa
Nyelengi Jadama. She was a woman queen residing at Jimansaar.
In Jarra you would find Mansa Jasey Wali; in Niamina you
would find Yareng Saweneh. He would live at either Pinyaye
or Kafamena.[15]

Q: How did Baddibu gain its independence from Jolof?

Samba: When Biran Njeme Kumba Njie died, that was when the Chiefs
         became free. Baddibu was the first to be freed from Jolof.
         When Sora Musa came from Manding to Jolof he greeted Jolof
         Mansa.[16] Jolof Mansa asked him where he was from.

         Sora Musa said, "I am from Manding."

         Jolof Mansa asked him who his ancestors were.

         Sora Musa told him, "I am from the same family as Sundiata."[17]

         Jolof Mansa asked him, "Where are you going?"

Sora Musa said, "Wherever Allah destined me to go, that is where I shall stay."

Jolof Mansa told him, "I want you to stay here and I will give you my daughter in marriage so that I can get somebody like you in my family."

Sora Musa said to him, "No, if you should give your daughter to someone, that person should stay with you. As for me, I cannot stay with anyone. I must find my own place to settle."

When Sora Musa left Jolof, he came to Kajor and found Damel Birema Faal there.[18] They greeted each other and the Damel said, "Where are you from?"

Here Samba repeats the same conversation between Sora Musa and Jolof Mansa as he encounters Damel Birema Faal of Kajor and Mansa Wali Jan of Siin. Both rulers wanted Sora Musa to remain there and marry one of their daughters. Sora Musa told each that he had to move on because he wanted to find his own place to settle. He then went through the same conversation with Wali Mbekam of Saloum, but at the end the story changes so that Samba can include something about the founding of the state of Saloum.[19]

Wali Mbekam said to him, "You can spend the night here and in the morning you can have a chat with the people of this country."

Sora Musa spent the night there. In the morning all the people assembled at Kahon. There was no Saloum then. The place was called Madi Mbai. The reason why it has a different name now, it was Saloum Suare who worked for Wali Mbekam, placing *juju* to protect the land. The holy water he gave him worked well, but Saloum Suare asked him not to pay him anything, but if he got his land to name it after him. Wali Mbekam said to him, "That's easy."

The reason why Saloum was very large was because of the holy water that Saloum Suare gave him and told him to mix it with sand. He told Mbekam to climb on his horse and wherever he threw this sand and wherever it touched would be the area he would rule. Saloum is larger than Jolof, larger than Siin, larger than Kajor, larger than Bawol, larger than Baddibu. All this was because of this trick.

In the morning the owners of horses shared the sand; everyone took his own and climbed on his horse. Some went this way and others went that way. They rode their horses and threw sand as they went. When the sand ran out the riders came back. When Wali Mbekam became ruler, he said, "I will name this land after my teacher." That teacher was Saloum Suare. That is why they called the land Saloum.[20]

It was that Wali Mbekam that Sora Musa found there. Then he left and crossed the river. When you left Saloum then, you came to Tubakuta. There was also a river there and Sora Musa crossed. He spent the night at Bajan, near where the Europeans came to meet Maba at Nioro--a place called Pate Bajan.[21] After he spent the night there his advisors told him that his country was still ahead of him. They said, "When you leave Pate Bajan there is a small village past Nioro; the place is called Diba Jajen."

Sora Musa spent the next night there. In the morning his advisors told him to go on a bit until he reached a *timpo* tree. He came to the tree at a place called Kande Kunola.

In that *timpo* tree were two male *jinn*.[22] After Sora Musa had spent the night there, he overslept. He awoke and told his followers, "Now I can stay here or our place is not very far from here."

The *jinn* got out and told him that this was indeed a place, but he had found it with its owners, but that they would show him a place and when he got there he would be able to stay there.[23] In the morning the *jinn* told him that there was a creek he must cross. Once he reached and crossed it, he then went upland to a place where there was a big *taba* tree. The *jinn* told him he could look there and build a fence and have that for his area of settlement.

At that time there was one *mansa* of Baddibu, a woman called Mansa Nyelengi.[24] This woman dreamed of Sora Musa. She dreamed that he was a middle-sized man, not tall and not short, not fat and not thin, and that he was a handsome man. She ruled for about seventy years. During the last seven of these years she dreamed of Sora Musa. In the mornings she would assemble all the people of Baddibu and tell them that she always dreamed about a man and that it worried her because she always dreamed that he would be her husband.

This took place not in Iliassa, which was not in existence then. It was only Jimansaar then that was in Baddibu.[25]

The people told her, "Mansa Nyelengi, please stop what you are saying about someone coming from outside of Baddibu to marry you rather than someone from Baddibu."

She told them, "I will stop what I am saying."

The following year, in the same month and at the same time she had dreamed about him before, she dreamed about Sora Musa again. The morning after she called all the people of Jimansaar and told them that she had dreamed it again. At that time Sora Musa was on his way.

When she told them, the people said to her, "Stop saying that. You said the same thing last year. You are a woman, but you are our *mansa*. None can marry you here."

She remained quiet, but she had dreamed about him for seven years. Sora Musa appeared in the seventh year. After he slept under the *taba* tree, he built a stockade around it. The *taba* tree is still there. *Taba* trees live a long time. When he came here, the period between then and now is about six hundred years.

The next morning Sora Musa heard the sounds of the *jung-jung*.[26] He said, "What do I hear in this country?"

His people said to him, "There is a queen in this country."

He said, "Hmm, that is serious. I have come to settle in this country and wherever I live, I must rule. Now it appears there is a ruler here. What do you know about that?"

His people said to him, "We await your decision. If you ask us to fight, we shall fight."

Sora Musa said, "I must send a messenger to the *mansa*, Nyelengi."

When the messenger reached her, he said, "I am sent by a *mansa* who sends his greetings to you."

Nyelengi asked, "Where did the *mansa* come from?"

"From Manding," replied the messenger.

Nyelengi said, "Is he from Manding? Is he a citizen of Manding? What is he like? I want to know what he looks like?"

The messenger described Sora Musa, telling her how tall and how heavy he was.

She said, "I hope he is not the man I have been dreaming about for the past seven years. Sit down and wait a while."

She called her people together and when they gathered she said to them, "I have received a messenger who informed me that a man sends his greetings to me. He is called Sora Musa. He is from Manding and has traveled through Mauritania; then through Jolof where he found Biran Njeme Kumba Njie. Biran wanted him to stay with him, but he refused. He then went to Damel Birema.[27] In all this he was hunting a place to settle. I once told you people that I used to dream about a man, middle-aged, not too fat, not too black in complexion, not too tall, and not too short. This messenger has come to tell me about him and he says he is greeting us. What have you to say?"

All the elders in Baddibu got together. They told her that they had heard of this man who had come to Siin, Jolof, Kajor, Bawol, and Saloum on his journey and had refused to stay in any of these places. "But before we do anything," they said, "we must decide something. We do not know

where this man is from, but we know we must fight him. If
he defeats us he can take over and rule us, but if we should
defeat him we can send him out of the country or kill him."

Nyelengi asked them to sleep overnight. In the morning she
called all her people together and told them, "The man I
used to see in my dreams will be my husband. He must marry
me, and I am the one in charge of Baddibu. Now I wish that
you would put off the war because everything we do in this
world will be recorded and recited."[28]

But the elders said, "If a man comes to your house, you must
do something to make him realize that he has come into a
house with someone living in it."

So the way they fought that war, they had guns but they did
not put anything inside the guns but gunpowder. By then
Mansa Nyelengi had talked to all her people. She showed
them that Sora Musa was to be her husband.

When Sora Musa had fought until the war was over, he married
Mansa Nyelengi.[29]

Over the years Sora Musa's advisers told him that either his
son or his grandson would meet a child of Saloum Mansa Biran
Njeme Kumba. Things started long ago. When the war came to
an end, Biran Njeme Kumba's daughter left Jolof and married
in Baddibu. That is why the people joined and became one.
Kasin Menje, Biren Menje, and Sabure Menje--these were all
in Saloum. They were rulers of Saloum in Kahon. Kasin Menje
was a woman. Biren Menje and Sabure Menje were both rulers
in Saloum. Any Menje you would hear of in Saloum was named
after Menje Ndure, the first ruler of Saloum, who was called
Wali Mbekan Ndure. His sister was Menje Ndure and this Menje
was named after her. Kasin Menje was a woman and he gave her
in marriage in Iliassa. She gave birth to Soremang Kasa.
Soremang Kasa begot Chukuli Salomang Kasa and Bambu Saremang
Kasa. You know, these are all Wolof.[30]

When Sora Musa married the woman *mansa* of Baddibu, she gave
birth to Musung Ndenki, and Musung Ndenki gave birth to Mansa
Musung Ndenki. Mansa Musung Ndenki gave birth to Sara Jimang,
and Sara Jimang begot Jata Metaba. Jata Metaba begot Biran
Njeme Samba. Then blessings came. Biran Njeme Samba's mother
came from Jolof. His surname was Jammeh. Biran Njeme Samba
begot Bambu Saremang Kasa and Chukuli Saremang Kasa, two sons.
Their mother came from Saloum in Kaimor.[31] Those who descended
from Chukuli Saremang Kasa and Fabi Saremang Kasa were Kuli-
bire, Aliwa Jammeh, Ali Meta Kumba, Jaju Jatela Kanku, and
Mo Joof. All were descended from him. Mo Joof was his name
but his surname was Jammeh. If you should hear Mo Joof, he
was the one who descended from Sora Musa.

When Sora Musa built Iliassa he said in the middle of one
night that he had dreamed about Kachakali here in Bakau.[32]

He said, "I must go and see Kachakali because what I saw in my dreams seems to be a place that would be good for settlement." In the morning when he gathered his followers, he said to them, "I am going to look at a bush which I saw in my dreams. It is a good bush and we must go back and look at it."

They asked him, "Where is it?"

He told them, "I do not know, but I know that I must cross the river." When he crossed at Kerawan he came to Jokadu. Sora Musa built Tambana in Jokadu. He left one of his followers there, whom they called "General Number One."[33] When he left Jokadu he went to build Niumi Sitanunku. When he left Niumi Sitanunku he built Niumi Jinak. Then he spent the night in Jinak, in the morning he crossed a river. By the time he reached Bakau it was evening.

At the same time the eldest in Kiang, Jannehba, also dreamed about Bakau Kachakali.[34] One of them came there in the evening, the other one in the morning. Madi Janneh came from Kiang Jannehba Kunda to Bakau here. In the evening, Sora Musa came also. They greeted each other. Sora told him, "I am an evening stranger." But he continued, "Normally a stranger in the afternoon can lodge a stranger in the evening,[35] but what I am coming to tell you is that we must share. You should take yours and I will take mine because I am not a stranger who should be stopped by anyone."

Janneh Keba said to him, "I will be the *Alkali* and you can be the Imam."[36] Sora Musa agreed, and this is how Bakau still is today. The Janneh people are the *Alkali* and the Jammeh people are the Imam. If you would go to Bakau and ask Mbalufele, this is what he would tell you.[37]

Q: Can you tell me something about a war that was fought between Saloum and Baddibu?

Samba: The Baddibu Mansa then was Mo Joof. Balen Dunku was ruling in Saloum. They called him Balen Dunku, but he was Balen Ndao. He was ruling in Saloum Kahon.[38] The reason they fought was that the Saloum ruler wanted to cut grass and take it away from Baddibu and Baddibu Mansa refused. Mo Joof told him, "The last time you were cutting grass here your nephew was the *mansa*, but now I am the *mansa* and the name of the grass is Jammeh, not Marong."[39] The war was really a fierce one. I know the battle was fierce because most of the *soninke* in Iliassa died. Siin Menke, who was the first son of the Saloum ruler died during that battle. The first son of Mo Joof also died in that battle.

There was another fight when Saloum and Baddibu came to Niumi Bato to help Demba Sonko.[40] There is a reason for everything. Demba Sonko gave his daughter in marriage to one of his war leaders. Now you know that *mansaya*[41] cannot be lent to anyone. If you lend it to someone, it is not safe. But when he gave his daughter in marriage, he shared the *coos* farm and gave part of Niumi over there to his son-in-law. Once this was done, his son-in-law got a lot of power and became very famous and the land remained in his hands. His son-in-law was called Ansuman.

Demba Sonko began to worry about this man his daughter married. But a daughter is closer to her father, and he worried about that. The things he gave Ansuman he began thinking how he could take them back. During this time of difficulty Demba Sonko's brother said to him, "Demba Sonko, to get someone to help you you should send a message to Iliassa, and they can get help from Saloum, and together they can come and help you. Otherwise you will not get your land back, for *mansaya* should not be lent."

When Demba Sonko slept, he dreamed that he should do as he had been told, so he sent messengers with presents and asked them to tell Mo Joof of his problem and his need for help. Demba suggested that Mo Joof's son, Yeramasang, would be the one to help. At that time Yeramasang, Jata Jimeseng, and Hantony Marameh Kekufa Mara were all there. But he said he wanted Yeramasang because he was brave. Mo Joof said, "All my sons are brave, but if he says he wants Yeramasang, then it is Yeramasang he can have."

Saloum Mansa heard that the Iliassa people would be going to a battle in Niumi. At that time they wanted to depose Ansuman Jaju and to drive him out of Niumi so that Demba Sonko could regain *mansaya*, but nobody could fight his own son-in-law. That was why we had Saloum Mansa and Iliassa Mansa come here. Saloum Mansa came through Iliassa and he joined the Iliassa people. They fought the first battle and won.

At one time Balen Dunku sent a message asking Yeramasang to come to Saloum and stay with him for a few days. Mo Joof told Yeramasang, "You know I am not speaking with Saloum Mansa and you want to go to him and be his stranger?"

Yeramasang told him, "Yes."

At that time my great grandfather, Makare Yasiu Kura—the man who begot my grandfather—was present. He was a very old *griot*. He told Mo Joof, "You are not on speaking terms with him and he has called your son to come see him. Go and tell him to come and be your stranger. I know about you—you are handsome, young, and brave. I have heard a lot about you, though this is the first time I have seen you."[42]

Mo Joof said to him, "No, let him go; they will not kill him."

It was after that time that they fought the war together until it ended, and they became friends. That was why when Saloum Mansa heard Yeramasang would be going to a war in Niumi to fight Ansuman Jaju, Saloum joined them, crossed into Niumi Bato, and fought.[43]

At the time of that war Asnuman Jaju was in Niumi Bakindiki. They went after him there. When the battle got fierce, he crossed the river at Albreda and went to Kiang, then Fogny, then to Jarra, and finally he came to settle in Niamina. Soon after he arrived there he married the daughter of the *mansa* of Niamina. That is why his relatives are still found there. After this was all over Mansa Demba got back Niumi Bato.

Q: Was there ever a *mansa* of Saloum who collected tribute from Niumi?

Samba: The *mansa* who asked Niumi for tribute, there was only one, he was called Biran Njeme Kumba. I told you that when Sora Musa came to this country he said no tribute would go to Jolof again. If you hear Jolof, that is Saloum. Jolof Mansa's sons parted and those were the Njie who are in Saloum. Even in Kairmor it is the same Njie. All the Njie descended from Njie Njau Njie. Wherever you see a Njie, he came from Jolof.[44]

Q: What can you tell me about a man named Yeli Bana?[45]

Samba: Yeli Bana? When Mbegane Ndure was coming he found Yeli Bana ruling in Saloum, in Kahon.[46] He was a Toranka.[47] His surname was Sowe. He came from Futa and became the *mansa* of Saloum. But during that time there were not enough people in Saloum--just a small group of Wolof. There were then a lot of Fula because they formed the majorities among all groups. When Yeli Bana came from Futa, he came to Kahon and it became the village of his large family. They were the leaders of that place. Then Kasingka came there.[48] Mbegane was a Kasingka. They used to drink wine; they never prayed. Yeli Bana built a small mosque and he and his people began to pray there. The Kasingka were really angry about all this. Mbegane said to his sister, "I want this *marabout* who is ruling us. He is a Muslim. He prays a lot, but I know what to do to him."

When they were praying, Yeli Bana and his followers went inside the mosque. Mbegane Ndure turned himself into a snake and went inside Yeli Bana's shoe and stayed there. His sister told him that if he bit Yeli Bana, poisoning him, and he happened to fall over, he could get out. She said, "If they come to kill you, I shall turn into a cat and pick you up and run away with you."

Inside the mosque Yeli Bana was surrounded by Toranka. He
was the Imam and *Alkali*, and he was also a great war leader.
But at that time there were not enough Toranka in Saloum,
but there were a lot of Kasingka and they did not like to
see the Toranka be *mansa* of Saloum. When Yeli Bana and his
followers entered the mosque and started to pray, Mbegane
turned into a snake and crawled inside the shoe of Yeli Bana.[4]
When they had finished praying and Yeli Bana went to put on
his shoe, the snake bit him and he threw off the shoe. The
snake went this way and the shoe went that way. His followers said, "It is a snake! It is a snake!" Then they saw a
white cat come and carry the snake away. They disappeared
without anyone seeing them again.

When Yeli Bana died, Mbegane Ndure became *mansa* of Saloum.
It was not the result of a war, for they did not know whom
to fight. The Toranka did not know that Mbegane Ndure was
the snake and the cat that took the snake was his sister.

When Yeli Bana died, the Toranka were afraid in Saloum.
They left and went to Futa. Others stopped in Walo but
they did not fight with Saloum. The Kasingka worked
their supernatural deeds and so killed him.

Q: I heard that Ndena Njie was the Saloum Mansa to whom Niumi
paid tribute. Do you know of a Saloum Mansa named Ndena
Njie?

Samba: The Ndena Njie that I know begot Bubacar Nene. The time of
Bubacar, from then to now is not a long period. Ndena Njie
Jobe was a *mansa* but he never fought with the Niumi people.
He was the one who built Ngogi. Ali Bure Njai, Ali Buri
Penda More, Ali Bure Sainbu. . . .But the Ali Buri that all
the people were familiar with, I know about him. Ali Buri
Njai, the Europeans found him here. He was the nephew of
Lajore. He never fought with the Niumi people. Those that
fought then were the Europeans. When the Europeans fought
with Kajor they killed Lajore; then they went after Ali Buri.
He went to seek help from Amadou Seku Njoro Lanujube.[50]

Q: Was there ever a state of Kular?

Samba: Kular? It was the place of the *nyancho*. When the *nyancho*
were coming from Kabu, they came here and built Kular first.
The *nyancho* in Siin and Saloum all came from Kular. Kular
is part of Saloum. The ancestors of Mansa Wali Jan lived
there.[52] Even today if you go to Kahon there is a certain
place where if you wanted to worship the idol there and you
did not speak Mandinka, the idol would not answer you. If
you should hear Mansa Wali, Wali Sanneh Wali--they came from
Kabu. They are Mandinka. The people of Mansa Wali Jan were
the leaders of Kular.

Q: Tell me something about the rotation of *mansaya* in Baddibu.

Samba: Four groups exchanged it: India, Jimansaar, Iliassa, and
            Kubendar. They exchanged it thusly: If the *mansa* died
            and they looked around for the eldest, wherever they found
            him, they would make him *mansa*. But the old *mansa* had to
            die first before they would make a new *mansa*.[53]

Q: What about rotation of *mansaya* in Niumi?

Samba: In Niumi? Bunyadu, Bakindiki--these are old towns--and
            Berending. They also looked for elders in any of those
            villages who could rule. It had to do with the oldest.
            If the *mansa* lived in Essau and died, if they found the
            eldest again in Essau, they would make him the next *mansa*.

Q: Can you tell me something more about the Sonko? Did they
            live in Saloum before they came to Niumi? Who were their
            ancestors?

Samba: Those who ruled in Niumi, you know, were a mixed group.
            The Sonko--we can just say they were Fula. The Fula ruled
            in Niumi. The Sonko that speak Mandinka here, they were
            Fula. The Jammeh found the Sonko here.[54] Labe Tengela, Bubu
            Tengela, and Sira Tengela. As for Koli Tengela,[55] the Koli
            Tengela that I know of, when he left Futa he went first to
            Saloum. This Koli Tengela begot Mapate Tengela; Mapate
            Tengela begot Njobu, and Njobu begot Mabajaku, the one who
            fought this country. He fought the *soninke* from Baddibu to
            Niumi Bato.[56] The Koli Tengela that came to Niumi is dif-
            ferent from the one I spoke to you about. The ancestor of
            the Sonko was Koli Tengela but the one I am speaking of was
            of the Nioro people of Maba.

Q: What do you know about the *dankuto*[57] between the Jola and
            Serer?

Samba: You know there is a reason for everything. Well, Serer and
            Jola were once all *soninke*. They all used to drink palm
            wine. The Serer are people who respect *dankuto*. To them
            it is no joke. I know these things about the Serer-Jola
            dankuto. A Serer was in his boat and a Jola joined him
            inside it. When they reached the middle of the river they
            spoke to each other. The Jola spoke in the Jola language
            and the Serer said to him, "What language are you speaking?"

            The Jola said, "I am a Jola."

            The Serer asked, "Why do you come into my boat?"

            The Jola answered, "I have no place to go. If I had one I
            would not have entered your boat."

The Serer got hold of him to throw him into the river, but they both ended up in the river. That was the day the Serer made *dankuto* with the Jola. That said that if any Serer should ever find a Jola and cause him any difficulty, he would die.

FOOTNOTES TO ABDOULIE SAMBA INTERVIEW

[1]This means, "I came from the village of Sarakunda in the Sanjal region of Baddibu."

[2]These are the empires, states, regions, or towns that Samba considers to be in his historical repertoire. Manding is what many Senegambian Mandinka call the old Mali Empire, though some use it more generally to refer to the traditional Mandinka homelands in the same upper Niger River region. Jolof is the former Wolof state, or empire, centered in central Senegal. There is reasonably good evidence that Jolof was the most powerful political unit in Senegambia some centuries ago, around the time of the first European contact with the region. Baddibu was the former Mandinka state east of Niumi on the north bank of the Gambia River. Sanjal was a semi-independent region of Baddibu. Interested Gambians still debate the extent of its independence. Saba is a village in the western part of old Baddibu. Siin was a predominantly Serer state that existed in western Senegal, north of the Saloum River, for several precolonial centuries. Kajor was a Wolof state along the Atlantic coast north of Cape Verde. Saloum was a Serer state immediately north of the lower Gambian Mandinka states of Niumi and Baddibu. Most of these states, perhaps all, were once part of the greater Jolof Empire. The best single source of the early history of these states is either Curtin, *Economic Change*, or Boulège, "La Sénégambie." For materials on the individual empires, states, or regions, see the bibliographical essay at the end of the second volume (Africa Series No. 38, 1979).

[3]Samba recites these names, seemingly without direct meaning to the narrative. However, they seem to serve to jog his memory for continued recitation.

[4]The political, social, and economic leader of the state; similar to the *mansa* in a Mandinka state; translated loosely as "king."

[5]Kahon, today a small village on the Saloum River just a few miles east of Kaolak, was the place of residence of the *bur* of Saloum. I do not know what Kanyimorijang is. Iliassa is a large village in The Gambia. It was one of the villages from which came the *mansa* of Baddibu.

[6]Of course, it always excites the historian whenever the *griot* says how many years ago someone lived. Many *griot*s tend to do this, some rather frequently. However, the historian must always temper his or her excitment long enough to find reasonable corroboration for the *griot*s' dating, for in many cases the numbers of years or dates recited are fabricated or, for other reasons, grossly inaccurate. In this instance, it was not difficult to attempt to corroborate Samba's word on when Biran Njeme Kumba lived because the historian Jean Boulègue, in a respected piece of research, collected a list of Saloum's

bur, forty-nine of them up to 1960, along with the number of years each held the position. By subtraction, Boulègue made a list of the *bur* with the dates each held the title. In his reading of European sources that mentioned the name of the *Bur* of Saloum in any given year, Boulègue found his list to be remarkably accurate. The tenth *bur* on Boulègue's list is "Biram Ndieme Coumba Ndiaye." He was the *bur* from 1615 to 1638, or thereabouts. If this is the Biran Njeme Kumba (my spelling) of Samba's recital, Samba says he lived some two-and-a-half centuries before Boulègue's list has him living. Furthermore, Boulègue suggests that the state of Saloum came into existence at the very end of the fifteenth century, a full century and more after Samba says Biran Njeme Kumba was alive. See Boulègue, "Contribution," pp. 657-665. For more on Boulègue's list and my recording of a recited list of Saloum's *bur*, see the interview with Samba Laoube and Boubacar Senn, following.

[7]Sora Musa is the same, largely mythical figure found in Unus Jata's narrative. See footnote 5 to the first Jata Interview.

[8]Futa refers to Futa Toro, a relatively dry pastoral and agricultural region along the middle Senegal River.

[9]This paragraph appears out of context in the narrative. Something he said or thought reminded Samba of the importance of marriage relationships among the different Senegambian states--probably just his naming several states and being aware of the interrelationships they had--and he felt it important to comment.

[10]*Tiligi* is "the West," the opposite of *Tilibo*, "the East."

[11]According to David P. Gamble in *The Wolof of Senegambia* (London, 1967), p. 58,

> The head of the women in the [Wolof] chiefdom had the title of *linger* ("Lynguere, Linguere"). She was normally the *bur*'s mother, or in some cases a sister. She had a number of dependent villages which cultivated her farms and paid tribute to her personal entourage, and her own court concerned with women's matters. . . .

[12]Walo Barob refers to the Wolof state of Walo or Waalo, located immediately north of Kajor and centered on the lower Senegal River.

[13]This payment of tribute in the major produce of the country is similar to Unus Jata's comments on Niumi's payment of tribute to Saloum in the form of thatching grass. It is unlikely, though not impossible, that Jolof ever held firm political authority over Jarra or Niamina, both Mandinka states on the south bank of the Gambia River.

[14]Samba seems to use Kelidibi to refer to the state of Jolof. I am not aware of a particular village of that name.

[15]These rulers mentioned, whether actual historical figures or fictional ones, appear to be symbols used by Samba to represent members of the ruling families of each of these states. Samba mentions that you would find Yareng Sawaneh living at either Pinyaye or Kafamena because political authority in the state of Niamina rotated between two families in these villages. At any given time the *mansa* of Niamina could be living in either place.

[16]Again, the ruler of Jolof was not called the *mansa*; he was the *burba* or *bur*.

[17]This is the famous Sundiata Keita. See footnote 6 to the first Unus Jata interview.

[18]The *damel* was the ruler of the state of Kajor--roughly equivalent to the *mansa* in a Mandinka state.

[19]The Wali Mbekam that Samba mentions may be the same figure that *griots* say was the first *bur* of Saloum, Mbegane Ndour. Boulègue estimates that Mbegane Ndour reigned in Saloum from 1494-1514. Boulègue, "Contribution," p. 657.

[20]Saloum Suare (Al-hajj Salimu Sware) is a controversial figure in West African history and among West African historians. Few agree about just when he lived or exactly what he did, but most agree that his impact upon the study and practice of Islam in the western portion of the Western Sudan was far reaching. Most historians accept the fact, too, that it was Saloum Suare's religious tradition that unified the group of related peoples who today call themselves Jahanke. Several oral traditions from the western Senegambian region have accounts similar to Samba's, saying that Suare came to Saloum, worked his magic, and gave the state his name. I know of no other evidence, however, that he ever traveled so far to the west. There are several recent studies on Suare and the Jahanke. See Curtin, *Economic Change*, pp. 75ff; Lamin Sanneh, "The Origins of Clericalism in West African Islam," *Journal of African History*, XVII (1976), pp. 49-72; and Thomas C. Hunter, "The Jabi Ta'rikhs: Their Significance in West African Islam," *International Journal of African Historical Studies*, IX (1976), pp. 437ff.

[21]Maba is the most celebrated figure in oral traditions of much of the lower Gambia-Saloum River region. He was a mid-nineteenth century Muslim warrior and social revolutionary who fought against the traditional ruling elites in several Senegambian states and, ultimately, against French incursion in the region north of the Lower Gambia. For information on Maba, see Quinn, *Mandingo Kingdoms*.

[22]A *jinn* is a spirit, usually found living in a tree or in a hole in the ground. It is most frequently translated as "devil."

[23]Note the similarity to the story in Unus Jata's narrative. "You have found a home, but you have found it with its owners" is a common Senegambian folklore motif.

[24]Many of the Mandinka states of The Gambia region have oral traditions that accord to women the first political leadership of the state. Different historians have speculated why this is so, one suggesting the possible existence of ancient Mandinka matriarchies or the influence of Serer matrilineal succession, and another considering the possibility of the influence of Bainounk women, who could succeed to village headship. See S. M. Cissoko, "La royauté (*mansaya*) chez les Mandingues occidentaux, d'aupres leurs traditions orales," *Bulletin de l'Institut Fondamental d'Afrique Noire*, Series B, XXXI (1969), pp. 332-333, and Galloway, "History of Wuli," p. 41. For the state of Kombo, across the river from Niumi, informants include women rulers seemingly to give the male Mandinka *mansa* a basis from which to claim legitimacy. The woman ruler married a Mandinka

and so yielded her family's claim to political leadership in the state. See Biddulph, "Memorandum on Native Custom."

[25]Jimansaar was one of the five villages in Baddibu wherein lived an extended family that provided Baddibu's *mansa*.

[26]A *jung-jung* is a drum associated with the *mansa* of a state. It is traditionally beaten only in the *mansa*'s presence and only on special occasions. When Sora Musa heard the *jung-jung* beating, he realized he was in a state that already had a *mansa*.

[27]I edited considerably here, for Samba once more goes through where Sora Musa traveled, the rulers he visited, and the conversations they had. This is indicative of how very repetitive are the tales of *griot*s.

[28]". . .everything we do in this world will be recorded and recited" is a comment on the role of the *griot* in Mandinka society. Presumbably, the implication of the sentence is that people will long know that Baddibu went to war against the man who was to become its *mansa*.

[29]This long story, culminating in Sora Musa's marriage to Nyelengi, is very likely a means of establishing the legitimacy of one or more families to rule in Baddibu. A number of Senegambian Mandinka oral traditions use the same motif--the marriage of a great male figure to a woman who is ruling a small, weak state--seemingly to ascribe legitimacy to a family to provide the *mansa* of the state.

[30]Samba's genealogical recitations are somewhat confusing, but in general they provide an idea of how important marriage ties among prominent people in the various Senegambian states were to residents of the region. Samba here seems to be stressing the marriage connections Baddibu had with Saloum and Jolof.

[31]Kaimor is a village in Senegal. It was once an important village in the eastern portion of the former state of Saloum. It is located about fifteen miles west and slightly north of the major soutward bend of the Gambia River some one hundred fifty miles (by river) from the Atlantic.

[32]Bakau is a large village near Cape St. Mary where the Gambia River enters the Atlantic. It is located about a dozen miles west of The Gambia'a capital of Banjul.

[33]"General Number One"--the phrase suggests that Samba is not completely unfamiliar with certain Western military concepts.

[34]Kiang was the Mandinka state located across the Gambia River from Baddibu. "Jannehba," "big" or "elder" Janneh, is simply referring to an important member of a prominent Gambian family, the Janneh.

[35]Normally, the people who settle in an area first have rights to the use and allocation of the land in Mandinka society. Thus, someone who arrives in the afternoon would have primacy over someone who arrives in the evening and would be in a position to tell the evening person where to settle. Samba

suggests, however, that in this case the two parties worked out a different arrangement.

[36]*Alkali* is the head of a Mandinka village; Imam is the Muslim religious leader of a village.

[37]Mbalufele refers to Mbalufele Janneh, a highly respected elder of the Janneh family of Bakau and a man known for his knowledge of the history of the lower Gambia. See the second volume (Africa Series No. 38) for my interview with Mbalufele Janneh.

[38]Boulègue's list of Saloum's *bur* shows Bale Ndoungou Ndao reigned from 1824 to 1852. The war Samba talks about, between the *mansa* of Niumi and Ansuman Jaju, occurred toward the end of his reign.

[39]Marong and Jammeh were two of the five families who provided the *mansa* for the state of Baddibu. Apparently, the Marong family had ties through marriage with the ruling family of Saloum; the Jammeh family did not. The story of the dispute over the cutting of grass is typical of the reasons found in oral traditions for the beginning of wars.

[40]Demba Sonko was *mansa* of Niumi from 1834 to 1862.

[41]Again, *mansaya* is the quality of being *mansa*, or, in free translation, kingship.

[42]Traditionally, the *griot* was one of the *mansa* advisors. Abdoulie Samba places his great grandfather in this role, though, interestingly, Mo Joof does not follow his advice.

[43]The story of Yeramasang going to Saloum to be Balen Dunku's "stranger" is an interesting one in the context of young male members of Mandinka *mansakunda* ("royal" families) and their aspirations to become *mansa* of their own state. Frequently, when they reached an age approaching manhood, these young men would leave their homes and travel to live with a *mansa* in another state. They served in something approaching an apprentice capacity, helping where they could but through it all learning the art of *mansaya*. Leaving home was often a good idea anyway, for it got the young men away from their brothers or other competitors who might try to ruin their opportunity to become *mansa* through magical means at best, or at worst try to kill them. The aspirants always left friends and relatives behind who would keep their names before the people--the *griot*s were important in these matters--and would see to it that magical practitioners did work on behalf of their candidate. Often the young men would remain away from their homes until they were actually selected to be the next *mansa*, then make the jubilant return. The odd aspect in this instance is noted clearly by Samba: Yeramasang went to live with Balen Dunku, who was not on good terms with his father. Normally the young men went to live with *mansa* who were relatives or close friends. Eventually, however, Yeramasang's residence with Balen Dunku led to the development of such a close friendship that when it became time for Baddibu to aid Niumi in its fighting, Saloum came to help, too. Obviously, Demba Sonko of Niumi knew of the relationship between Baddibu and Saloum, through Yeramasang, when he asked specifically for Yeramasang to help him fight against Ansuman Jaju.

I treat these matters and similar ones in my "Niumi: The History of a Western Mandinka State," pp. 209ff.

[44]See footnote 6 above for Biran Njeme Kumba. This is another example of a *griot* not knowing the answer to a question but providing one anyway. I have edited extensively here, for Samba repeats quite a bit of his original tale of Sora Musa and the ceasing of tribute from Baddibu, Niumi, and other Gambian states to Saloum.

[45]In an earlier interview an informant mentioned the name of Bana in association with one of the families of Niumi. I thought there might be some connection between the family and Yeli Bana, a prominent figure in Saloum traditions. Therefore, I posed this question to Samba.

[46]See footnote 19, above, for Mbegane Ndure.

[47]A "Toranka" is a person from Futa Toro, the region along the middle Senegal River.

[48]A "Kasingka" is another name for a member of the Serer ethnic group.

[49]When a Muslim enters a mosque, he leaves his shoes by the door and goes in barefooted.

[50]Boulègue's list of the *bur* of Saloum has several named Ndena Njie or something approaching that, but none of these has the surname Jobe. In fact, there is not a Jobe--a common Wolof surname--on the entire list. Also, there is no Ali Buri nor is there an Amadou Seku. Perhaps Samba is speaking of persons who were not Saloum's *bur*, or he may be referring to leaders of the state of Kajor.

[51]See the second interview with Unus Jata, footnotes 31 and 43.

[52]Most oral traditions say that Mansa Wali Jan was the man who led the *nyancho* out of Kabu, northward across the Gambia River into the regions that would become the states of Siin and Saloum.

[53]Most informants from Baddibu say there were five extended families in five villages that provided the *mansa* of that state. The village of Jajerre is included along with the four villages Samba mentions.

[54]This statement is contrary to what most informants say about the primacy of the Jammeh family over the Sonko in Niumi. It is indicative of the contradictions found in oral traditions and it brings out, once again, the difficulties one encounters in trying to determine historical truth from oral testimony.

[55]Compare Samba's account of Koli Tengela with Unus Jata's account in the first interview.

[56]Samba is referring to Ma Ba, or Maba Kiakou, the mid-nineteenth-century religious and military leader who overcame the secular state of Baddibu and led wars in a wider region between the lower Gambia and Saloum Rivers.

[57]A *dankuto* is a mutually accepted, special relationship, similar to what is commonly called a "joking relationship," among two individuals, families, villages, states, or ethnic groups. A *dankuto* entails reciprocal obligations for both parties. For most such relationships in the western Mandinka region, there are allegorical stories about how the *dankuto* came about.

SAMBA LAOUBE AND BOUBACAR SENN

ONE INTERVIEW: February 4, 1975.

GENERAL SUBJECT MATTER: History of the group of people called *guelowar* and
their role in the founding of Saloum; history of the
state of Saloum before the colonial period; Saloum
relations with the Mandinka states of Niumi and
Baddibu.

LOCATION OF RECORDING: Indiana University Archives of Traditional Music,
Access numbers 4387 and 4388.

The Informants.   Samba Laoube and Boubacar Senn call themselves "court *griot*s."
They are the eldest members of *griot* families that the ruling families of the
state of Saloum patronized.   Laoube, sixty-eight years old, is especially important as a court *griot* for he is one of the few permitted to play the *jung-
jung*, the "royal" drum, which was traditionally beaten only in the presence of
the *bur*, the sovereign ruler, of Saloum.   Senn, fifty-four years old, plays the
halam, a stringed instrument.   When asked their occupations, both men said they
were farmers and weavers as well as *griot*s.   They grow millet, primarily, in
fields around Kahon.   I did not ask about their weaving, though I suspect the
art is associated with the occupational grouping of *griot*s.

Laoube and Senn reside in Kahon, their home throughout most of their lives.   They
command a considerable amount of respect among residents of the community, who still
recognize their position as court *griot*s and holders of considerable knowledge about
the former state of Saloum.

The Interview.   By the end of January 1975 I had collected a great deal of oral
data relating to Niumi and some of the other Gambian Mandinka states.   I was eager,
then, to interview knowledgeable informants in other regions over a wider area,
to ask these informants about their own histories, indeed, but also to ask them,
as outside sources with fewer (or different) reasons for distorting the truth,
about Niumi and the surrounding area.   It is important to know what people in
Saloum know about, and consider important in, Niumi's history.   With this in mind,
I arranged with B. K. Sidibe to obtain a government Land Rover for approximately
ten days.   I agreed to provide food (where necessary), payment for informants
(again, where necessary or advisable), and blank magnetic tapes for the interviews, which Sidibe would copy for the Gambia's Cultural Archives oral data collection upon our return.   So on February 3, after several annoying delays, we
left Banjul for a week and a half of traveling (pretty much where I wished to go)
and collecting oral traditions.   Besides Sidibe and myself, we traveled with
Dembo Manneh, the driver of the Land Rover and an extremely pleasant individual,
who helped me obtain interviews on several occasions, and Omi Awa Bah, a woman
who would cook for the four of us and assist in interpreting when informants
spoke Wolof only.

From the outset I knew I wanted to go to Kahon to interview one or more of the court *griot*s residing there. Kahon was the capital of the precolonial state of Saloum; I knew from Jean Boulègue's work that there were *griot*s there who had one or more lists of Saloum's *bur*, and I figured these *griot*s would be good informants on Saloum's history and individuals likely to know something about the history of surrounding states.

We entered Kahon around noon on February 4 and we went more or less directly to the compound of the village head, Malik Sarr. Kahon is a small village today--much smaller than it once was, one suspects--located just five kilometers east of Kaolack, a city of 100,000 and one of Senegal's regional capitals. It lies on the north bank of the Saloum River at a point that is the head of navigation for ocean-going vessels of fairly light draught. Because of this, before the rapid growth of Kaolack in the last century, Kahon was a commercial hub with a fairly large hinterland. In the dry season--and February was in the heart of that period--Kaolack is notoriously hot; Kahon is, too. As we pulled across the open, sandy square area in the center of the village I remember thinking Kahon to be somewhat desolate. Malik Sarr welcomed us and said he thought two *griot*s in Kahon would be happy to speak with us. However, these men were working or visiting somewhere and would have to be summoned. We decided to fix our lunch while we waited, so we found a shady spot near Sarr's compound and proceeded to do so.

After about forty-five minutes the two *griot*s came walking across the open square toward us. One was dressed in a long, off-white, ankle-length gown, the other in a similarly cut gown of light blue--nearly aqua. Both wore stocking caps. Sarr introduced us and we sat down to discuss the interview I wanted. Both men were quite used to being recorded. They let us know they expected payment for their services, but left the amount up to us. Sidibe explained to them my interests; both felt they could add to the information I had, so the interview proceeded. Samba Laoube, the elder, spoke first, but throughout the rest of the interview each took his turn, deferring to the other when he thought the other could provide a better answer to our specific question. On several occasions Malik Sarr added something he knew, and the *griot*s welcomed his comments. It was altogether a professional session.

Toward the end of the interview Samba Laoube agreed to play the *jung-jung* and to let me record his playing. Therefore, the last ten minutes or so of the second cassette consists of Laoube's drumming on the revered royal drum.

Sidibe and Omi Awa Bah acted together as interpreters. Binta Jammeh translated the interview about two weeks after its recording. The informants spoke in Wolof.

Q: We would like to begin by having you tell us something
        about the first *guelowar* people who came to this area.

Laoube: The first *guelowar* who came to Saloum was Yande Kamal.
        He came with Oufu Jabun, Cherno Mbaye, Bherno Jonay, Siin
        Mengen, Tegi Yab, and Niooro Were. These were the first
        people who came to Saloum.

Q: Where did they come from?

Laoube: They came from Mekka.

Q: Mekka?   Which Mekka?

Laoube: The Mekka where people go to pray.   That was a long time
          ago.   During the war between Nabet Bunkanala and Sara Bagii,
          that was when these people came to Saloum, looking for a
          place to rest and to gain their independence.   That is how
          they founded Kahon.   There was nobody here then.   They
          were the ancestors of the *guelowar* and they gave birth to
          the *guelowar*.

Q: How long ago was that?

Laoube: Some six hundred years or more.

Q: Through which lands did they pass when coming?

Laoube: They came through Futa and when they became powerful they
          came to Jolof.

Q: Is that Futa Toro or. . .

Laoube: Yes, they passed through Futa Toro.   No, I am sorry, it was
          Futa Hai, and they came directly to Saloum.   They were
          divided into two groups.   The first consisted of Oufu Jabun
          and his followers.

Q: Whom did they find here?

Laoube: They did not find anyone here.   Yande Kamal first stopped
          between Kaur and Kuntaur.[1]   He stayed in Kaur for a long
          time and he had a son called Saloum whose mother was Kumba.
          It was Saloum who founded Saloum in Jolof.   Cherno Mbaye
          was the first to come here.   Siin Mengen went to Siin to
          a village called Mbissel.   It was Yande Kamal who directed
          them to go to these places.   Kung Kumba was also Yande's
          son.   I do not know his relationship with Cherno Mbaye,
          but they came together.   Siin Mengen built Siin and the
          village was named after him.   Cherno Mbaye was here. Saloum
          was at Saloum and Siin Mengen was at Siin, which is near
          the river, and he was put in charge of all the things that
          arrived from the boats.   Cherno Mbaye was here at Kahon.
          These were the Njob.[2]   Cherno Jonai came to a village called
          Njegen, and he founded a village at Ila.   The other *guelowar*
          also founded Gapah.   These were the *guelowar* who came here
          first before any other *guelowar*.

Q: How did they come to be called *guelowar*?

Laoube: The *guelowar* were followers of a holy prophet.   They fought
          for the prophet until the war ended.   During the war they
          proved themselves to be brave and strong men.   After the

war the prophet said, "These people are very brave men and they should be promoted to high positions. These people are *guelowar*; they should be given respect."

That is the meaning of *guelowar*. The *guelowar* here and those of Kabu are all the same. When Yande Kamal died, Kuyang Keita succeeded him. He lived during the time of Sumanguru Keita. Kuyang Keita left Mali and came to Saloum. He came here to seek his fortune because people rested during the dry season.[3] He lived near the river. You can see it easily behind Kaolack. After he came, Saloum Suare came. He also has descendants here.[4] After Saloum came Yeli Bana Musa Sallah. He was the *marabout*. He quarreled with Koli Jam Sundiata of Futa. Yeli Bana was defeated by Koli and he left Futa. Koli gave him a leaf and told him that wherever the leaf dried he should settle. It would also mean that Koli had left him in peace. He assured him that if he settled somewhere before the leaf was dry there would still be war between them. When Yeli brought the leaf to Njob, which was the name of Kahon at that time. . . . That was when the *guelowar* of Kabu left Kabu. Sino Meo and Kularo Meo were the *guelowar* who came from Kabu. The time between these *guelowar* of Kabu and the others was long. The time of Yande Kamal, Kuyang Keita, and Saloum Suare and Yeli Bana came to about two hundred years. Yeli Bana was the last to come. It was he whom the *guelowar* of Kabu met here. They fought with Yeli Bana and killed him.

Q: What happened after these events--on toward the present?

Laoube: A *guelowar* called Mbegane Ndure came from Siin. His mother came from here. His father lived in Siin. Mansa Wali Jan[5] was his grandfather. His mother and his father, Marfasak, lived here.

Here there was a brief discussion between Laoube and Senn. They decided that Senn knew this story better than Laoube, so he began to narrate in his own fashion.

Senn: I will tell you about the *guelowar* from the time they were in Kabu up to the time when they were here as it was told me by my ancestors. There was a *guelowar* who lived in Kabu called Mansa Wali Jan. He was not yet named Jan then. He was only called Mansa Wali and that meant king in Mandinka. He fought in Kabu with a king called Bamba Siteh, who drove him away from Kabu. He left there and sought a place to settle until he arrived at Siin Saloum. He rested for a while at Girof and then came to Kular, where he stayed for a while. His real village in Siin is Mbissel. There was no king in Siin Saloum when he came to Mbissel. We

counted four to five villages and appointed someone to
rule those four or five villages. We called him a *laman*.
He would settle our disputes and carry out our administration. They called this person the *laman* in both Wolof
and Serer.[6]

When Mansa Wali came and saw those *laman*. . . .He came at
a time when there was famine in this land, which caused
great difficulty. In that same year the head of a family
died and he left his son, a nephew, and a lot of cattle.
This caused Mansa Wali Jan to become the *bur* of Siin.
They tried to divide the cattle between the son and the
nephew, but they were unable to settle on a fair division.
They tried to divide it seven times. Mansa Wali said to
the *laman*, "I will divide your cattle fairly without any
quarrels."

The *laman* replied, "If you are able to succeed in dividing
the cattle equitably, we will all unite and make you our
leader because we are presently tired of it."

Mansa Wali called the son and nephew of the deceased and
he said to the son, "Did you say that you should inherit
the herd of cattle?"

The son replied, "Yes, I worked with my father and helped
him have a good herd."

He said to the nephew, "Have you heard what the son has
said--that he was all the time working with his father?"

The nephew replied, "No, these cattle are inherited matern-
ally and by rights I should have them because I am his
sister's son."

Each one insisted on inheriting the cattle. Mansa Wali
took two boxes large enough to hold young men and he put
a man who was very wise in each box. Whatever was said
within range of the boxes, the men inside would be able
to hear and tell what was said. He gave a box to the son
and one to the nephew and told them to come and see him
in the morning so that he could judge between them. He
did not tell them that people were in the boxes. He just
said that his clothes were in the boxes and they were to
take the boxes home and bring them back the next morning.
They loaded the boxes and went, each going with his wife.

When he got a distance away, the son told his wife to help
him put down the box because it was getting very heavy.
The man inside the box heard it. They put the box down
under a shade tree and began to chat. The wife said to
the husband, "If I were you I would give up the cattle.
You now look tired and you are sweating profusely. The
cattle belong to the maternal line anyway. Your father
inherited them through his mother and he is now dead.
Leave the cattle affair and we can go and seek our fortune
elsewhere."

The son replied, "I will not leave this cattle dispute. If I try to get the cattle, then my maternal lineage will prosper. I do not care. I shall never leave it."

The nephew also got tired and his wife said to him, "If I were you I would forget about the cattle. They are yours, but when a person trusts in Allah he will prosper."[7]

The nephew replied, "They are my property, which was owned by my grandmother and then by my uncle and my other uncle. It is my uncle who died recently. He had the cattle and now I should have them. I do not know what to say in the next world, but I shall not live to see cattle that are mine given to someone else."

The man in the box was hearing the conversation. In the morning both men returned the boxes and greeted Mansa Wali. He returned their greetings and reminded them of his promise. He told them to open their boxes and they saw the men. Each man told what he had heard from the two opponents. That was how the cattle were handed over to the nephew.

Thus, all the *laman* decided to install Mansa Wali as their king and they handed over all their land to him. After that, Mansa Wali had a sister who was called Ngila Faye. From this arises the story of Mbegane and the *marabout*, about which you were asking--why he came to Kahon and why he left there.

Mansa Wali's sister had a bad sore on her foot and was getting treatment here at Mbudai Kebe's.[8] A man called Burey Kulema married her. The begot a son called Mbegane. Mbagane went home to Siin. When he became an adult, Mansa Wali's sons occasionally said malicious things about him. They said, "He has refused to go to his father. Here is our father's kingdom. We will have to look after our father. He knows what he is up to."

When Mbegane heard this, he decided to try to obtain his father's land. He was very angry. When he came here he found Yeli Bana Musa here. He found no king here because Yeli Bana was not a king, he was a *marabout*. Mbegane told Yeli that he had come to take his father's land. Yeli replied that in order to have it, he would have to win it in a fight. They fought for seven years, but it ended in a stalemate.

Mbegane had a sister called Menge Ndure, who said to him, "Mbegane, you really surprise me."[9]

Mbegane said, "What have I done to surprise you?"

She answered, "This *marabout* will never be killed by fighting him in person."

He asked, "Then what kind of fight will kill him?"

She answered, "Fighting by magic!"

He said, "That worries me very much. I can turn into an elephant and when I run and strike I will kill him, but the Tukulor will kill me.[10] If I turn into a lion and kill him, the Tukulor who have guns will kill me. After all, one should live long enough to enjoy one's success in gaining kingship. If I should kill Yeli and not live to be king then what use is it to kill him?"

Blacksmiths and cobblers also lived here.[11] One of them was called Ngoyan Sarr. He said to them, "What you are saying is very brutal. Have you no other means of killing the Tukulor than these brutal methods?"

Menge replied, "We asked Mbegane and he said that he could turn into a snake."

Ngoyan asked Mbegane, "Could you turn into a snake and bite him?"

Mbegane replied, "Yes."

Ngoyan asked, "How will you prevent the people from killing you?"

Mbegane answered, "I will just make a cat carry me and the people would believe that the cat was killing me and then we would have our kingdom."

By seven o'clock, when prayers were being called,[12] Yeli Bana went into the mosque and started praying. While he was praying Mbegane, in the form of a snake, and his sister, in the form of a cat, went inside the mosque. Mbegane waited in the right-hand corner. When Yeli had finished praying and was about to put on his shoes at the door, saying "*Bismilahi*,"[13] Mbegane bit him. Yeli told the Tukulor that a snake had bitten him. When the Tukulor were about to intervene, the cat pretended to kill the snake and take it away. Yeli told his people that they should not worry since the cat had gone with the snake to kill it. The cat took it to a nearby village called Chawando. People in those days possessed magical powers. Yeli Bana died on that day and Mbegane established a real kingdom for the first time in Kahon. Before him, all those who had come to Kahon were just *marabout*s who spent their time preaching to the people. When there were wars against enemies, the *marabout*s just gave them *juju*[14] and told them ways of conquering their enemies. After Mbegane ruled he established a dynasty and this man here [motioning toward Malik Sarr, the *Alkali* of Kahon] is, till now, the last of that dynasty.

Q: Was Yeli Bana a Fula?

Senn: Yeli Bana Musa was a Tukulor. He came from Futa in a village called Haireh. He was not originally a Tukulor.

Koli Tengela drove him away from Futa. He was only a
follower of the teaching of the Koran. He was a devout
Muslim. Koli was a *cheddo*[15] who was only after kingship.
Futa was the first to have a king. Koli said to Yeli,
"Since you are a Muslim and I am not on good terms with
the Muslims, quit my land."

They fought a war between them and after that Yeli Bana
left and came here. The people here were not yet con-
scious of Islam. We knew nothing about the Koran or any
other books. Yeli Bana came here with his Koran and tried
to teach the people, helping them to be successful in their
wars. But there was no centralized government here before
the time of Mbegane Ndure.

Malik Sarr, village head of Kahon, interrupted, saying he had something
to add about the *guelowar*. The two *griot*s deferred to him:

Sarr: In those days only the true *guelowar* were installed as *bur* in
Saloum. This is how it all was done. A *guelowar* was a *guelowar* because of his mother. When a *guelowar* had a child,
he would give his child to the *jaraf*,[16] who trained the
child and taught him along strict lines, developing in him
a clean mind and teaching him how to administer. He showed
him the importance of self-respect and of judging people
properly. Besides the *jaraf*, the *jarad*, and the *bisak*, and
the *faraba* helped train the young *guelowar*.[17] The *jarad* was
an elder who was very intelligent and capable of teaching
others. All these were the same category as the *jaraf*.
Three different young *guelowar* would be taught by these
people and each one would teach the *guelowar* his own way.
They would teach about habits, knowledge, and *juju*.[18] The
young *guelowar* was called *lawah*. They taught the *guelowar*
satisfactorily and they always had confidence that any
guelowar who listened to their teachings and put them into
practice would never humiliate them.

When all the people of Kahon met together, each *jaraf* would
bring his *guelowar* and say, "I have brought my adopted child,
he whom I have trained and given much knowledge, in whom I
have developed good habits, and whom I have protected with
juju. If I give you this young man, he will be able to
administer this land effectively and peacefully."

Afterwards the people competed for the kingship because
there were many *guelowar* families and each wanted it. For
example, Koldu Bijay's family is here; Honoja Bijay's
family is here; and Dijen Bijay's house is here. All these
are *guelowar*. Anyone born in each of these families is a
guelowar. If you are born by a female in one of these
families, then you are a *guelowar*.

Q: What are *guelowar* surnames?

Sarr: The *guelowar* surnames are Mbodj, Njie, Ndow, Joof. . .

Q: How many *guelowar* families are there?

Sarr: I told you, we have five.

Q: What is the surname of Keke Bijay's family?

Here Samba Laoube reenters the conversation.

Laoube: Mbodj. But you see, the *guelowar* were women and they had
            different surnames: Jeng, Job, Faal, Joof, and so on. All
            brave men had *guelowar* surnames. They did not have any
            fixed names. Kordu Bijay's surname was Njie. They are
            descended from Sengan. The founders of these five families
            were of the same mother and father. They were all Njie.

Q: Were men *guelowar* as well as women?

Laoube: The women were the *guelowar*. A man became a *guelowar*
            through his mother. The children of a woman *guelowar* be-
            came *guelowar* and the father's children became kings but
            not *guelowar*.

            At a gathering of people in Kahon, *jaraf*, *fara jung-jung*
            (the leader of the *griot*s), *parr* (another head *griot*),
            fara tega (leader of the blacksmiths), *farawudeh* (leader
            of the leather-workers), *lawah* (the young *guelowar*), and
            the *bisak* (the person who spoke for the king) got together.
            The *bisak* told the people the intentions of the king. *Fara
            tega* made the king's weapons when he was preparing for war.
            Before the rains he made the king's hoes, plows, and other
            tools. *Farawudeh* coated with leather the king's *juju*
            that he was to wear in wars, and he made the king's saddle
            and horse bits. *Jaraf* in today's government would be the
            leading minister. The *faraba* would be like the *ministre
            de l'interieur*. He settled disputes between different
            people in the state. He kept the weapons, too, which he
            divided among the people when wars were to be fought. The
            jaraf ruled the world of Saloum--even the *bur*. If the
            bur of Saloum did anything that the *jaraf* did not like,
            he would depose the *bur*.

Q: What were the names of the *jaraf*?

Laoube: Some were Njie, Ndure, Sarr, Fye, Nyang, and so on.

Q: If there was no *bur* for a time was the *jaraf* made *bur*?

Laoube: If there was no *bur* the *jaraf* acted as *bur* and stayed in the *bur*'s house until the next *bur* was installed.

Q: Tell us about the installation of the *bur*.

Laoube: After the *jaraf* would bring his adopted *guelowar* and show him to the people, telling them that he was fit to be king, the *guelowar* would walk up to the middle with a sword. He would thrust the sword into the ground and say, "Kahon, make me *bur*! If I am made *bur* I will rule the land without any complaints and you will all be happy with my rule. There will be peace and prosperity, no illnesses, no deaths."[19]

Q: Who told him to stand and proclaim these things in the middle of the group?

Laoube: The *jaraf* ordered him to do so. After that the people who belonged to the family of the *guelowar*'s mother would get up and say, "*Jaraf*, the magnificent, install this *guelowar*. If you do we shall give you so many slaves."

There would have been another young *guelowar* beside the one to be installed. He would also have lived with the *jaraf*. He, too, would get up and put his sword in the ground and say, "*Jaraf*, magnificent *jaraf*."

All the maternal relatives of this *guelowar* were present: his uncles, his brothers of the same mother, his maternal grandparents, his paternal uncles. They would get up and say, "*Jaraf*, magnificent *jaraf*, we want you to make this your *guelowar*. If you make him *bur* the land will prosper and we will give you twenty horses,[20] thirty male slaves, forty female slaves, and so on."

There would be great competition and the young men would tell things to each other that were not true just because of the great rivalry that existed between them. The one who was successful in becoming *bur*. . . .

When the elders went home the *jaraf*, *faraba*, *bisak*, *fara jung-jung*, and *parr* would sit in their own hut and discuss the selection. They would say to each other, "Now, in truth, this one, the son of ___, is very fortunate. They have a large family and they are very influential. You, *faraba*, you have adopted this other one, and you liked him, but honestly, this one is more qualified to be our *bur*."

Faraba would say, "I have come to an agreement with you since he is the elder[21] and he is most qualified. I am not angry."

Q: What would they have done if they had quarreled and the *faraba* had refused?

Laoube: They consulted their fetish. It was called *saltigi*.

Q: What was it?

Laoube: It was a person who was very knowledgeable and intelligent.
When they consulted *saltigi*, he told them to go home and
the next morning he told them the one who would be the next
bur.

Q: Did the *saltigi* not merely judge by age?

Laoube: No, he chose the person he foresaw as the most dynamic
ruler. He did not tell the people in public. He called
the *jaraf* and the others into his hut and told them who
would be the next *bur*. The *jaraf* would then tell the
bisak, "Go and get the *jall*."

There was a kind of sand we called *jall*, which we used to
install the *bur*. The man to be installed faced the east.
He was held by the shoulders and rubbed with the *jall*
seven times. The *jaraf* then walked to the people, followed by the *bisak* and the *lawah*, who would be the next
bur. The public would then know who would be their next
bur.

When they arrived at the place where the *bur* was to be
installed, the *bisak* would put *jall* on the ground, chew
some leaves seven times, spit them onto the *jall*, and put
it on the piece that was put on the *bur*'s head as a sign
that he was the one.

Q: What was that like?

Laoube: It was a hat made of woven cloth.

Q: What color was it?

Laoube: White. The *lawah* would face the east and they would place
the hat on his head, give him a hand, and tell him, "How
successful you are." They sounded guns and beat the *jung-
jung*, and the *griot*s sang. The *bur* gave the *jaraf* what he
had promised beforehand. He gave gifts to the *fara jung-
jung*, *bisak*, *farawudeh*, and all the other people who
brought about his installation. He gave them horses and
slaves. Each of the relatives of the mother and father
rewarded these officials. That was how a *guelowar* was
installed in Kahon.

Q: Did you have many horses in Saloum?

Boubacar Senn speaks again.

Senn: Yes, we owned many horses. Have you not seen how vehicles
           are plentiful now? We owned horses in the same way.

Q: Where did you get your horses?

Senn: From *Denku* in Hai.[22]

Q: Where was Saloum's boundary in the east?

Senn: It was at Makakui, behind Kungel, through Kuntaur. In
           this area it went as far as Barra.[23]

Q: Was Niumi part of Saloum?

Senn: Yes. That was a long time ago. You know *mansa* were in-
           stalled at Essau.

Q: Did your boundary extend to Baddibu?

Senn: It went as far as Farafenni.[24] Baddibu was part of Saloum.
           It was afterwards that Baddibu got her independence. Essau
           also joined Banjul and the other states gained their inde-
           pendence.[25]

Q: With whom did the people of Kahon marry regularly?

Senn: With people of Siin, Kajor, Jolof, Bawol, Ndukomar, and
           Baddibu.

Q: Did you intermarry with people from Niumi?

Senn: Niumi? Oh, yes. Ebrima Ndow's father, Saidou Ndow, lives
           here but he is from Jolof from the Njie family. Saidou
           Ndow begot Ebrima. Saidou Ndow is a politician from Sinn-
           Saloum.

Q: Did Saloum ever pay any tax or tribute to anyone?

Senn: No, that never occurred here. We were all once ruled by
           Jolof and we paid tribute to them. Ngai, Kungai, Jilor,
           Njafe-Njafe, Kajawan, Bofi, Kagmar, Jokol, Ganye, Seringe
           Pakala Njoteh, and Sering Taga paid tax to the *bur* in
           Kahon.[26] These are all that paid tribute here. It should
           also include Kanyai.

           Samba Laoube adds:

Laoube: Siin and Kahon were not part of the same kingdom. The *bur*
           of Saloum fought Siin. Sajuka was the first to fight Siin.
           Sajuka Mbodj fought against Salmone Faye and Saloum over-
           came Siin.[27]

Q: What brought about that war?

Laoube: Salmone was very cruel to the poor *guelowar* and he killed
          them in great numbers, so Sajuka intervened because the
          guelowar of Siin and Saloum were all the same--mainly from
          the same mother. Sajuka sent three legates--Biran Yassin,
          Han, and Bumi Fode--to tell Salmone that the wicked crimes
          he was committing by killing the people were too much,
          since he owed his position to the people. It was not be-
          cause of the trees or houses that he was ruling; it was be-
          cause of the people, so he should have had pity on the people
          and should have passed better judgment on them than killing
          the *guelowar*. If it continued, Sajuka warned, the *guelowar*
          would not only no longer become rulers, but the Faye, too,
          would no longer become rulers because it would be said that
          the Faye were of the same unkind nature as Salmone.

          Faye, Joof, Njie, and Mbodj ruled in Saloum. The three
          legates set out for Siin. Now you know that a ruler wants
          to be told the truth but he does not want to tell the truth.
          Salmone Faye had a wolf that ate people and the wolf killed
          people for him. This meant that Salmone was an absolute
          despot. The legates were sent to tell Salmone that what he
          was doing was not right because since the time of their an-
          cestors who left Kabu and went to Mali and then Futa and
          then came there, that such brutality had never been prac-
          ticed. Salmone was told to stop what he was doing.

          Salmone replied, "What you have said is not true. The *bur*
          of Saloum should have no interference in the affairs of Siin.
          I will kill to show that you have insulted my dignity."

          Salmone killed Biran Mbodj and the rest came back to Saloum.
          That was the cause of the war. Sajuka overcame Salmone in
          the war. Salmone was killed.

          The next war was fought by Sajuka's younger brother, Yegal
          Mbodj,[28] who was then the *bur* of Saloum succeeding his
          brother. Yegal fought with the *bur* Siin called Mbaki Njie--
          Mbaki Kod Njie. Hamadi Barrow was to succeed Salmone Faye.
          Mbaki Njie and Hamadi Barrow competed for rule; they were
          both princes with the right to rule. They struggled by
          fighting physically. The *jaraf* talked to them, but they
          still did not come to an agreement. The Joof family refused
          to back down and so did the Njie, so war resulted. Hamadi
          Barrow defeated Mbaki Njie. Mbaki then came to Saloum and
          found Yegal Mbodj ruling. Mbaki came to seek help from
          Yegal. Yegal discussed it with the elders of Saloum--*jaraf*
          and *faraba*. These two made the decisions and whatever they
          decided was accepted by the leaders of Jilor, Njafe-Njafe,
          Banyar, Mandari, Seringe Pakala, and Alwali Ndemen. The
          people of Saloum allied with Mbaki Njie and fought Hamadi
          Barrow of Siin. Hamadi Barrow was killed by Yegal Mbodj
          and Mbaki Njie was restored to rule.[29]

Boubacar Senn asks to speak:

Senn: You said you wanted to know about Essau and how they were able to gain their independence and begin installing their own *mansa*?[30] Well, we were all related because our *guelowar* were Mandinka. When they settled here, they discussed with their relatives who were in other places and gave them power to rule in their areas. When those relatives refused to pass their orders along, war resulted.

Q: How did the people of Niumi manage to get their independence? Was there not any war fought between Niumi and Saloum?[31]

Senn: A native of Saloum, Waji Njie Wai Bak, once fought with Jata Selang.[32] The people used to pay tribute here and it was during Jata Selang's time that they abolished it. I have heard that the *bur* of Saloum then was Ndena Njie Marong.[33] For three years Jata Selang refused to pay tribute.

But you have asked how the people of Niumi managed to gain their independence. That was in the time of Yande Kamal, when he came with all the different peoples. When Yande Kamal came, people did not know if he was a Serer or a Mandinka. That was about six hundred years ago. Our history is not written in a book. It is just in the form of oral traditions, so we cannot remember it all.[34]

Ndena Njie Marong of the Njie family fought with Jata Selang of Iliassa. I will also tell you about Balay Ndow's war. Jata Selang refused to pay tribute to Ndena Njie Marong for three years. In the end Ndena sent the Ndow to collect the tribute and the Mandinka refused, saying, "Tell him '*Mbang*'." If a Mandinka says "*Mbang wuleng*," then he will never agree to do what is asked.

Jata Selang was Ndena Njie's nephew and Jata was a Mandinka. When Balay Ndow heard Jata and the Baddibunka say "*Mbang*," Ndow said, "I do not know what *mbang* means, but whenever I ask the Mandinka, they say it to me."

Ndow sent his people to Ndena Njie to tell him that he would come after collecting the taxes. But Ndena said that he would collect the taxes himself from Jata Selang. Ndena went and called Jata a chameleon, but still Jata Selang refused. So the people of Saloum prepared for war, walking both day and night because Baddibu is a long way from here. Both horses and people got hungry. When they came the war was a stalemate, because Baddibu was very powerful. They came upon Baddibu at night and in the morning they told Jata Selang, "Your uncle has come to collect tribute and you should come and talk with him."

The Mandinka told him to refuse and he listened to their advice. Ndena Njie promised to take the taxes by force and the two enemies began fighting. From sunrise to sunset they fought. Much was spoiled in the fight. They all got tired and hoisted a white flag as a sign that they should rest. The people of Saloum went to rest under a tree near a village. The *guelowar* here were of the same mother as the Mandinka *guelowar*.

Ndena Njie Demba said, "If we wait until the people of Iliassa have had their meals and drunk their water and we remain hungry and thirsty, when we fight again they will kill us without any difficulty. I suggest that as soon as we kill their king, we will be successful."

His people said to him, "How can you kill the king when you will be unable to see him and if you go to his court his bodyguards will kill you?"

He replied that he would only have to ride his horse, Sawtah, which is the name we call our slaves. He saddled Sawtah and went up to Jata Selang's court, calling, "Jata Selang, Jata Selang. Tell him that I, Ndena Njie Demba, want to fight with him."

Jata used to come to Kahon and used to see Ndena Njie Demba, so he was able to determine whether he would be able to defeat Ndena or not. When people told him that Ndena was waiting for him outside and that only the two of them were to fight alone in the woods, Jata told his men to prepare his horses. Ndena Njie said that the war would end if the king were able to defeat him.

Jata went to Samarama, the one who was to witness the fight. Jata told him that nobody was to interfere, that only the two of them were to fight. Since Ndena was alone, he also would be alone. Jata was very powerful, a warrior. He came quickly and anxiously, riding his horse. The two horses and riders faced each other and the two enemies began threatening each other with their swords. Jata said to Ndena, "You have no manners because fighters should not throw harsh words at people. You are shameless. You know I can defeat you easily."

Ndena said, "Do not predict what will happen."

Ndena brought out his gun and wanted to shoot Jata. The latter said, "Shoot me and I will catch you."

Ndena shot but nothing came out. He continued to try, but nothing happened. Then Ndena told Jata to do the same thing. Jata fired at Ndena but it ended the same way. They abandoned their weapons and fought hand to hand. Jata was more powerful than Ndena. He held Ndena's hands and they started fighting until Jata showed that he was going to get the better of it. Jata had a cutlass that he kept secretly. Jata's horse and Ndena's horse were also fighting. Ndena had a half-brother called Ma Marama Demba.

People began to say, "Jata Selang will kill Ndena Njie Demba."

As soon as Ma Marama heard that he galloped his horse quickly. Whenever Jata tried to stab Ndena with his cutlass, the latter's horse intervened and prevented him from doing as he wished. Ma Marama came up and hit Jata twice with a sword and Jata fell from his horse. Ndena Njie Demba told Jata to get up and he would go tell Ndena Njie Marong that he had been defeated by Jata. Jata Selang was killed in that battle, but it was the same year the Iliassa gained her independence. This is what my elders told me.

Q: How did Niumi gain her independence from Saloum?

Senn: Through the same way, during the time of Maraba, Maraba Usuf, Dienda, and so on. All these *bur* ruled as far as Niumi and Baddibu. This one sitting here [pointing to Malik Sarr], his family ruled over all these places.

Through some discussion, we next learned that the *griot*s had a list of the *bur* of Saloum, from beginning to Fode Ngui Joof, who held at least the titular office down into the 1960s. It was the same list, or one similar to it, that Jean Boulègue used in his "Contribution." Realizing the value of such a list, I asked if they would read what was on it into the microphone. Samba Laoube said he would read it. The list was written with French orthography, though when translating the tape from Laoube's reading Binta Jammeh used the English spellings with which she was most familiar. I have retained these spellings.

Laoube read slowly, saying first the name of the *bur*, then the number of years or, in a few instances, days, that the *bur* reigned. He read:

Laoube: Lists des reis Saloum par ordre de chronologie:

1.	Jateret Tambedu	19 years
2.	Yeli Bana	7 years
3.	Mbegane Ndure	2 years
4.	Giranunka Ndong	7 years
5.	Latmingue Gillen	2 years
6.	Samb Lambour Njie	6 days
7.	Saine Njeme Joof	9 years
8.	Latilor Bajan	7 years
9.	Makodu Njie	no days or years mentioned.
10.	Walbumi Jeleng Njie	7 years
11.	Malieu Tane Njie	7 years
12.	Sambareh Jobe	6 days
13.	Biran Njeme Kumba Njie	11 days
14.	Ndena Njie Marong	28 years
15.	Mbanjemel Njie	9 years
16.	Wal Jojo Njie	7 days

17.	Makodu Njie.....................	6 years
18.	Ama Fal Fall....................	6 years
19.	Ama Joof Joof...................	5 years
20.	Sengan Kebe Njie................	7 years
21.	Latilor Ndong...................	7 years
22.	Anna Sega Secka.................	3 years
23.	Bigan Hureja Secka..............	6 years
24.	Njemeh Bigay Njie...............	4 years
25.	Mbang Job Job...................	20 years
26.	Mbang Nob Njie..................	7 years
27.	Sang Neneh Kodu Faal Ndow.......	23 years
28.	Sengan Jogob Mbodj..............	4 years
29.	Ndene Jogob Mbodj...............	4 years
30.	Sengan Ndengen Njie.............	9 years
31.	Sanneneh Kodu Faal Ndow.........	8 years
32.	Birang Njeme Njahamet Ndow......	5 years
33.	Ndene Mbaru Njie................	23 years
34.	Birang Hureja Njie..............	2 years
35.	Ndene Mbaru Njie................	6 years
36.	Balay Ndow......................	35 years
37.	Balay Adam Njie.................	6 years
38.	Sosi Bigay Njie.................	6 years
39.	Kumba Dama Mbodj................	6 years
40.	Samba Laube.....................	30 years
41.	Safuteh Mbodj...................	2 years
42.	Sajuka Mbodj....................	2 years
43.	Myawud Mbodj....................	4 years
44.	Gedal Mbodj.....................	19 years
45.	Semon Gimut Joof................	3 years
46.	Ndene Jemun Ndow................	33 years
47.	Ndena Jogob Joof................	10 years
48.	Semu Ngui Joof..................	2 years
49.	Gori Dioro Joof.................	6 years
50.	Ma Awa Dioro Jogob Joof.........	16 years
51.	Fode Ngui Joof..................	25 years[35]

Q: Who recorded this list?

Laoube: I told you before that we cannot write. This list is just
         about the *bur* of Kahon. When one died another succeeded
         him. We wrote their names down to avoid forgetting them.

Q: When were they written here?

Laoube: A long time ago. It has been copied and recopied. We
         wrote this when very little French was spoken in Kahon.[36]

     Malik Sarr interrupted, saying he had a similar list that he had made by
asking his elders. We recorded his reading of his list, too. It was different
from the list Laoube read in only a very few instances.

Q: Tell me the names of the elders you took it from.

Sarr: My grandfather, Waldaribaw Secka of Kahon; Jaraf Njuma
            Njie, who was becoming a *jaraf*; and a *faraba* in Kahon;
            from Ndena Ndure, who was a *jaraf* in Kahon; and from my
            father, who was called Faraba Mu Kumba Sarr.

Q: What is the meaning of *faraba*?

Sarr: *Faraba* is just like *ministre de l'interieure* in the
            Senegalese government.

Q: Was the *faraba* not a leatherworker?

Sarr: No, the leatherworkers whom Mandinka call *faraba* are dif-
            ferent from this *faraba*. A *faraba* in the past was like a
            permanent secretary of the *jaraf*. He was a middleman be-
            tween the *bur* and his subjects. Whatever the *faraba* and
            the *jaraf* disagreed about, they told the *bur*. The *faraba*
            was the first to discover grievances of the people, and
            when he learned of these things, he told the *jaraf*, who
            in turn told the *bur*. The *jaraf* was the minister next to
            the *bur*. If they ever decided to overthrow the *bur*, it was
            decided by the *jaraf* and *faraba*.

            The other *faraba* was the leader of the leatherworkers. He
            was appointed by the people and was made the leader of all
            the leatherworkers in the state. If the *bur* needed his *juju*
            coated with leather, it was the *faraba wide*'s responsibility
            to see that it got done.

            A *faraba* was not a slave. He could give the hand of his
            daughter to the *bur*, or vice versa. The same also applied
            to the *jaraf*.

Q: Can you tell me something about Niumi Bato?

      Samba Laoube begins speaking again.

Laoube: I know the Manneh who lived there were Arafang Manneh,
            Bubacar Manneh, and others.

Q: Did the Sonko ever settle there?

Laoube: Yes, the original settlers there were the Sonko and Manneh.
            It was under the rule of Ndena Njie that the Mandinka gained
            independence. Ndena was killed by the Mandinka and the Bad-
            dibunka abolished payment of tribute to Kahon. The king who
            managed to kill Ndena was really very powerful. I think his
            name was San Ndene, or. . . .It was after Jata Selang's death
            that the Baddibunka last paid tribute to Saloum.

Q: What about Niumi?

Laoube: It was the same for Niumi. It was in that year that
            Essau, Barra, Jarra, and Kiang gained their independence.[37]
            This did not mean that these independent lands would not
            marry women from here. It was just like separating our
            farms. I took mine and you took yours. It was as if this
            was owned by your father and it was my uncle who begot your
            father. If we quarreled over it and I was unable to defeat
            you, you would take your father's plot of land and I would
            take my father's, leaving my uncle's alone. All the *guelowar*
            were of the same mother. The *guelowar* of Kabu who came to
            Siin were all Mandinka. If a Mandinka gave the hand of his
            daughter in marriage to a Serer, the daughter in the end
            would be able to speak Serer and their children would be-
            come Serer. The same applies to any other groups.

            Boubacar Senn wants to add something:

Senn: What we know about the Jammeh and Sonko is that they lived
            in Tubakuta, Sandikoli, and Sanguako.[38]

Q: When Niumi gained her independence, who was the *mansa*
            in Niumi?

Senn: Before the Europeans came,[39] Mandinka ruled at Kawas in
            Nioro.[40] Jereba ruled there. Sukari ruled at Kular, and
            Mandinkas lived at Tenku.[41] These Mandinka had Serer
            fathers. That is why people like Sajuka Mbodj and others
            had Mandinka names. Those Mandinka are descended from
            Sakuja Mbodj and others. They came there and settled. Be-
            fore the coming of the Europeans those Mandinka and the
            Serer were in the same state. They then migrated to Jarra,
            Dankunku, Jarome, and other areas. They came from here.
            Kaur, Kuntaur, Balewo, and the upper river were all part
            of Saloum. When Mansa Wali left Kabu and came here he
            found these villages already established. It was three
            hundred years after they were founded that Mansa Wali
            came.[42]

Q: Did you ever have women rulers here?

Senn: Here in Saloum? Yes, we had a woman ruler, She was called
            Sira Bajal Ndong. She was the only woman ruler in Saloum.

Q: Why was she the only one?

Senn: Because she came together with Mansa Wali. When they came
            to Djilor, Sira was the elder and she ruled there. This
            caused Mansa Wali to travel until he came to Siin. It was
            there he judged between the son and nephew as we told you.
            Sira was a Mandinka.

Q: Have you ever heard of Sora Musa?

      Laoube answers.

Laoube: We do not know about him and it is not good to tell lies.
            This is our custom. This *jung-jung*, we play it for the
            men. Those who narrate the genealogies of people are
            *griot*s. If they are educated from European schools they
            write the genealogies of the different families; those
            who read Arabic do likewise.

Q: What was the general occupation of the Niuminka and of
            the people of Saloum a long time ago?

Laoube: The Niuminka wove mats because they had a tree from which
            they got the materials for them. The Niuminka brought
            mats and traded them to the people of Saloum. They got
            palm oil, too, the red and the colorless kind. The Niumi-
            nka were good sailors. They brought fish, salt, oysters,
            and other seafoods.[43]

Q: What did the people of Saloum trade for these things?

Laoube: You know money was not abundant then--not until the Euro-
            peans came. We traded millet and woven cotton cloth for
            them. In those days there were no beds or mattresses.
            The Niuminka brought fine woven mats and we obtained the
            mats with slaves. The slaves had to be young children be-
            cause when you offered adult slaves to the traders, they
            refused to go or they escaped on the road.

Q: How did they obtain slaves?

Laoube: From wars. If we defeated our enemies, we captured their
            women and boys and took them as slaves. When you have
            women slaves they were easily sold because they did not
            try to escape. The young boys were also unaware of con-
            ditions and they were easily captured. That is how we
            obtained them. When the *bur* of Saloum went to Siin and
            killed the *bur* of Siin, he captured the women and young
            boys and took them to Saloum. If the traders brought
            horses we obtained them with slaves. Sometimes a horse
            was worth three, four, or five slaves. Especially good
            and strong horses were sold for six slaves each.

Q: There is a family living between here and the Gambia
            River named Manneh. Were there Manneh here before the
            guelowar?[44]

Laoube: The Manneh came here before the Njie, Joof, Mbodj. . . .
            The Manneh were the original settlers of this place.

Q: What about the Manneh of Niumi?

Laoube: The Manneh of Niumi and these Manneh around here are all
            of the same ancestors. They were numerous when they came
            and they lost each other. The Sanneh and the Manneh were
            guelowar.

Q: Which came first, the Manneh here or the Manneh of Niumi?

Laoube: We do not know of the two families. All Manneh are the
            same.

Q: Can you tell me how Saloum got its name?

Laoube: As far as I know, Saloum was named after Saloum Suare.
            Yande Kamal, as I was told, was Saloum Suare's father.
            He gave this land to Saloum Suare and named it after him.
            They told me something else about Saloum Suare, too. When
            Yeli Bana Musa was coming to this land he brought Saloum
            Suare with him as his *marabout*. When Mbegane Ndure quar-
            reled with Yeli Bana and succeeded in killing him, Saloum
            Suare led the bereaved family at night, using a lighted
            piece of wood to guide them. Yeli Bana did not have a
            chance to say whether he was to be buried here or there.
            Saloum Suare tied Yeli Bana with a rope and threw him into
            the bush. Then he took a route which led to the upper
            river, going to a village called Ngach. The people of
            Kahon went after him but were unable to get him. When he
            reached Ngach he came upon an animal called "*ratan refet
            jatara*." The animal was surrounded by water and it was
            a very white creature. When the people of Kahon were
            about to get him, he went into the water and people still
            worship the place at Ngach where this took place. I my-
            self went there to worship last Friday.[45]

            In those days the Tukulor disliked the Serer. Nobody was
            able to say that he saw Yeli Bana's grave. The people of
            Kahon followed Yeli Bana's family through Ndofan to Ngach.
            At the river called "Mabange" *jatara tambedu* performed his
            magic. There was an animal in the river and the place was
            white. He disappeared at that spot and people still wor-
            ship it.

Q: In these days were you people Muslims?

Laoube: No, I told you before that we were not Mulsims. We did
            not know anything about Islam then. The Serer did not
            pray in those days. Yeli Bana Musa became the object of
            awe when he prayed; they sat and watched him. His Tukulor
            friends asked him why the Serer never married. Yeli Bana

said to them that the Serer worshipped idols. It became
a *dankuto* between the Tukulor and Serer.[46] Idols were
very important to the *bur* of Kahon. All people were the
same, we just lived in different places and adapted to
different conditions.

When our women married foreigners their sons came here
and ruled. Mbegane Ndure allowed his sister to marry in
Jolof, where she begot Latmingue Gilen, who became *bur*
here. You have asked us about the Sanneh and Manneh, of
whom we know very little. If you had asked us about the
Njie or any *bur* of Kahon, we would have been able to tell
you whether his reign was successful or not and what he
did during his reign. When a woman *guelowar* left here
to marry a foreigner, she was followed to see if she was
living happily.

Q: I heard that Latmingue Gilen fought eight wars. Can you
          tell me who these wars were against?[47]

Laoube: He fought eight wars here. I have not heard of any wars
          fought by Latmingue. I am an elder's son, this Chief
          is an elder's son, and he is an elder's son. We were not
          told of such things.

Q: For how many years did he rule?

Laoube: He ruled for eight years in Kahon. When he died his brother,
          Walbumi succeeded him.[48] I can show you where he was buried.
          I have not heard that he fought any wars; I know only that
          the *jung-jung* sounded for him.[49] He was a very fortunate
          bur.

Q: Was Siin under your government?

Laoube: Two *bur* existed in Siin who once governed both Siin and
          Saloum. Siin was a separate state. Kular was also inde-
          pendent of Siin. Siin and Saloum were once under the
          rule of one *bur*; that is why people still say "Siin-
          Saloum." Kular had been an independent state for a
          long time.

Q: When did Kular last have a *mansa*?

Laoube: The people of Kular were affected by Jata Selang's demand
          for independence. They declared Kular independent of Saloum.
          Saloum was left with only Nioro Deri Yassin. The people of
          Kular were very powerful. They were surnamed Manneh. They
          ruled at Tunku, Rawosalew, and Nioro Mamundari. They were
          Mandinka. When Nioro was not yet independent, Jereba paid
          tribute to Balang, the *bur* of Saloum.[50] Raad Jahor paid
          tribute to us in Saloum before the Europeans came. There

were wars then, but when the Europeans came they maintained law and order and abolished slavery and people
gained their independence from their African overlords.
In those days we did not give the Europeans our children,
we gave them our slaves.[51]

    At this point the formal part of the interview ended. We spoke to Laoube
about his playing of the *jung-jung*--the royal drum--and he volunteered to play
the drum for us. When he went to get his *jung-jung* he returned with another
jung-jung player and two drums. Both drums were about two-feet high and fifteen
inches in diameter. Straps passed over the drummer's shoulders to hold the drums
in playing position. The remainder of tape number 4388, then, consists of Laoube
and another man playing the *jung-jung*.

FOOTNOTES TO THE SAMBA LAOUBE AND BOUBACAR SENN INTERVIEW

[1]Kaur is a village located near the Gambia River at the end of its major northward bend about one hundred miles inland from the Atlantic. Kaur was, roughly speaking, the easternmost village of the old state of Saloum. Kuntaur is about thirty miles upriver from Kaur.

[2]Njob (Job, Jobe) is a common surname in Wolof-speaking areas.

[3]I can only assume Laoube means here that during the dry season people did not--indeed, could not--work in their fields. It was during the dry season that young men traveled widely in search of adventure and good fortune.

[4]This can be compared with Abdoulie Samba's account of Saloum Suare, Yeli Bana, and others, above.

[5]Mansa Wali Jan (Dione) is often said to be the man who led several families of *nyancho* out of Kabu, up across the Gambia River, and into the region of the lower Saloum River. Whereas Mandinka call these people *nyancho*, Wolof- and Serer-speakers call them *guelowar*.

[6]Curtin includes the following discussion of the office of *laman* in his *Economic Change*, pp. 25-26:

> Wolof land tenures bore a family resemblance to others in Sene-Gambia, but with their individual peculiarities. The primary claim came through descent from the man who had first settled and cleared it. This claim, however, was held by the lineage, not the individual, and it usually included much more land than a single family could work. The head of that lineage held a claim called *borom dai* (the right of fire) and his office of *laman* (often translated as master of the land) also included obligations to the earth deities--obligations that have often disappeared in recent centuries with the progressive introduction of Islam. The *laman* who held *borom dai* collected customary payments from each of the families that actually worked the land, though these payments were usually more nearly a ritual token of recognition than an economic rent. . . .
>
> It is usually assumed that the *laman*ate preceded the establishment of states. When higher authorities like the Burba of Jolof, the Damel of Kajor, and the Teen of Bawol came on the scene, they simply superimposed their power, leaving the *laman* in office with their old functions. But the state needed to reward loyalty, and it began granting tracts to those it favored. . . .Many of the grants covered areas that had no pre-existing *laman*. . . .Later grants were in the core areas of the various kingdoms, but they

tended more often to extinguish the rights of the existing
laman than to impose a second layer over him.

Senn's story that follows seems to express in typical *griot* fashion this supression of the *laman*'s authority by a higher office--here symbolized by Mansa Wali Jan.

[7]Senn's use of the name of Allah here does not necessarily mean the people were Muslims. Senn is a Muslim, so he refers to the deity as Allah. It could probably be translated "the gods" or "the spirits" if one wished to do so.

[8]Stories of persons, usually women, having sores, usually on their feet, and visiting someone for a cure abound in Senegambian oral traditions. If it is a woman, the man usually cures her sore and they eventually marry. The common folklore motif is an attempt to explain how two families came together and developed close relations through long periods of time.

[9]Senn's story that follows about Mbegane, his sister, and Yeli Bana is a somewhat more embellished version of that narrated by Abdoulie Samba. See Samba's interview, above.

[10]Senn calls Yeli Bana a Tukulor rather than a Fula or Fulbe. The difference is a slight one. English-speakers in The Gambia call Fulbe "Fula." French-speakers in Senegal call agricultural Fulbe "Tukulor" and pastoral Fulbe "Peul." They are all Fulbe, speakers of Pular. See Curtin, *Economic Change*, pp. 18ff.

[11]Blacksmiths and cobblers were two occupational groupings--some refer to them as castes, though the term in its usual sense is hardly appropriate--in Senegambian society whose members were long thought to have special relationships with the spirits of the ground and trees. Because they dealt with these spirits regularly, making charcoal and tanning ingredients or extracting ores from the earth, people often consulted them when magic was to be employed. It seems to be such advice that Ngoyan Sarr is giving Mbegane and his sister.

[12]Muslims pray regularly, five times per day. When each time for prayer arrives a call goes out from the mosque, summoning people to come to pray.

[13]"*Bismilahi*" means "In the name of Allah." This shortened form of the phrase, "*Bismilahi-Rahmani-Rahim*," meaning "In the Name of Allah, the Merciful, the Compassionate," is the opening invocation in the first *sura* (chapter), *al-Fatihah*, in the Koran. It is used by Muslims to dedicate each of their undertakings--even such mundane tasks as putting on one's shoes--to God.

[14]*Juju* are protective amulets, usually worn on the body or affixed to weapons or saddlery. Good *marabout*s, who could make effective *juju* and help a warring party defeat the enemy, were extremely valuable.

[15]*Cheddo* means different things in different places. Among speakers of Wolof and Serer, and some speakers of Pular (Fulbe), it was the name for royal slaves that rulers used as professional military or administrative corps. But

in Futa Toro, and seemingly in this instance as Senn uses the term, it refers to free men of a particular royal dynasty, the Denyanke dynasty, of which Futa Toro's noted leader, Koli Tengela, was indeed a member.

It is interesting to note the chronological congruence of what Senn is saying here. Koli Tengela established the Denyanke dynasty in Futa Toro in the last third of the fifteenth century. If he did indeed expel Yeli Bana, the latter could have gone to Kahon and lived there a decade or more before Mbegane Ndure, by Jean Boulègue's estimate, founded the state of Saloum in 1494. For the latest work on Koli Tengela see Person, "Nyani Mansa Mamadu." See Boulègue, "Contribution," p. 656 for dates of Mbegane Ndure's reign as *bur* of Saloum.

[16] According to Gamble in *The Wolof of Senegambia*, p. 57, the *jaraf au rei*, or "Grand Jaraf," represented the freeborn people of the Chiefdom and was their protector. He was freeborn himself, though not of a *guelowar* lineage, and he acted as an elector of the *bur* and as the *bur*'s advisor. "He was also a judge with power to impose the death penalty," writes Gamble, and "should the occasion arise he could depose the *bur*." There were lesser *jaraf*, too, such as the *jaraf bekaneg*, a sort of chamberlain, either freeborn or slave, who looked after the *bur*'s household.

Curtin, in *Economic Change*, refers to a "Great Jaraf of Sinn" (p. 115), but he notes (p. 39) that the Great Jaraf was elected by an assembly of village heads called *jaraf*.

[17] The *faraba* in Saloum was in charge of the *bur*'s slaves. He directed the military forces. Gamble notes lesser *faraba*, also of slave origin.

Samba Laoube notes later that the *bisak* was a person who spoke for the king—a sort of intermediary between the people and the king. I cannot find a reference to the duties of an officer called the *jarad*.

[18] Oral traditions throughout Senegambia place great emphasis on the importance of young hopefuls for kingship learning about the powers of magic and dealing with spirits. Learning ways to protect oneself from others' magic was equally importnat. Several Mandinka informants spoke as if "finding *juju*" was the most important part of preparation for eventual rule.

[19] Throughout many of the Serer, Wolof, and Mandinka states of the Senegambia the person who was to become the next ruler had to predict what would happen during his reign. His prophesy seemed to form something like a contract between the ruler and the powerful lineages of the state (here represented by the *jaraf*). It was when the ruler did not do the things he said he would do, or did not come near expectations of him, that the other freeborn families of the state would depose him. Laoube says the *jaraf* could depose the *bur* of Saloum, but surely when he did so he was acting in the capacity of representative of the powerful, freeborn lineages of the state and was deposing a *bur* who had taken some of the power away from these non-royal lineages. See Curtin's discussion of government in *Economic Change*, p. 37ff, or Quinn, *Mandingo Kingdoms*, pp. 11-17.

[20] Horses were an extremely valuable commodity throughout the Senegambia. The elite, warrior class that provided rulers for the Mandinka, Wolof, and Serer states took great pride in their horsemanship and in fighting on horseback. Horses did not have long life spans in all parts of the region, however,

because of tsetse fly infestation in certain areas. In Saloum and points north they bred and traded for horses; then, in turn, they traded horses to the Mandinka states to the south, where there were more tsetse flies. If a family did indeed offer the *jaraf* twenty horses, it would have been no small offering.

[21]Though Laoube says below that age was not a significant factor in selecting the next *bur* of Saloum, I found in many instances that age was critical, and that persons deciding upon the next ruler of a Senegambian state often had to have an extremely good reason why they selected a younger individual over an elder.

[22]*Denku* is the Wolof equivalent of the Mandinka *tilibo*. It means the land of the sun (rise), or the east, Haire is a semi-desert region north of the upper Senegal, in what is today part of Mauritania. Since this region was a probable source of horses for Saloum,Haire may be what Senn means when he says "Hai."

[23]Maka Goui is a village in Senegal on The Gambia border about ten miles north of Kuntaur on the Gambia River. Kounghel is a larger Senegalese town about fifteen miles northeast of Maka Goui. In maps I have seen, I do not remember noting Saloum's borders stretching so far east. State borders were often less formally recognized than today. Residents of Saloum may indeed have considered Maka Goui as part of Saloum. Barra is another name for Niumi.

[24]Baddibu was the Mandinka state on the Gambia River directly east of Niumi and south of Saloum. Farafenni is the major town in Baddibu today. It is located about sixty-five miles southeast of Kaolack.

[25]Essau joined Banjul in the sense that they both became part of the British colony of The Gambia rather than part of French Senegal. Senn is speaking of colonial times here.

[26]Although I cannot identify each one, I can tell from the ones that are identifiable that these are villages within a reasonable distance of Kahon.

[27]Boulègue's list of the *bur* of Saloum has "Sadiouka Mbodj" as the *bur* from 1876 to 1879. Boulègue, "Contribution," p. 657.

[28]Boulègue lists "Guedal Mbodj" as the successor to Sadiouka. Guedal reigned from 1879-1896.

[29]Someone keenly interested in these wars would, of course, be well advised to find out what informants in Siin said about them. It would be good, too, to ask informants who were less involved about them. And, finally, since the wars took place in the last third of the nineteenth century, when there was an increasingly strong French presence in this part of Senegal, interested students of these wars could very likely find mention of them in the French records in the Archives Nationales du Sénégal.

[30]Essau is one of the villages in Niumi in which resided two families that provided Niumi's *mansa*. Senn refers to Niumi as Essau on occasion.

[31]This is one of the main questions I wanted to ask. Several sources, written and oral, said that Niumi long paid tribute to Saloum. One English factor in The Gambia in the 1730s, Francis Moore, who knew the area well, said that Niumi was tributary to Saloum. I wanted to know from Saloum sources about the tributary arrangement and how the arrangement ended. I was disappointed with the answers I got.

[32]Jata Selang lived in Iliassa and was apparently a *mansa* of Baddibu.

[33]Boulègue's list has "Ndene Ndiaye Marone Ndao" as the eleventh *bur* of Saloum, reigning from 1638 to 1640.

[34]Senn is either being apologetic that he does not know about Niumi's tributary relationship with Saloum and any wars the two states fought, or else he is getting perturbed at my continual questioning about Niumi when he knows more about other things.

[35]It is interesting to compare this list with the one Boulègue copied in Kahon about a decade earlier. Laoube's list and Boulègue's list differ in many instances over specific lengths of reign. Laoube's list, too, has four names that Boulègue's does not, and Boulègue's has two that Laoube's does not. However, when omitting the first two names on Laoube's list and beginning with Mbegane Ndure, the first name on Boulègue's list and the individual most informants call the first true *bur* of independent Saloum and adding the lengths of time all the *bur* on each list reigned, the sum of one list differs from the other by only two years. Boulègue's list has Mbegane Ndure reigning from 1494; Laoube's has him becoming *bur* in 1492.

[36]This could have been a long time ago. Saloum had contact with French traders from the seventeenth century. From time to time from then into the mid-nineteenth century the trade between Saloum and the French was heavy. Then, increasingly after 1850, the French presence in the Saloum River grew until the official colonial takeover of Saloum in 1891.

[37]Jarra and Kiang were Mandinka states on the south bank of the Gambia, I have never before heard that they were subject to political dominance of Saloum.

[38] These are villages in what is called Niumi Bato, the ocean-oriented region along the Atlantic stretching north from Jinak Creek in The Gambia through the maze of mangrove islands and adjacent coastline northward toward the mouth of the Saloum River.

[39]In nearly every instance, the phrase "before the Europeans came" means before the actual colonial takeover of the European powers, or, speaking generally, before about 1890 in the Senegambia region.

[40]Nioro is a Senegalese village located some forty miles southeast of Kaolack in what was the Mandinka state of Baddibu. Jereba refers to a nineteenth century *mansa* of Baddibu, Jereba Marong.

[41]Kular is a village--it may once have been a state or at least have had political authority beyond the village level--in Senegal, forty miles due south

of Kaolack. It is located at the head of the Miniminiyang Creek, a tributary of the Gambia River. I am not familiar with a village called Tenku.

[42]This evidence suggests that Mandinka had been in the area for some time prior to the arrival of the *guelowar*. See my, "Niumi: The History of a Western Mandinka State," pp. 27ff., for discussion of the settlement of this area.

[43]The Niuminka are a fascinating group of people who seem to be something of ethnic and cultural hybrids. They inhabit many of the islands and the coastal region of Niumi Bato. Claiming to be both Serer and "Soce" (as they call the Mandinka), these people are excellent boatsmen and they still make much of their livings from produce of the sea. For more information on the Niuminka see F. Lafont, "La Gandoul et les Niominkas," *Bulletin du Comité d'Etudes Historiques et Scientifiques de l'Afrique Occidentale Française*, XXI (1938), pp. 385-458.

[44]I ask this question because the Manneh family of Niumi claims that its ancestors were *nyancho* (or *guelowar*) who came from Kabu. It is interesting that these informants say that the Manneh were the original settlers of the area. Whenever one person says that an unrelated family lived in the area before the informant's family, there is more likelihood that it is so than if the informant says *his* family came first.

[45]Saloum Suare is one of the most widely known Muslims in the Western Sudan. A place where people say he entered the water would indeed be celebrated as a holy place for Muslims.

[46]See Abdoulie Samba interview, footnote 57.

[47]Martin Klein of the University of Toronto had collected some traditions in Djilor, which referred to eight wars which were fought by Latmingue. I read this in an unpublished paper written by Klein. Of course, it is interesting that the *griot*s from Kahon know nothing about any wars fought by Latmingue. This is odd, for Klein's sources refer to Latmingue as a successful warrior, and successful wars are typically the kind that *griot*s remember.

[48]Laoube did not refer to his written list when asked this question. On the list, when he read it, Latmingue supposedly reigned for two years, and four *bur* separate Latmingue from Walbumi.

[49]This means "I know only that he was the *bur*," because the *jung-jung* sounded only for the *bur*.

[50]This refers to the middle of the nineteenth century. Balang is either Bale Ndoungou Ndao, who reigned as *bur* of Saloum from approximately 1824 to 1852, or Bala Adama Njie, who reigned from 1852 to 1855.

[51]I assume Laoube is talking about the days of the slave trade. One would not sell one's children to the Europeans, and, generally speaking, one would not sell household or family slaves.

AFRICA PROGRAM
CENTER FOR INTERNATIONAL STUDIES
OHIO UNIVERSITY
ATHENS, OHIO 45701

ORDER FROM:
Ohio University Press
Scott Quad, Ohio University
Athens, Ohio 45701

Out of Print volumes (marked with an *) can be obtained in microfilm or xerographic copies from University Microfilms International, at Box 1467, Ann Arbor, Michigan 48106 or 18 Bedford Row, London WCIR 4EJ, England.

Publication Number:

1 - THE NEW ENGLISH OF THE ONITSHA CHAPBOOKS. By Harold Reeves Collins. 1968. 22 pp. $1.75

2 - DIRECTIONS IN GHANAIAN LINGUISTICS: A Brief Survey. By Paul F.A. Kotey. 1969. 20 pp. $1.75

3 - DEFINING NATIONAL PURPOSE IN LESOTHO. By Richard F. Weisfelder. 1961. 39 pp. $2.25

4 - RECENT AGRICULTURAL CHANGE EAST OF MOUNT KENYA. By Frank E. Bernard. 1969. 41 pp. $2.75

5 - THE STRUGGLE AGAINST SLEEPING SICKNESS IN NYASALAND AND NORTHERN RHODESIA, 1900-1922. By Norman H. Pollock. 1969. 21 pp. $1.75

6*- BOTSWANA AND ITS SOUTHERN NEIGHBOR: The Patterns of Linkage and the Options in Statecraft. By Richard Dale. 1969.

7 - WOLF COURTS GIRL: The Equivalence of Hunting and Mating in Bushman Thought. By Daniel F. McCall. 1970. 24 pp. $1.75

8 - MARKERS IN ENGLISH-INFLUENCED SWAHILI CONVERSATION. By Carol M. Eastman. 1970. 25 pp. $2.00

9*- THE TERRITORIAL EXPANSION OF THE NANDI OF KENYA, 1500-1905. By Bob J. Walter. 1970.

10 - SOME GEOGRAPHICAL ASPECTS OF WEST AFRICAN DEVELOPMENT. By R.J. Harrison Church. 1970. 34 pp. $2.75

11 - THE IMPACT OF THE PROTÉGÉ SYSTEM IN MOROCCO, 1800-1912. By Leland Bowie. 1970. 21 pp. $1.75

12 - MARKET DEVELOPMENT IN TRADITIONALLY MARKETLESS SOCIETIES: A Perspective on East Africa. By Charles M. Good. 1971. 39 pp. $3.00

13 - SOUTH AFRICA'S OUTWARD STRATEGY: A Foreign Policy Dilemma for the United States. By Larry W. Bowman. 1971. 1973 reprint. 32 pp. $2.50

14 - BANTU EDUCATION AND THE EDUCATION OF AFRICANS IN SOUTH AFRICA. By R. Hunt Davis, Jr. 1972. 60 pp. $3.50

15 - TOWARD A THEORY OF THE AFRICAN UPPER STRATUM IN SOUTH AFRICA. By Thomas E. Nyquist. 1972. 66 pp. $3.50

16 - THE BASOTHO MONARCHY: A Spent Force or a Dynamic Political Factor? By Richard F. Weisfelder. 1972. 66 pp. $4.50

17*- YORUBA PROVERBS: Translation and Annotation. By Bernth Lindfors and Oyekan Owomoyela. 1973.

18 - POST-MILITARY COUP STRATEGY IN UGANDA: Amin's Early Attempts to Consolidate Political Support. By Jeffrey T. Strate. 1973. 65 pp. $3.75

19 - HIGHLAND MOSAIC: A Critical Anthology of Ethiopian Literature in English. Compiled by Paul E. Huntsberger. 1973. 133 pp. $4.75

20 - THE KENYA NATIONAL YOUTH SERVICE: A Governmental Response to Young Political Activists. By Richard L. Coe. 1973. 39 pp. $2.50

21 - CONSTRAINTS ON THE EXPANSION OF COMMERCIAL AGRICULTURE: Iringa District, Tanzania. By Marilyn Silberfein. 1974. 59 pp. $3.50

22 - ECHO AND CHORUSES: "Ballad of the Cells" and Selected Shorter Poems. By Cosmo Pieterse. 1974. 75 pp. $3.75

23 - THE NIGER-NIGERIAN BOUNDARY, 1890-1906: A Study of Ethnic Frontiers and a Colonial Boundar. By Derrick J. Thom. 1975. 49 pp. $3.25

24 - A COMPREHENSIVE PERIODICAL BIBLIOGRAPHY OF NIGERIA, 1960-1970. Compiled by Edward Baum. 1975. 261 pp. $6.00

25 - ABYSSINIA TO ZONA AL SUR DEL DRAA: A Guide to the Political Units of Africa in the Period 1950-1974. Second Edition. By Eugene C. Kirchherr. 1975. 50 pp. $3.50

26 - THE ORIGINS AND DEVELOPMENT OF EFIK SETTLEMENTS IN SOUTHEASTERN NIGERIA. By Kannan K. Nair. 1975. 42 pp. $3.00

27 - MOUNTAIN WARRIORS: The Pre-Colonial Meru of Mt. Kenya. By Jeffrey Fadiman. 1976. 82 pp. Bib. $4.00

28 - DEPENDENCE AND UNDERDEVELOPMENT: The Development and Foreign Politics of Zambia. By Timothy M. Shaw. 1976. 67 pp. Bib. $3.75

29 - CHIEF EXECUTIVES IN BLACK AFRICA AND SOUTHEAST ASIA: A Descriptive Analysis of Social Background and Characteristics. By Edward Baum and Felix Gagliano. 1976. 43 pp. App. $3.00

30 - FEARS AND WORRIES OF NIGERIAN IGBO SECONDARY SCHOOL STUDENTS: An Empirical Psycho-Cultural Study. By Sadek H. Samaan and Anne J. Samaan. 1976. 90 pp. App., Bib. $4.50

31 - ISLAND OF THE BLEST: Islam in a Libyan Oasis Community. By John P. Mason. 1977. 173 pp. Index, Photos, Glossary. ISBN 0-89680-063-6. LC 77-620016. $6.00

32 - THE EARLY HISTORY OF NIUMI: Settlement and Foundation of a Mandinka State on the Gambia River. By Donald R. Wright. 1977. 122 pp. Maps, Glossary. ISBN 0-89680-064-4. LC 77-620032. $5.50

33 - DEFENSE LEGISLATION AND COMMUNAL POLITICS: The Evolution of a White South African Nation as Reflected in the Controversy over the Assignment of Armed Forces Abroad, 1912-1976. By Kenneth W. Grundy. 1978. 157 pp. ISBN 0-89680-065-2. LC 77-620051. $3.50

34 - COMMUNICATION FOR NEW LOYALTIES: African Soldiers' Songs. By Anthony Clayton. 1978. 64 pp. Photos. ISBN 0-89680-069-5. LC 78 1-17653. $4.00

35 - DRUG USE AND SOUTH AFRICAN STUDENTS. By Brian M. duToit. 1979. 135 pp. ISBN 0-89680-076-8. $6.00

36 - THE MOMENT OF CONQUEST: MERU, KENYA, 1907. By Jeffrey Fadiman. 1979. 70 pp. ISBN 0-89680-081-4. $4.00

37 - ORAL TRADITIONS OF THE GAMBIA: Volume I--Mandinka *Griot*s. Collected, edited, and introduced by Donald R. Wright. 1979. 189 pp. ISBN 0-89680-083-0. $7.50

ALSO: WEST/AFRICAN PIDGIN-ENGLISH: A Descriptive Linguistic Analysis with Texts and Glossary from the Cameroon Area. By Gilbert D. Schneider. 1969. 256 pp. $6.00

This book is an attempt to apply the basic principles of structural linguistics to West African Pidgin-English. After an introductory chapter which deals with the general characteristics of the language as spoken in the Cameroon area, the author proceeds to the treatment of sounds, meaningful units, and sentence patterns. A glossary and bibliography are included.

LATIN AMERICA PROGRAM
CENTER FOR INTERNATIONAL STUDIES
OHIO UNIVERSITY
ATHENS, OHIO 45701

ORDER FROM:
Ohio University Press
Scot Quad, Ohio University
Athens, Ohio 45701

Publication Number:

1 - THE MANDATE OF HISTORY AND CHILE'S FUTURE. By Eduardo Frei M. Translated
   by Miguel d'Escoto, M. M. Edited and Introduced by Thomas W. Walker.
   1977. 85 pp. ISBN 0-8214-0334-6. LC 77-620018. $4.00

2 - MULTINATIONAL CORPORATIONS IN LATIN AMERICA: Private Rights and Public
   Responsibilities. Edited by Donald P. Irish. 1978. 135 pp. ISBN 0-89680-
   067-9. LC 77-620055. $5.50

3 - MULTINATIONAL CORPORATIONS AND INTERNATIONAL INVESTMENT IN LATIN AMERICA:
   A Selected and Annotated Bibliography. Compiled by Harold Molineu. 1978.
   105 pp. ISBN 0-89680-068-7. LC 77-620052. $5.00

4 - THE CENTRAL AMERICAN SOCCER WAR: Historical Patterns and Inernal Dynamics of
   OAS Settlement Procedures. By Mary Jeanne Reid Martz. 1979. 118 pp. ISBN 0-
   89680-077-6. $6.00

5 - CRITICAL ELECTIONS AND CRITICAL COUPS: State, Society, and the Military in
   the Processes of Latin American Development. By Howard J. Wiarda. 1979. 83 pp.
   ISBN 0-89680-082-2. $4.50

6 - POLITICAL PARTICIPATION IN A NON-ELECTORAL SETTING: The Urban Poor in Lima,
   Peru. By Henry A. Dietz and Richard Moore. 1979. 100+ pp. ISBN 0-89680-085-7.
   $6.00 (tentative).

SOUTHEAST ASIA PROGRAM
CENTER FOR INTERNATIONAL STUDIES
OHIO UNIVERSITY
ATHENS, OHIO 45701

ORDER FROM:
Ohio University Press
Scott Quad, Ohio University
Athens, Ohio 45701

Out of Print volumes (marked with an *) can be obtained in microfilm or xerographic copies from University Microfilms International, at Box 1467, Ann Arbor, Michigan 48106 or 18 Bedford Row, London WCIR 4EJ, England.

Publication Number:

1 - TREASURES AND TRIVIA: Doctoral Dissertations on Southeast Asia Accepted by Universities in the United States. Compiled by Lian The and Paul W. van der Veur. 1968. 155 pp. $5.00

2 - PUBLIC PROTEST IN INDONESIA. By Ann Ruth Willner. 1968. 21 pp. $1.75

3*- DEVELOPMENTAL CHALLENGE IN MALAYSIA. By Siew Nim Chee. 1968.

4 - THE USE OF HISTORY. By Wang Gungwu. 1968. 24 pp. $1.75

5*- THE TRADITIONAL USE OF THE FORESTS IN MAINLAND SOUTHEAST ASIA. By James L. Cobban.

6*- CONFLICT AND POLITICAL DEVELOPMENT IN SOUTHEAST ASIA: An Exploration in the International Implications of Comparative Theory. By Gerald S. Maryanov.

7*- SRI PADUKA: The Exile of the Prince of Ayondha. Translated by S.M. Ponniah.

8 - AGRARIAN UNREST IN THE PHILIPPINES: Guardia de Honor--Revitalization within the Revolution; Rizalistas--Contemorary Revitalization Movements in the Philippines. By David R. Sturtevant. 1969. 1973 reprint. 44 pp. $2.75

9 - PANDANGGO-SA-ILAW: The Politics of Occidental Mindoro. By Remigio E. Agpalo. 1969. 32 pp. $2.00

10*- REPRESSION AND REVOLT: The Origins of the 1948 Communist Insurrection in Malaya and Singapore. By Michael R. Stenson.

11 - RUBBER AND THE MALAYSIAN ECONOMY: Implications of Declining Prices. By Tan Sri Lim Swee Aun. 1969. 36 pp. $2.50

12 - EDUCATION AND SOCIAL CHANGE IN COLONIAL INDONESIA: I. Progress and Procrastination in Education in Indonesia prior to World War II; II. The Social and Geographical Origins of Dutch-Educated Indonesians. By Paul W. van der Veur. 1969. 62 pp. $3.50

13*- COMMUNAL VIOLENCE IN MALAYSIA 1969: The Political Aftermath. By Felix V. Gagliano.

14*- SOVIET AND AMERICAN AID TO INDONESIA 1949-1968. By Usha Mahajani. 1970.

15*- POLITICS AMONG BURMANS: A Study of Intermediary Leaders. By John Badgley. 1970.

16 - TRADE AND EMPIRE IN MALAYA AND SINGAPORE, 1869-1874. By D. R. SarDesai. 1970. 22 pp. $1.75

17*- EXPANSION OF THE VIETNAM WAR INTO CAMBODIA: Action and Response by the Governments of North Vietnam, South Vietnam, Cambodia, and the United States. By Peter A. Poole. 1970.

18 - THE PRE-WORLD WAR II PERANAKAN CHINESE PRESS OF JAVA: A Preliminary Survey. By Leo Suryadinata. 1971. 44 pp. $2.75

19*- A REVIEW OF COMMUNITY-ORINETED ECOLOGICAL RESEARCH IN THE PHILIPPINES. By Robert A. Bullington. 1971.

20*- A BIBLIOGRAPHY OF PHILIPPINES LINGUISTICS. By Nobleza C. Asuncion-Landé. 1971.

21*- THE BURMA-YUNNAN RAILWAY: Anglo-French Rivalry in Mainland Southeast Asia and South China, 1895-1905. By J. Chandran.

22*- THE NORTH BORNEO CHARTERED COMPANY'S ADMINISTRATION OF THE BAJAU, 1878-1909: The Pacification of a Maritime, Nomadic People. By James F. Warren.

23*- PROMINENT INDONESIAN CHINESE IN THE TWENTIETH CENTURY: A Preliminary Survey. By Leo Suyandinata.

24 - PEACOCKS, PAGODAS, AND PROFESSOR HALL: A Critique of the Persisting Use of Historiography as an Apology for British Empire-Building in Burma. By Manuel Sarkisyanz. 1972. 68 pp. $3.50

25 – IMBALANCES IN DEVELOPMENT: The Indonesian Experience. By Selo Soemardjan. 1972. 26 pp. $2.00

26 – THE VERHANDELINGEN VAN HET BATAVIAASCH GENOOTSCHAP: An Annotated Content Analysis. Compiled by Lian The and Paul W. van der Veur. 1973. 150 pp. Index. $5.00

27 – JAPAN'S SCHEME FOR THE LIBERATION OF BURMA: The Role of the *Minami Kikan* and the "Thirty Comrades." By Won Z. Yoon. 1973. 65 pp. Bib. $3.50

28 – EDUCATIONAL SPONSORHIP BY ETHNICITY: A Preliminary Analysis of the West Malaysian Experience. By Yoshimitsu Takei, John C. Bock, and Bruce Saunders. 1973. 44 pp. $3.00

29 – BLOOD, BELIEVERS, AND BROTHER: The Development of Voluntary Associations in Malaysia. By Stephen A. Douglas and Paul Pederson. 1973. 119 pp. App. $4.50

30*– THE DYNAMICS OF POLITICS AND ADMINISTRATION IN RURAL THAILAND. By Clark D. Neher.

31 – PEASANT CITIZENS: Politics, Religion, and Modernization in Kelantan, Malaysia. By Manning Nash. 1974. 1977 reprint. 179 pp. Bib. $7.00

32 – MARGINAL MAN IN A COLONIAL SOCIETY: Abdoel Moeis' *Salah Asuhan*. By David de Queljoe. 1974. 43 pp. $3.00

33*– THE NEUTRALIZATION OF SOUTHEAST ASIA: An Analysis of the Malaysian/ASEAN Proposal. By Marvin C. Ott. 1974.

34 – THE LAND-TO-THE-TILLER PROGRAM AND RURAL RESOURCE MOBILIZATION IN THE MEKONG DELTA OF SOUTH VIETNAM. By C. Stuart Callison. 1974. 48 pp. $3.00

35 – THE FUTURE OF BURMA IN PERSPECTIVE: A Symposium. Edited and with an Introduction by Josef Silverstein. 1974. 104 pp. $4.50

36 – INDOCHINE: Perspectives for Reconciliation. Edited and with an Introduction by Peter A. Poole. 1975. 92 pp. $4.25

37 – THE COMINTERN AND VIETNAMESE COMMUNISM. By William J. Duiker. 1975. 48 pp. $3.25

38 – BROKER, MEDIATOR, PATRON AND KINSMAN: An Historical Analysis of Key Leadership Roles in a Rural Malaysian District. By Connor Bailey. 1976. 89 pp. Bib. LC 75-620141. $4.25

39 – CHIEF EXECUTIVES IN BLACK AFRICA AND SOUTHEAST ASIA: A Descriptive Analysis of Social Background and Characteristics. By Edward Baum and Felix Gagliano. 1976. 43 pp. App. $3.00

40 – FREEMASONRY IN INDONESIA FROM RADERMACHER TO SOEKANTO, 1762–1961. By Paul W. van der Veur. 1976. 42 pp. $3.25

41 – CULTURAL-ECOLOGICAL PERSPECTIVES ON SOUTHEAST ASIA: A Symposium. Edited and with an Introduction by William Wood. 1977. 192 pp. ISBN 0-8214-0322-2. LC 76-620062. $8.00

42 – SOUTHEAST ASIA, AN EMERGING CENTER OF WORLD INFLUENCE? ECONOMIC AND RESOURCE CONSIDERATIONS. Edited and introduced by Wayne Raymdond and K. Mulliner. Comments by Laurence D. Stifel. 1977. 136 pp. ISBN 0-8214-0324-9. LC 76-620090. $6.00

43 – POLLUTION AND POLITICS IN THE PHILIPPINES. By Ross Marlay. 1977. 131 pp. ISBN 0-8214-0325-7. LC 76-620091. $6.00

44 – INCOME, EMPLOYMENT, AND FOOD SYSTEMS IN JAVANESE COASTAL VILLAGES. By William L. Collier, Harjadi Hadikoesworo, and Suwardi Saropie. 1977. 160 pp. Maps, Tables, Glossary, Bib. ISBN 0-89680-031-8. LC 77-620017. $7.00

45 – FOREVER PLURAL: The Perception and Practice of Inter-Communal Marriage in Singapore. By Chew Sock Foon and John A. MacDougall. 1977. 67 pp. Tables, Bib. ISBN 0-89680-030-X. LC 77-620031. $3.75

46 – THAILAND, DOMINO BY DEFAULT? The 1976 Coup and Implications for United States Policy. With an Epilogue on the October 1977 Coup. By William Bradley, David Morell, David Szanton, and Stephen Young. 1978. 67 pp. ISBN 0-89680-032-6. LC 77-620050. $3.75

47 - COSMOLOGY AND SOCIAL BEHAVIOR IN A WEST JAVANESE SETTLEMENT. By Robert Wessing. 1978. 200 pp. ISBN 0-89680-072-5. $8.00

48 - SOUTHEAST ASIAN REFERENCES IN THE BRITISH PARLIAMENTARY PAPERS, 1801-1972/73: An Index. Compiled, Edited, and Introduced by Thomas F. Willer. 1978. 106 pp. ISBN 0-89680-033-4. LC 77-620064. $5.00

49 - AGRICULTURAL PRODUCTION AND HOUSEHOLD BUDGETS IN A SHAN PEASANT VILLAGE IN NORTHEASTERN THAILAND: A Quantitative Description. By E. Paul Durrenberger. 1978. 154 pp. Tables. ISBN 0-89680-071-7. $6.50

50 - Robustiano Echaúz' SKETCHES OF THE ISLAND OF NEGROS. Translated by Donn V. Hart with an Introduction by John A. Larkin. 1978. 174 pp. Glossary, Bib., Index. ISBN 0-89680-070-9. LC 78-13403. $7.00

51 - MAYORS AND MANAGERS IN THAILAND: The Struggle for Political Life in Administrative Settings. By Ronald L. Krannich. 1978. 139 pp. ISBN 0-89680-073-3. $6.00

52 - WHAT IS MODERN INDONESIA CULTURE?: Proceedings of the Indonesian Studies Conference, 1976. Edited by Gloria Davis. 1979. 300+ pp. ISBN 0-89680-075-X. $10.00 Prepublication.

53 - ART, RITUAL, AND SOCIETY IN INDONESIA: Proceedings of the Indonesian Studies Conference, 1977. Edited by Ed Bruner and Judy Becker. 1979. 175 pp. ISBN 0-89680-080-6. $7.00

54 - THE STUDY OF THAILAND: Analyses of Knowledge, Approaches, and Prospects in Anthropology, Art History, Economics, History, and Political Science. Edited by Eliezer B. Ayal. 1978. 250 pp. ISBN 0-89680-079-2. $10.00

ALSO: INTERNATIONAL BIOGRAPHICAL DIRECTORY OF SOUTHEAST ASIA SPECIALISTS. Compiled by Robert O. Tilman. 1969. 373 pp. Special price: $1.25

SEARCH FOR NEW GUINEA'S BOUNDARIES: From Torres Strait to the Pacific. By Paul W. van der Veur. ANU Press, 1966. 176 pp. $10.00

Ohio University

AFRICAN STUDIES PROGRAM

The African Language and Area Center, established in 1965 with the aid of an NDEA Title VI grant from the U.S. Office of Education, forms an important part of the Center for International Studies. In addition to assisting in the coordination and development of new courses and expansion of library resources, the Center also supports faculty and student field research and sponsors the African Publication Series. It provides a forum for lectures by distinguished Africans and specialists on Africa, and helps to bring African cultural attractions to the Athens campus. As a supplement to undergraduate academic degrees, students may select African studies as an area of concentration and by meeting specified course and language requirements, be awarded an area certificate. Similarly, the Center for International Studies offers an interdisciplinary master of arts in international affairs degree with emphasis on African studies.

Faculty:

Edward Baum
Political Science

Frank E. Bernard
Geography

Alan R. Booth
History

Edwin G. Charle, Jr.
Economics

Gifford B. Doxsee
History

John Hunter
Economics

James A. Lee
Management

Gertrude Linnenbruegge
Africana Bibliographer Emeritus

Marianne M. J. Maghenda
Swahili

Suzanne Miers
History

Judith M. Perani
Art

Cosmo G. Pieterse
African Literature

Sadek H. Samaan
Education

Arthur Saxe
Anthropology

Gilbert D. Schneider
Linguistics

Bob J. Walter
Geography

Mohamed Yamba
Hausa

H. Marshall Carter
Political Science/Criminal Justice